American Catholic History

American Catholic History

A Documentary Reader

EDITED BY

Mark Massa, S.J., with Catherine Osborne

New York University Press

NEW YORK AND LONDON

NEW YORK UNIVERSITY PRESS
New York and London
www.nyupress.org

Library of Congress Cataloging-in-Publication Data
American Catholic history : a documentary reader / edited by Mark Massa
with Catherine Osborne.
p.   cm.
Includes bibliographical references and index.
ISBN-13: 978-0-8147-5745-1 (cl : alk. paper)
ISBN-10: 0-8147-5745-6 (cl : alk. paper)
ISBN-13: 978-0-8147-5746-8 (pb : alk. paper)
ISBN-10: 0-8147-5746-4 (pb : alk. paper)
1. Catholic Church—United States—History.   2. United States—Church
history.   I. Massa, Mark Stephen. II. Osborne, Catherine.
BX1406.3.A489 2008
282'.73—dc22   2007043267

New York University Press books are printed on acid-free paper,
and their binding materials are chosen for strength and durability.

Manufactured in the United States of America

c 10 9 8 7 6 5 4 3 2 1
p 10 9 8 7 6 5 4 3 2 1

To old and dear friends, Ruth and Mike Lipper,
who supported me in this project as in so much else that
has made the Curran Center possible.   —M.M.

For my parents.   —C.O.

Contents

Acknowledgments

At the Francis and Ann Curran Center for American Catholic Studies at Fordham University, we thank Jim Fisher, Maria Terzulli, Jack Downey, and especially Alex Sacco for his assistance on this project.

Robert McClory and Jaime Vidal generously provided photocopies of otherwise unobtainable documents. Many individuals and institutions graciously granted us permission to reprint documents and photographs not in the public domain. We would especially like to acknowledge the work of the editors of the two major multi-volume collections of American Catholic primary sources: John Tracy Ellis's essential *Documents of American Catholic History* and the far more wide-ranging and up-to-date *American Catholic Identities: A Documentary History*, edited by Christopher J. Kauffman along with many other scholars.

We are grateful for the comments of three anonymous readers on our prospectus. Finally, we thank our editor, Jennifer Hammer of New York University Press, and her assistant, Emily Park, as well as the editorial and production staff of the press.

Introduction

It is difficult to date precisely the arrival of Catholicism in what is now the United States: we might choose one of the early Spanish exploratory journeys, or the founding of St. Augustine, Florida (the first permanent settlement in present-day U.S. territory), in 1565, or the 1634 arrival of the ships *Ark* and *Dove* in the new colony of Maryland, conceived partly as a safe haven for Catholic colonists, or the ordination of John Carroll as the first bishop of the United States in 1790. It is equally difficult to chart a single "American Catholic history," no matter which beginning we might choose. The traditional approach to the American Catholic experience broke its history into five periods. The first era, the "colonial," lasted from 1492 to the 1660s. The second was the "penal period," so-called because new laws passed by the British Parliament deprived Catholics of basic civil rights, such as the right to serve on juries, carry firearms, or hold certain public offices; this stage lasted from the 1660s to the American Revolution. The "national" period refers to the years between 1776 and the 1830s, when native-born leaders like John Carroll oversaw the construction of new institutions and dioceses. The era of the "immigrant church," from the 1830s to the 1940s, was regarded as a century during which immigrants overwhelmed Anglo-American Catholics and *became* the church, due to a massive influx of Irish, German, Italian, and Eastern European Catholics. Finally, the traditional model referred to the period from World War II to the present as the era of "modern American Catholicism."

These five stages of American Catholic history make sense from the perspective of strictly institutional history, but there are a number of problems with its presuppositions—problems which the new discipline of American Catholic Studies tries to address. The five-periods approach presupposes that the Catholic Church in the United States is primarily composed of institutions: bishops appointed, new dioceses created, Catholic colleges founded, orders of sisters invited to run schools, etcetera. It ignores or minimizes the perspective of the vast numbers of Catholics who did not hold positions of decision-making power. American Catholic Studies, without ignoring institutional history, also considers the concerns and beliefs of the majority of American Catholics who were and are lay-people and whose Catholicism has been focused primarily on practice and prayer. In particular, this updated approach of American Catholic Studies tends to make a special effort to look at the history of women and ethnic minorities, who have been almost invisible in the accepted story (with the exception of mother foundresses of religious orders), despite the fact that the majority of American Catholics have always been women and despite the significant presence (even before the massive influx of Latino and Asian immigration in the latter part of the twentieth century) of non-European Catholics. Given the complexity that American Catholic Studies is bringing to the foreground, it makes sense for students to ask: what (and who) do we mean when we say "American," "Catholic," and especially "American Catholic"? Does a single historical narrative, neatly divided into five parts, continue to make sense of the data available?

In the past—and even today—answering these questions might have meant taking courses in a wide variety of university departments: history, literature, sociology, religious studies, and theology, to name a few. Each course might have understood the heart of American Catholic identity to lie in a different area—theology focusing on the distinctive belief systems of the church; sociology on the actual practice and worship habits of Catholics; history on the church's structural characteristics, or its immigrant identity, or the biographies of bishops. It is the contention of this volume that *all* of these approaches have merit.

The relatively new interdisciplinary field known as Catholic Studies conceives of Catholicism as something like a "solid state system." That is, rather than understanding Catholic identity as *primarily* about theology, or *chiefly* about worship, or *really* about the way the church is structured, Catholic Studies approaches Catholic Christianity as a densely interrelated network of beliefs, practices, church structures, and cultural artifacts that form one "field"—all the parts of which are related to all the other parts. From this perspective there is not so much a center to American Catholic identity as a collection of tightly interwoven multiple centers.

According to this interdisciplinary approach, then, one cannot really understand Catholic theology without also understanding liturgical worship, and the historical context in which that worship took place. Likewise, this approach suggests that a careful analysis of the literature produced by Catholics offers an important lens for viewing what Catholics believe about right and wrong (ethics), about the "end" or meaning of things (called "teleology" in theology), and about Catholic identity in a pluralistic culture. In short, Catholic Studies believes that everything is related to everything else, and to understand one thing well, scholars must study a host of other things related to it. Literature, history, social science, and popular culture, as well as theology and philosophy, have much to contribute to a full understanding of the term "American Catholicism." This documentary reader, then, draws on a wide variety of sources to help students develop this more extensive vision of Catholic history, culture, and identity in the United States.

This collection is focused on texts produced in North America from the earliest missionary voyages to North America in the sixteenth century up to the present day. A very small percentage of texts are European in origin, but have been included because they had an outsized impact on the American scene. We have selected and introduced particular texts in the belief that the best way for students to understand the complex history, beliefs, and practices of what became North American Catholicism is for them to grapple directly, and without elaborate introductions and interpretations, with important texts from American Catholicism's past. Thus our introductions to the texts are brief, offering historical and biographical data to help students understand the context and cultural significance of each text, but minimizing editorial judgment. We have sought both to provide maximum space for the actual texts and to invite readers to interpret these texts for themselves. As you read, you might keep in mind a variety of questions. First and foremost, *what "question" is this document addressing?* That is, in what historical circumstances did the writer feel the need to put these words to paper? Second, *what is the argument of the document and how is it constructed?* That is, what is the point the writer is making and what evidence does he or she advance to support the point? Third, *how does the social location of the writer affect his or her "answer"?* That is, what are the circumstances of the writer (in terms of nationality, race, class, gender, job description, etc.) and how do these circumstances affect the viewpoint he or she offers in response to the issue addressed? Finally, of course, we should ask of any document in this collection, *how can we apply this document to an understanding of "American Catholic identity"?* That is, if someone asked you tomorrow to tell them what it means to be American and Catholic, how might you refer to this document in giving your answer? What does this document suggest about the ways American Catholics have conceived of their own and others' identities? Do you think this document even *has* such an application, or is it only an example of the writer's personal circumstances and agenda?

Students of the American Catholic past and even present must sometimes wrestle with dense but significant letters, diaries, newspaper articles, and theological reflections—sometimes in obscure and initially hard-to-understand language—to get a sense of what real Catholics in this country have thought, believed, feared, and dreamed in the past. We believe that it is important to go directly to the sources, in addition to looking at culture at one remove, through the words of historians or teachers. Scholars sometimes use the term "distanciation" to describe the strange and salutary sense of disorientation that may come over us on reading directly words written by others, strangers. This term refers to the belief that people in the past were as different from us ("distant") as they were similar. Inexperienced students of history often believe that the people of the past were just like us, but dressed differently; or that they shared the same worldview as contemporary people, but used different words to describe that world. Most Catholic Studies scholars would disagree with such a belief: sixteenth-century Catholic explorers, or nineteenth-century nuns opening schools on the prairies of the American Midwest, actually saw the "real world" in a different way from contemporary Catholics, and we hope that the texts offered here will help students to understand both the similarities and the differences—the cultural "distance" as well as the closeness—between us and them.

Although this reader does take an interdisciplinary approach, we understand the texts here as historically conditioned (colloquially, we might say that they were products of their times.) Thus the volume has been broken up into sections that are *internally* chronological. This internal chronological approach within each of the five sections is balanced by a larger set of thematic concerns that shapes the entire work and has shaped our choice of selections. This thematic approach to American Catholic thought and culture argues that to really understand the past, it is necessary to offer much more than a simple narration of "this happened then, followed by that." Such an approach to the past is chronology, but hardly "history" in its deepest and most important sense.

The final presupposition of this reader is that history cannot be understood as a single, unified stream, all flowing in the same direction. Rather, certain themes—like the problem of being "outside" mainstream culture, explored in Part B of this reader—defy a neat historical resolution, for they are never solved or understood in any definitive way. Certain historically specific forms of the problem might be resolved, but larger questions and patterns reappear in new dress later on. "Outsiderhood" as a locus of identity—which for American Catholics has been a result of being a religious minority within an overwhelmingly Protestant culture—has not disappeared in the twentieth century after a series of battles fought in the eighteenth and nineteenth centuries. Rather, "outsiderhood" has manifested itself in different ways in the twenty-first century, even with Catholics representing the single largest religious group in the United States. Hispanic Catholics—now the single largest non-European group within American Catholicism—perceive themselves as "outsiders" within their own church, forcing the American Catholic community to re-examine what being "inside" the church is about. Meanwhile, in the early 1980s two important pastoral letters from the U.S. Catholic bishops (attacking both the use of nuclear weapons and devotion to "pure" capitalism) reminded all American Catholics that, as Catholics, they should avoid feeling too comfortable within mainstream American culture, "as we have here no lasting city, but seek one which is to come."

The remaining four sections of this reader offer students an opportunity to explore several other long-term themes in American Catholicism. Part A surveys the problem of the "frontier," referring to frontiers both territorial (the new lands and peoples encountered by European explorers and missionaries) and intellectual (the reconceptualizing of an ancient faith in new ways as European practices and answers came to seem inadequate in a new setting). Part A suggests that religious pluralism itself is an important contemporary "frontier" with which Catholics are presently grappling. Following Part B, on "outsiderhood," Part C, "Catholicism and the Intellectual Life," explores important currents within the American Catholic community as it sought to make sense of its ancient intellectual tradition within a democratic culture the French visitor Alexis de Tocqueville called "the first new nation." Older intellectual approaches inherited from Europe came to be applied in exciting new ways to interpret and defend American "inventions" like the separation of church and state and freedom of conscience—inventions that the older forms of Catholic thought condemned outright. Part D brings a variety of historical and contemporary approaches to bear on the knotty problems of Catholicism and politics. What kind of relationship should Catholicism have to American politics, laws, and justice? What about to the social politics of gender, race, and sexuality? What approach, if any, should Catholics take to economic issues? This section pays special attention to the theological and legal politics of birth control and sexuality in general. Finally, Part E gathers sources on worship and spirituality, with the understanding that, in the traditional phrase, *lex orandi lex credendi*—the law of prayer is the law of belief. In other words, if you want to get to the heart of what American Catholics have believed and do believe, what they were and are, it is crucial to examine the ways in which they have prayed.

Part I

Frontiers and Encounter

"Frontiers and Encounter" serves as an introduction to the study of an old faith on new shores. European Catholic explorers and missionaries reached what was then known as the "New World" in the sixteenth century, and shortly thereafter set up settlements in what is today Quebec, Florida, the American Southwest (Texas, New Mexico, Arizona), and California. The Roman Catholic Church came to play an important role in these European settlements very early on.

European Catholic missionaries arrived with the first explorers, and began a discussion within the Church about how best to go about making the native "heathens" into European-style Christians. Both the role of the Church in those early settlements and the missionary debates about native conversion have elicited much contemporary scholarly debate, in theology and in the fields of history, cultural anthropology, and cultural theory. Readers of the primary documents collected in this volume might find it useful to keep an eye on both the ethnocentric presuppositions of those early explorers and missionaries (i.e., their fairly uncritical presupposition that Europe was the center of the civilized world and carried beliefs and values that "others" needed), and on our own contemporary—and problematic—tendency to practice historical anachronism (i.e., our tendency to judge earlier or foreign civilizations by our own cultural standards).

The "frontiers" referred to in this section are both geographical and ideological: thus, some of the documents in this section deal with cultural frontiers, as illustrated for example in European encounters with Native Americans (Nos. 2, 4, 6, and 11); other documents refer to the ideological "frontier" of having to re-conceive a Christian tradition largely shaped by European culture in a wholly new set of cultural circumstances, where European precedents were either unwelcome or irrelevant (Nos. 5, 8, 9, 10, and 13). Still other frontiers refer to what the historian Arthur Schlesinger Jr. referred to as "America's oldest prejudice," anti-Catholicism (No. 7), a frontier that challenged Catholic Christians in America well into the twentieth century. Yet another frontier was embodied in the ways in which a young and activist Catholic community forced women religious to rethink their traditional ("cloistered") role within a Church with very immediate needs in schools, hospitals, and orphanages (No. 14).

The various "frontiers"—and the encounters they brought about—guaranteed that North American Catholicism would not simply be European Catholicism on new shores: as the historian Frederick Jackson Turner argued more than a century ago, the frontier itself played a major role in defining American civilization (and religion), and forced a Eurocentric form of Christianity to adapt in (and adopt) ways unforeseen in the "Old World."

1. "Sublimus Deus": Bull of Pope Paul III (1537)

In this extraordinarily important papal letter, Pope Paul III answered a request to pronounce on whether the natives "discovered" in the Americas were human beings capable of receiving the Catholic faith. Charles V, emperor of the Holy Roman Empire, feared that any recognition of the natives in the New World as fully human would hamper the territorial and mercenary goals of his European "envoys" by recognizing the natives' fundamental human rights. Charles therefore forced the pope to revoke "Sublimus Deus" and issue another bull in 1538 that allowed the emperor freer reign in his American colonies by downplaying the natives' essential humanity. While that later bull included significant concessions to Charles's imperial designs, the pope refused to totally revoke his declaration that the Native Americans were human beings capable of conversion. Nevertheless, the pope's partial bowing to political pressure from the emperor seriously hampered the efforts of Franciscan and Dominican missionaries to fight the rapacity of the conquistadores in dealing with the natives.

Paul III, Pope: To all faithful Christians to whom this writing may come: health in our Lord Jesus Christ and apostolic blessing.

The sublime God so loved the human race that He [*sic*] created man [*sic*] in such wise that he might participate, not only in the good that other creatures enjoy, but endowed him with capacity to attain to the inaccessible and invisible Supreme Good and behold it face to face; and since man, according to the testimony of the sacred scriptures, has been created to enjoy eternal life and happiness, which none may obtain save through faith in our Lord Jesus Christ, it is necessary that he should possess the nature and faculties enabling him to receive that faith; and that whoever is thus endowed should be capable of receiving that same faith. Nor is it credible that any one should possess so little understanding as to desire the faith and yet be destitute of the most necessary faculty to enable him to receive it. Hence Christ, who is the Truth itself, that has never failed and can never fail, said to the preachers of the faith whom He chose for that office: "Go and teach all nations." He said all, without exception, for all are capable of receiving the doctrines of the faith.

The enemy of the human race, who opposes all good deeds in order to bring men to destruction, beholding and envying this, invented a means never heard of before, by which he might hinder the preaching of God's word of Salvation to the people: he inspired his envoys who, to please him, have not hesitated to publish abroad that the Indians of the West and the South, and other people of whom We have recent knowledge, should be treated as dumb brutes created for our service, pretending that they are incapable of receiving the Catholic Faith.

We, who though unworthy, exercise on earth the power of our Lord and seek with all our might to bring those sheep of His flock who are outside into the fold committed to our charge, consider however that the Indians are truly men and that they are not only capable of understanding the Catholic Faith but, according to our information, they very much desire to receive it. Desiring to provide ample remedy for these evils, We define and declare by these our letters, or by any translation of them signed by any notary public and sealed, to which the same credit shall be given as to the originals, that—whatever may have been or may be said to the contrary notwithstanding—the said Indians and all other people who may later be discovered by Christians, are by no means to be deprived of their liberty or the possession of their property, even though they are outside the faith of Jesus Christ; and that they may and should, freely and legitimately, enjoy their liberty and the possession of their property. Nor should they be in any way enslaved: should the contrary happen, it shall be null and void.

2. Meeting of a Spanish Missionary with a Navajo Apache Chief (1630)

In 1630, Spanish Franciscan Alonso de Benavides published a memoir about his missionary work among the indigenous peoples of New Mexico. In this selection Benavides recounts his first meeting a Navajo Apache "chief" at a pueblo near Santa Fe. The Franciscan converted this leader with the help of already converted Indian "captains" present for the initial meeting.

I awaited him at the church, which on my instructions had been arranged nicely, with many lights burning because it was already night when they arrived. And as this nation is proud and spirited, I judged it better to receive this captain and those accompanying him in a manner different from that in which we received other nations, with whom, at the beginning, we sit on the ground, thus conforming ourselves to their simple ways until we can teach them better manners. But since the Apache nation is so haughty, I thought it better to deviate from this practice. So I ordered a chair placed on a rug close to the altar, and, seated there, I received him.

All the people of the pueblo came along ahead of him, and among the Christian captains came the Apache captain with four other of his captains. As soon as they had entered the church and recited a prayer at the altar, the chief captain of the Christians came up to me and kissed my feet —a thing which did not much displease me, although I had not anticipated it—and the strangers, following his example, did in like manner. After greeting me, the chief said that those (our) captains had gone to offer him peace on my behalf and on behalf of their own captains; and to be more certain of this, he had come personally to investigate. Immediately the chief captain of the pueblo arose and offered his own bow and arrows to the Apache, saying that there—before God present on that altar and before me, his priest—he was giving him those weapons as a pledge of his word that he would never violate the peace; and so he placed them on the altar. In order that he (the Apache) might see that all were of like opinion, he (the chief captain) asked the people if they all agreed to what he had said. With a loud cry, they replied that they did. Then the Apache captain selected from his quiver the arrow he considered most suitable, made of white flint and very sharp; and in the presence of all he pronounced these words in a loud voice: "I do not know who this one is whom you call God, but since you invoke him as witness and assurance of your promise that you will not, under any condition, break your word, he must be person of great power, authority, and goodness. So to that God, whoever he may be, I also, with this arrow in the hands of this priest, give my word and promise in the name of all my people, that on my part and on the part of my people peace and friendship will never be lacking." Accepting the arrow from him, I said that if he wished me to tell him who God was, he would enjoy hearing me, and all the more so after pledging to Him his word. He told me that he would.

So in very few words and in his own manner, I explained who God was: the Creator and Lord of all created things, Who had died on the cross in order to redeem us from eternal sufferings. I demonstrated all this to him by means of the painting on the altar, and I told him that whoever did not adore Him and was not baptized would be condemned and go to burn in those eternal torments. Because the word of God is so efficacious, and because it touched his heart so deeply, he turned with great emotion toward all the people; heaving a deep sigh, he said to them in a very loud voice: "O Teoas, how I envy you! You have here one who teaches you who God is, and things so good; while we have no such one, but live and die, going about these fields and mountains like deer and jackrabbits. Herewith I declare that I adore this God of Whom this priest speaks; and now that I know him, I offer peace and give my word that I shall maintain it with greater determination."

Tears flowing from his eyes, he fell upon his knees to kiss my feet. Whereupon I raised him up and embraced him with all the kindness I could, and then all the Christian captains also embraced him. I took this opportunity to have the bells rung and the trumpets and flageolets sounded—a thing which he enjoyed very much because it was the first time he had heard it. I immediately hung those arrows there on the altar as trophies of the divine word, even though it was announced by so humble a minister, and in this manner I declared it to the people of the pueblo so that they might render thanks to the divine Majesty for everything. Then the Christian captains took the guests away in order to lodge them in their homes, and I gave them what gifts I could.

3. THE ENGLISH JESUITS ESTABLISH THE MISSION OF MARYLAND (1634)

The three English Jesuits—John Altham, Thomas Gervase, and Andrew White—who wrote the account below left England by evading the authorities, seeking to establish a colony in "Virginia" [now the state of Maryland] where English Catholics could practice their faith. From the first the colony was made up of both Catholics and Protestants, so that the Jesuits had to proceed with both care and prudence, lest their efforts attract the attention of neighboring [Protestant] Virginia. The following report was written by White from St. Mary's City [now Annapolis] in April 1634, to the General Superior of the Jesuit order in Rome.

On the 22nd day of the month of November, in the year 1633, being St. Cecilia's Day, we set sail from Cowes, in the Isle of Wight. And after committing the principal parts of the ship to the protection of God especially, and of His most Holy Mother, and St. Ignatius, and all the guardian angels, we stopped opposite Yarmouth Castle, which is near the southern end of the same Island. Here we were received with a cheerful salute of artillery. Yet we were not without apprehension; for the sailors were murmuring among themselves, saying that they were expecting a messenger with letters from London, and from this it seemed that they were contriving to delay us. But God brought their plan to confusion. For that very night a strong wind arose; and a French cutter, which had put into the harbor with us, being forced to set sail, came near running into our pinnace. The latter, therefore, to avoid being run down, having been cut away and lost an anchor, set sail without delay; and since it was dangerous to drift about in that place, made haste to get farther out to sea. And so that we might not lose sight of our pinnace, we determined to follow. Thus the designs of the sailors, who were plotting against us, were frustrated. This happened on the 23rd of November, St. Clement's day, who—because he had been tied to an anchor and thrown into the sea, obtained the crown of martyrdom. . . .

We had delightful weather for three months, so that the captain and his men declared they had never seen it calmer or pleasanter; for we suffered no inconvenience, not even for a single hour. However, when I speak of three months, I do not mean that we were that long at sea, but I include the whole voyage, and also the time we stopped at the Antilles. For the actual voyage occupied only seven weeks and two days: and that is considered a quick passage. . . . If you except the usual sea-sickness, no one was attacked by any disease, until the Feast of the Nativity of our Lord. In order that that day might be better kept, wine was given out; and those who drank of it too freely were seized the next day with a fever; and of these, not long afterwards, about twelve died, among whom were two Catholics.

[Stops were made at Barbados and Virginia.] After being kindly treated for eight or nine days, we set sail on the third of March, and entering the Chesapeak Bay, we turned our course to the north to reach the Potomeack River, which we named after St. Gregory. Having now arrived at the wished-for country, we allotted names according to the circumstances. And indeed the Promontory, which is toward the south, we consecrated with the name St. Gregory [now Smith Point], naming the northern one [now Point Lookout] St. Michael's, in honor of all the angels. Never have I beheld a larger or more beautiful river. . . . Just at the mouth of the river, we observed the natives in arms. That night, fires blazed through the whole country, and since they had never seen such a large ship, messengers were sent in all directions, who reported that a "Canoe" like an island had come with as many men as there were trees in the woods. We went on, however, to Heron's Islands, so called from the immense numbers of these birds. The first island we came to [we called] St. Clement's Island, and as it has a sloping shore, there is no way of getting to it except by wading. Here the women, who had left the ship to do the washing, upset the boat and came near being drowned, losing also a large part of my linen clothes, no small loss in these parts. . . .

On the day of the Annunciation of the Most Holy Virgin in the year 1634, we celebrated mass for the first time. This had never been done before in this part of the world. After we completed the sacrifice, we took upon our shoulders a great cross, which we had hewn out of a tree, and—with the assistance of the Governor and his associates—we erected a trophy to Christ the Saviour, humbly reciting, on our bended knees, the Litanies of the Sacred Cross, with great emotion.

Now when the Governor had understood that many Princes were subject to the Emperor of the Pascatawaye, he determined to visit him, in order that, after explaining the reason for our voyage, and gaining his good will, he might secure an easier access to the others. And when he had learned that the Savages had fled inland, he went on to the city which takes its name from the river, being also called Potomeack. [The natives] willingly listened to Father John Altham [S.J.] who had been selected to accompany the Governor. And when the Father explained, as far as he could through the interpreter Henry Fleet, the errors of the heathen, he would every little while acknowledge his own; and when he was informed that we had come thither, not to make war, but out of good will towards them, in order to impart civilized instruction to his ignorant race, and show them the way to heaven, and at the same time with the intention of communicating to them the advantages of distant countries, he gave us to understand that he was pleased with our coming. The interpreter was one of the Protestants of Virginia. And so, as the Father could not stop for further discourse at the time, he promised he would return before very long. "That is just as I wish," said Archichu [the King's guardian], "we will eat at the same table; my followers too shall go to hunt for you, and we will have all things in common. . . ."

On account of our ignorance of their language, it does not yet appear what ideas they have besides, about Religion. We do not put much confidence in the Protestant interpreters: we have only hastily learned these few things. They acknowledge one God of Heaven, yet they pay him no outward worship. But they strive in every way to appease a certain imaginary spirit, which they call *Ochre,* that he may not hurt them. They worship corn and fire, as I hear, as Gods that are very bountiful to the human race. Some of our party report that they saw the following ceremony in the temple at Barchuxem. On an appointed day, all the men and women of every age, from several districts, gathered together round a large fire; the younger ones stood nearest the fire, behind these stood those who were older. Then they threw deer's fat on the fire, and lifting their hands to heaven, and raising their voices, they cried out *Yaho, Yaho.* Having completed the circuit, the pipe is taken out of the bag, and the powder called *Potu* is distributed to each one, as they stand near; this is lighted in the pipe, and each one, drawing smoke from the pipe, blows it over the several members of his body, and consecrates them. They were not allowed to learn any more, except that they seem to have some knowledge of the Flood, by which the world was destroyed, on account of the wickedness of mankind.

4. Jean de Brebeuf, S.J., "Instructions to the Fathers of Our Society Who Shall Be Sent to the Hurons" (1637)

French missionary Jean de Brebeuf wrote home in 1637, offering advice to fellow Jesuits undertaking the arduous mission of working among the native peoples of North America. As part of a much broader effort by Europeans to convert the natives from their tribal religions to Christianity, Brebeuf nonetheless embodied what is now termed the "indigenist" approach to mission work: that is, he advocated translating as much of the Christian message as could be done in local idioms and customs. For Breubeuf, this approach began with "externals"—such as how to behave in a canoe—a new experience for the aristocratic French Jesuits who peopled the mission.

The Fathers and brethren whom God shall call to the Holy Mission of the Hurons ought to exercise careful foresight in all the hardships, annoyances, and perils that must be encountered in making this journey, in order to be prepared for all emergencies that may arise.

You must have sincere affection for the Savages—looking upon them as ransomed by the blood of the son of God, and as our brethren with whom we are to pass the rest of our lives.

To conciliate the Savages, you must be careful never to make them wait for you in embarking. You must provide yourself with a tinder box or with a burning mirror, or with both, to furnish them fire in the daytime to light their pipes, and in the evening when they have to encamp; these little services win their hearts.

You should try to eat their sagamite or salmagundi in the way they prepare it, although it may be dirty, half-cooked, and very tasteless. As to the other numerous things which may be unpleasant, they must be endured for the love of God, without saying anything or appearing to notice them.

It is well at first to take everything they offer, although you may not be able to eat it; for, when one becomes somewhat accustomed to it, there is not too much. You must try to eat at daybreak unless you can take your meal with you in the canoe; for the day is very long, if you have to pass it without eating. The Barbarians eat only at Sunrise and Sunset, when they are on their journeys.

You must be prompt in embarking and disembarking; and tuck up your gowns so that they will not get wet, and so that you will not carry either water or sand into the canoe. To be properly dressed, you must have your feet and legs bare; while crossing the rapids you can wear your shoes, and in the long portages even your leggings.

You must conduct yourself as not to be at all troublesome to even one of these Barbarians. It is not well to ask many questions, nor should you yield to your desire to learn the language and to make observations on the way; this may be carried too far. You must relieve those in your canoe of this annoyance, especially as you cannot profit much by it during the work. Silence is a good equipment at such a time.

You must bear with their imperfections without saying a word, yes, even without seeming to notice them. Even if it be necessary to criticize anything, it must be done modestly, and with words and signs which evince love and not aversion. In short, you must try to be, and to appear, always cheerful. Each one should be provided with half a gross of awls, two or three dozen little knives, called jambettes [pocket knives], a hundred fishhooks, with some beads of plain and colored glass, with which to buy fish or other articles when the tribes meet together, so as to feast the Savages; and it would be well to say to them in the beginning: "Here is something with which to buy fish." Each one will try, at the portages, to carry some little thing, according to his strength: however little one carries, it greatly pleases the Savages, if it be only a kettle.

You must not be ceremonious with the Savages, but accept the comforts they offer you, such as a good place in the cabin. The greatest conveniences are attended with very great inconvenience, and these ceremonies offend them.

Be careful not to annoy anyone in the canoe with your hat; it would be better to take your nightcap. There is no impropriety among the Savages.

Do not undertake anything unless you desire to continue it; for example, do not begin to paddle unless you are inclined to continue paddling. Take from the start the place in the canoe that you wish to keep; do not lend them your garments unless you are willing to surrender them during the whole journey. It is easier to refuse at first than to ask them back, to change, or to desist afterwards.

Finally, understand that the Savages will retain the same opinion of you in their own country that they will have formed on the way; and one who has passed for an irritable and troublesome person will have considerable difficulty afterwards in removing this opinion. You have to do not only with those of your own canoe, but also (it must be stated) with all those of the country; you meet some today and others tomorrow who do not fail to inquire from those who brought you what sort of man you are. It is almost incredible, how they observe and remember even the slightest fault. When you meet the Savages on the way, as you cannot yet greet them with kind words, at least show them a cheerful face, and thus prove that you endure gaily the fatigues of the journey. You will thus have put to good use the hardships of the way, and already advanced considerably in gaining the affection of the Savages.

This is a lesson which is easy enough to learn, but very difficult to put into practice; for leaving a highly civilized community, you fall into the hands of barbarous people who care little for your Philosophy or your Theology. All the fine qualities which might make you loved and respected in France are like pearls trampled under the feet of swine, or rather of mules, which utterly despise you when they see you are not as good pack animals as they are. If you go naked, and carry the load of a horse upon your back, as they do, then you would be wise according to their doctrine, and would be recognized as a great man, otherwise not. Jesus Christ is our true greatness; it is He alone and His cross that should be sought in running after these people, for if you strive after anything else you will find naught but bodily and spiritual affliction. But having found Jesus Christ in His Cross, you have found the roses in the thorns, sweetness in bitterness, all in nothing.

5. Maryland's Act of Religious Toleration (1649)

The "Act Concerning Religion," published in April 1649 in the colony of Maryland, certainly deserves its place among the most famous documents of American colonial history. While Cornelius Calvert, the second Lord Baltimore and first governor of the colony, had maintained religious freedom for all Christians, Puritan settlers in the colonies had grown bolder in attacking their Catholic neighbors, especially after the triumphs of Oliver Cromwell's Puritan "Roundheads" in England. Lord Baltimore thus sought in this act of expediency to ensure that his policy of toleration would find legal establishment in one of the most liberal acts of religious toleration of the seventeenth century.

Fforasmuch as in a well governed and Christian Common Wealth matters bee taken into serious consideration and endeavored to bee settled. Be it therefore ordered and enacted . . . that whatsoever person or persona within this Province shall from henceforth blaspheme God or deny our Saviour Jesus Christ to bee the sonne of God, or shall deny the holy Trinity the ffather sonne and holy Ghost, or the Godhead of any of the said Three persons of Trinity or the Unity of the Godhead, shal be punished with death and confiscation or forfeiture of all his or her lands and goods to the Lord Proprietary and his heires . . . And bee it also enacted by the Authority and with the advise and consent aforesaid: That whatsoever person or persons shall from henceforth use or utter any reproachful words or Speeches concerning the blessed Virgin Mary the Mother of our Saviour or the holy apostles or Evangelists or any of them shall in such case for the first offence forfeit to the Lord Proprietary and his heirs the sume of ffive pound Sterling or the value thereof to be Leveyed on the goods and chattels of every such person soe offending. And be it also further Enacted by the same Authority that whatsoever person or persons shall from henceforth uppon any occasion of Offense or otherwise in a reproachful manner or Way declare call or denominate any person or persons whatsoever inhabiting within the Province an heritick, Schismatic, Idolator, puritan, Independent, Presbiterian popish priest, Jesuite, Lutheran, Calvenist, Anabaptist, Brownist, Antinomian, Roundhead, Separatist, or any other name or terme in a reproachfull manner relating to matter of Religion shall for every such Offence forfeit and loose tenne shillings sterling or the value thereof to bee leveyed on the good and chattels of every such Offender. . . . And whereas the inforceing of the conscience in matters of Religion hath frequently fallen out to be of dangerous Consequence in those Commonwealths where it hath been practiced. And for the more quiett and peaceable government of this Province, and the better to preserve mutuall Love and amity amongst the Inhabitants thereof. Be it Therefore enacted (except as in this present ct is before Declared and sett forth) that noe person or persons whatsoever within this Province, or the Islands, Ports, Harbors or Creekes, or havens thereunto belonging professing to believe in Jesus Christ, shall from henceforth bee any waies troubled, Molested or discountenanced for or in respect of his or her religion nor in the free exercise thereof within this Province or the Islands thereunto belonging nor any way compelled to the belief or exercise of any other Religion against his or her consent, soe as they may not be unfaithfull to the Lord Propriatory, or molest or conspire against the civill Government established or to bee established in this Province under him or his heires. And that all & every pson or psons that shall presume contrary to this Act and the true intent and meaning thereof directly or indirectly either in person or estate willfully to wrong disturbe trouble or molest any person whatsoever within this Province professing to believe in Jesus Christ for or in respect of his or her religion or the free exercise thereof within this Province other than is provided for in this Act that such pson or psons soe offending, shalbe compelled to pay trebble damages to the party soe wronged or molested, and for every such offence shall also forfeit 20s sterling in money or the value thereof.

6. Louis Hennepin's "Description of the Missionary Difficulties in Converting the Native Americans" (1697)

Louis Hennepin, a missionary belonging to the Recollects, a French Catholic order, accompanied the explorer La Salle in 1679 in exploring the western Great Lakes; in 1680 it was Hennepin himself who discovered and named St. Anthony's Falls in what is now Minneapolis, Minnesota. After these explorations Hennepin published an account of the difficulties both he and other missionaries encountered in attempting to convert the natives to Catholic Christianity.

Chapter XII: What Method Is Proper to Convert the Savages

Our ancient Missionary Recollects of Canada, and those that succeeded them in that work, have always given the opinion, and I now own 'tis mine, that the way to succeed in converting the Barbarians, is to endeavor to make them men before we go about to make them Christians. Now in order to civilize them, it is necessary that the Europeans should mix with them, and that they should dwell together, which can never be done for certain until the Colonies are augmented; but it must be acknowledged that the Company of Canada Merchants have made great Obstacles to the increasing of the Colonies; for out of greediness to keep all the Trade in their own hands, these gentlemen would never permit any particular Society to settle themselves in the Country, nor suffer the Missionaries to perswade the Barbarians to dwell constantly in one place. Yet before this be done, there's no way to convert these Unbelievers. Thus the covetousness of those who are for getting a great deal in a short time has mightily retarded the establishment of the Gospel among the Savages.

Hence it is manifest that the office of a Missionary is very troublesome and laborious amongst these numerous Nations, and it must be granted that it is necessary to spend many Years, and undergo a great deal of pains to civilize People so extremely stupid and barbarous.

And therefore, one should not venture without much caution, to administer the Sacraments to adult Persons who pretend themselves Converts; for we see that after so many Years of Mission, there has been but little progress made, though no pains have been wanting on the Missionary's hands.

So that Christianity is not like to gain much ground among the Savages until the Colonies are strengthened by a great Number of Inhabitants, artisans, and Workmen, and then the Treaty betwixt the Barbarians and us should be freer, and extend to all Europeans. But chiefly it should be endeavoured to fix the Barbarians to a certain dwelling Place, and introduce our Customs and Laws amongst them, furthered by the assistance of zealous People in Europe. Colleges might be founded to breed up the young Savages in the Christian Faith, which might in time contribute very much to the Conversion of their Country-men. This is a very proper Method without doubt, to strengthen the Temporal and Spiritual Interests of the Colonies. But the generality of Mankind are bent upon Gain and Traffick, and are little concerned to procure God's Blessing upon them, and endeavor the advancement of his Glory.

God is often pleas'd to prove his Children, and amongst them those that employ themselves in saving souls, by those means that most afflict them, but Dangers, Labors, Sufferings, and even Death it self would be welcome to them, provided in sacrificing themselves for the Salvation of their brethren, God would afford them the Consolation to see their Undertakings Crown'd with success to his Glory, and the Conversion of Infidels.

It is impossible for us to look upon so great a number of People as this relation mentions, and consider the little progress Religion has made among the Savages of these vast Countries, but we must needs admire the inscrutable Decrees of God, and cry out with the Apostle, "O the Depth of the Riches of the Wisdom and Knowledge of God!" A great number of learned secular priests, and zealous Religious men of our Order, have carried the light of the Gospel into all Parts of the Earth, and labor'd hard in the Lord's Vineyard. But God would have us know, that the Conversion of Souls is the Work of his Grace, the blessed Moments of which are not yet come. . . .

These miserable dark Creatures listen to all we say concerning our Mysteries, just as if it were a Song; they are naturally very vitious, and addicted to some superstitions that signifie nothing; their customs are savage, brutal and barbarous; they will suffer themselves to be baptized ten times a Day for a Glass of brandy, or a Pipe of tobacco, and offer their children to be baptiz'd, but without any Religious Motive. Those that one takes the pains to instruct, for a Winter together, as I my self taught some of them while I dwelt at Fort Frontenac, give no better sign of edification, than others in our Articles of Faith: so wrapt up are they in Insensibility to what concerns Religion, which occassion'd terrible Checks of Conscience in our Religious, in the beginning of their Mission among the People of Canada; they saw that the few Persons of years of Discretion that they had instructed and afterwards admitted to Baptism, soon fell again into their ordinary indifference for Salvation, and that the Children follow'd the unhappy Example of their Parents, insomuch that it was no better than a plain profanation of Baptism to administer it to them.

Chapter XIII: The Barbarians of North-America Don't Acknowledge Any God

Our ancient Missionaries Recollects were acquainted with several different Nations within the compass of 600 leagues in North-America. And I have been among many more, because I went farther than any of them, having made a Voyage all along the River of St. Lawrence. I observed, as [did] my predecessors, that the Savages don't want good sense in what concerns the general and particular Interest of their Nation. . . . But what I am astonished at, that whilst they are so clear sighted in their common Affair, they should have such extravagant notions of the concerns of Religion.

We must all of us own that almost all the Savages in general have no Belief of a Deity, and that they are incapable of the common and ordinary Arguments and Reasonings that the rest of Mankind are led by upon this Subject; so dark and stupid are their Understandings. At the same time we may acknowledge that now and then in some of them we discover some glimmerings of a confused Notion of God. Some will confess, but very cloudily, that the Sun is God. Others say that it is a Genius that rules the Air. Some again look upon the Heavens as a kind of Divinity. But these only make a shew of believing something that we can hardly guess at: we can't fix them to any settled Principle. The Nations Southward seem to believe [in] an Universal Spirit that governs all: they imagine, after a fashion, that there's a Spirit in every thing, even in those that are inanimate; and they address themselves to it sometimes, and beg something of it. . . .

All these Nations don't profess their belief of a Deity out of any respect to Religion: they talk of it ordinarily, as a thing they were prepossessed with, or frolicksomly, not regarding any thing they say themselves as otherwise than as a kind of Fable. They have no outward Ceremony to signify that they worship any Deity: there's no Sacrifice, Temple, nor any other Token of Religion amongst them. Their Dreams are to them instead of Prophecy, Inspiration, Laws, Commandments, and Rules. In all their Enterprizes in War, Peace, Commerce and Hunting, they regard them as Oracles. The Opinion they have of their Dreams draws them into a kind of necessity to be ruled by them, for they think it's an Universal Spirit that inspires them by Dreams, and adviseth them what to do. And they carry this so far that if their Dream orders them to kill a Person, or commit any other wicked Action, they presently execute it, and make satisfaction for it afterwards, as we shall show anon. The Parents dream for their Children, the Captains for their Village. There are some among them that take upon them to interpret Dreams, and explain them after their own fancy or inclination; and if their Interpretations don't prove true, they are lookt upon as Cheats ere the more for that.

Chapter XIV: Of the Great Difficulty in Converting the Savages

The great Insensibility of these Barbarians is caused principally by their Carelessness and neglect to be thoroughly instructed. They come to us, and attend to what we say, purely out of Ideleness, and natural Curiosity to converse with us, as we are with them; or rather they are tempted to follow us, by the Kindness and Flatteries we express towards them, or because of the Benefit their sick receive from us, or out of hope to gain by trafficking with us; or lastly, because we are Europeans, and they think us stouter than themselves, and hope we will defend them from their Enemies.

We teach them Prayers; but they repeat them like Songs, without any distinction by Faith. Those we have catechized a long time are very wavering, except some few. They renounce all, return into their Woods, and take up their old Superstitions upon the least Crotchet that comes into their Heads.

I don't know whether Predecessors had any Knowledge of a God, but it is certain their Language, which is very natural and expressive in every thing else, is so barren on this subject that we can't find any expression in it to signify the Deity, or any one of our mysteries, not even the most common. This gives us great perplexity when we would convert them. Another great Obstacle to their Conversion is this: most of them have several wives, and in the Northern parts they change them as often as they please. They can't conceive how people can tie themselves indissolubly to one person in Marriage. See how silly you are, cry they, when we argue with them about it. . . .

Another hindrance lies in a Custom of theirs, not to contradict any Man. They think every one ought to be left to his own Opinion, without being thwarted. They believe, or make as if they believed all you say to them; but it is their Insensibility and Indifference to every thing, especially Matters of Religion, which they never trouble themselves about. America is no place to go out of a desire to suffer Martyrdom, taking the Word in a Theological Sense: The Savages never put any Christian to death upon the score of his Religion; they leave every body at liberty in Belief. They like the outward Ceremonies of our Church, but no more. These Barbarians never make War, but for the Interest of their nation. They don't kill people, but in particular quarrels, or when they are brutish or drunk, or in revenge, or infatuated with a Dream, or some extravagant vision. They are incapable of taking away any Person's Life out of hatred to his Religion. . . . They are naturally Inconstant, Revilers, scoffers, and Lascivious. In short, among all the Vices they are addicted to, we can perceive no Principle of Religion or Morality; and to be sure this needs must render their Conversion extremely difficult.

7. Massachusetts's "Act Against Jesuits and Popish Priests" (1700)

In 1697, Earl Richard Coote, son of a famous English Protestant commander who persecuted Catholics in Ireland under Oliver Cromwell, was appointed governor of the colonies of Massachusetts, New York, and New Hampshire. Personally anti-Catholic, Coote believed that European Jesuits and other Catholic missionaries sought to stir up native peoples against British settlements in North America. The 1700 act reprinted here, which Coote published, followed an earlier such act of 1647, but this act was more severe in its lists of punishments of "Jesuits and Popish priests."

Whereas diverse Jesuits, priests, and popish missionaries have of late come, and for some time have had their residences in the remote parts of this province, and other his majesty's territories near adjacent, who by their subtile insinuations industriously labour to debauch, seduce, and withdraw the Indians from their due obedience unto his majesty, and to excite and stir them up, to sedition, rebellion, and open hostility against his Majesty's government; for the prevention whereof:

Be it enacted by His Excellency the Governor, Council, and Representatives in General Court assembled, and it is enacted by the authority of the same.

1) That all and every Jesuit, seminary priest, missionary or other spiritual or ecclesiastical person made or ordained by any authority, power or jurisdiction derived, challenged or pretended from the pope or see of Rome, now residing within this province or any part thereof, shall depart from and out of the same at or before the tenth day of September next, in this present year one thousand and seven hundred.

And be it further enacted by the authority aforesaid,

2) That all and every Jesuit, seminary priest, missionary, or other spiritual or ecclesiastical person made or ordained by any authority, power or jurisdiction, derived, challenged, or pretended from the pope or see of Rome, or that shall profess himselfe or otherwise appear to be such by practicing and teaching of others to say any popish prayers, by celebrating masses, granting of absolutions, or using any other of the Romish ceremonies and rites of worship, by or of what name, title or degree soever such person shall be called or named, who shall continue, abide, remain or come into this province, or any part thereof, after the tenth day of September aforesaid, shall be deemed and accounted an incendiary and disturber of the publick peace and safety, and an enemy to the true Christian religion, and shall be adjudged to suffer perpetual imprisonment; and if any person, being so sentenced and actually imprisoned, shall break prison and make his escape, and be afterwards re-taken, shall be punished with death.

And further it is enacted,

3) That every person which shall willingly receive, harbour, conceal, aid or succour any Jesuit, priest, missionary or other ecclesiastical person of the Romish clergy, knowing him to be such, shall be fined two hundred pounds, one moiety thereof to be unto his majesty for and towards the support of the government of this province, and the other moiety to the informer; and such person shall be further punished by being set in the pillory on three several days, and also be bound to the good behaviour at the discretion of the court. . . .

And further be it enacted by the authority aforesaid,

5) That it shall and may be lawful to and for every justice of the peace to cause any person or persons suspected of being a Jesuit, seminary priest, or of the Romish clergy, to be apprehended and convented before himself or some other of his majesties justices; and if such person do not give satisfactory account of himself, he shall be committed to prison in order to a tryal. And it shall and may be lawful to and for any person or persons to apprehend without a warrant any Jesuit, seminary priest or other of the Romish clergy as aforesaid, and to convent him before the governour or any two of the council, to be examined and imprisoned in order to a tryal, unless he give satisfactory accompt of himselfe. And as it will be esteemed and accepted as a good service done for the king by the person who shall seize and apprehend any Jesuit, priest, missionary, or Romish ecclesiastic as aforesaid, so the governour, with the advice and consent of the council, may suitably reward him as they think fit; provided this act shall not extend or be construed to extend to any of the Romish clergy which shall happen to be shipwrackt, or through other adversity shall be cast on shore, or driven into this province, so as he continue or abide no longer within the same than until he may have opportunity of passage for his departure; so also as such person immediately upon his arrival shall forthwith attend the governor, if near to the place of his residence, or otherwise on one or more of the council or next justices of the peace, and acquaint them with his circumstances, and observe the directions which they shall give him, during his stay in the province.

8. FERDINAND FARMER'S REPORT ON CATHOLICISM IN THE ENGLISH COLONIES (1773)

Farmer, a Jesuit living and working in colonial Philadelphia in the years leading up to the American Revolution, wrote the following letter to fellow Jesuit Bernard Well in Canada regarding the state of Catholicism in the English colonies. Behind the proper phrases of Farmer's letter lay a tense religious and political situation: the American colonies had no resident Catholic bishop, answering rather to the distant Vicar Apostolic in London in the place of a local bishop. In 1771, officials in Rome suggested that the Bishop of Quebec, Joseph-Olivier Briand, take responsibility for the American colonies, visiting them to perform the sacrament of confirmation and to formally dedicate churches. After conferring with the other members of the Society of Jesus who made up the great majority of priests in the colonies ["our society"], Farmer penned this report.

Reverend Father in Christ,

Your Reverence desires to know the state of our Missions. I shall describe them briefly. In only two of the several English Provinces or Colonies is the Catholic religion tolerated, namely in Maryland and Pennsylvania; in the latter in virtue of a Royal Charter given to the founder of the Colony; in the former more from ancient possession than owing to any right. In Pennsylvania, by virtue of a Royal deed, all religions are tolerated, not that each one is free to publicly perform the rites of his religion, but in this sense that he may accomplish them in private, and that he may be in no way compelled by anyone to share in any exercise whatsoever of another Religion than his own.

As, however, the oath must be exacted of all such as desire to be numbered among the born subjects of the Kingdom, or hold divers offices in the Commonwealth, contains a renunciation of the Catholic religion, none of our faith can obtain the like favors. In Pennsylvania there are presently five Missionaries, one Englishmen and four Germans, who attend with no mean labor to small congregations of men nearly all poor and widely scattered throughout the Province. In Philadelphia, however, where reside two missionaries, there is a greater number of souls comprising men of different nationalities. In Maryland, there are both more missionaries and a greater and better number of faithful, but, as I already mentioned, they enjoy less liberty than that which we here enjoy. All of these Missionaries are of our society; the Superior resides in Maryland. . . .

From the foregoing it is easy to see that the Catholic Religion is practiced with far greater authority and freedom in Canada than in our own country. Wherefore it is most certain that the advent in our midst of the right Reverend and Illustrious [Bishop of Quebec] would create great disturbances, with the danger of depriving us of the paltry privileges we are now enjoying, especially in Maryland where, as already mentioned, the exercise, even in private, of our Religion rests upon no authority. For the same reason, when several years ago the Vicar Apostolic of London intended to send some one hither for the purpose either of visiting or of giving Confirmation, the gentlemen of Maryland placed under our care, by a letter to the right reverend Vicar, informed him of the danger to which they were exposed; wherefore the said Vicar, under whom are all these colonies, gave up his intention.

I do not wish you to understand by this that we are not greatly desirous of having Confirmation administered to those of our flock born in this country, but that it is plain to our eyes, being given especially the character of Americans, that such rite could not safely be conferred by a person established in dignity. For it is incredible how hateful to non-Catholics in all parts of America is the very name of Bishop, even to such as should be members of the Church which is called Anglican. Whence many considered it a most unworthy measure that a Bishop be granted to the Canadians; and, as for several years past the question is being agitated in England of establishing in these Provinces a Protestant Bishop of the Anglican Communion, so many obstacles were found, due especially to the character of the Americans (of whom most of the early colonists were dissidents from the Anglicans, not to mention such as left our own faith) that nothing has as yet been effected. Hardly can I persuade myself that the Right Reverend [Bishop] might succeed in obtaining from the Governor of Canada or from the King, the faculty of exercising his power beyond the limits of the Provinces belonging formerly to the Canadian government, and lately ceded by treaty to the English.

From Europe we have received no letters for several months past, so that we are ignorant as to what may be the state of our society. However, from what we learned last year from Ours, and also from what the newspapers announce, we justly infer that our interests in Rome are not succeeding favourably, though that doth succeed favourably whichsoever it pleaseth Divine Providence to ordain.

Your Reverence will excuse me for not having written this more neatly, as in this city, especially at the present time, we are very busy with various labors of our ministry. I urgently recommend myself in all holy intentions.

Of Your Reverence the most humble servant in Christ,

Ferdinand Farmer, S.J.

9. The First American Report to Propaganda Fide on Catholicism in the United States (1785)

In March 1785, Jesuit John Carroll, the superior in charge of the "American mission"—and destined in 1790 to become America's first Catholic bishop— wrote a report to the Roman office in charge of Catholic missionary activity, the Propaganda Fide. The specific event that demanded Carroll's report was a scurrilous accusation brought against American Catholics by an ex-priest, Charles Wharton. The subtext of Carroll's report, then, was the effort to explain the New World context of Catholicism to Roman officials who misunderstood and/or distrusted separation of church and state, the voluntary nature of religion in the new United States, and so forth.

Concerning the State of Religion in the United States of America

1. Of the Number of Catholics in the United States

There are in Maryland about 15,800 Catholics; of these there are about 9,000 freemen, adults or over twelve years of age; children under that age, about 3,000; and above that number, of slaves of all ages of African origin, called negroes. There are in Pennsylvania about 7,000, very few of whom are negroes, and the Catholics are less scattered and live nearer each other. There are not more than 200 in Virginia who are visited four or five times a year by a priest. Many other Catholics are said to be scattered in that and other States, who are utterly deprived of all religious ministry. In the State of New York I hear that there are at least 1,500. (Would that some spiritual succor could be afforded them!) They have recently sent for a Franciscan Father from Ireland, and he is said to have the best testimonials as to his learning and life. . . . I was for a time in doubt whether I could properly approve this priest for the administration of the sacraments. I have now, however, decided, especially as the feast of Easter is so near, to consider him as one of my fellow-priests, and to grant him faculties, and I trust that my decision will meet your approbation.

As to the Catholics who are in the territory bordering on the river called Mississippi and in all that region which following that river extends to the Atlantic Ocean, and from it extends to the limits of Carolina, Virginia, and Pennsylvania—this tract of country contains, I hear, many Catholics, formerly Canadians, who speak French, and I hear that they are destitute of priests. Before I received your Eminence's letters there went to them a priest, German by birth, but who came last from France; he professes to belong to the Carmelite order: he was furnished with no sufficient testimonials that he was sent by his lawful superior. What he is doing and what is the condition of the Church in those parts, I expect soon to learn. The jurisdiction of the Bishop of Quebec formerly extended to some part of that region; but I do not know whether he wishes to exercise any authority there now, that all these parts are subjects to the United States.

2. On the Condition, Piety, and Defects of Catholics

In Maryland a few of the leading more wealthy families still profess the Catholic faith introduced at the very foundation of the province by their ancestors. The greater part of them are planters and in Pennsylvania almost all are farmers, except the merchants and mechanics living in Philadelphia. As for piety, they are for the most part sufficiently assiduous in the exercise of religion and in frequenting the sacraments, but they lack that fervor, which frequent appeals to the sentiment of piety usually produce, as many congregations hear the word of God only once a month, and sometimes only once in two months. We are reduced to this by want of priests, by the distance of congregations from each other and by difficulty of traveling. This refers to Catholics born here, for the condition of the Catholics who in great numbers are flowing in here from different countries of Europe, is very different. For while there are few of our native Catholics who do not approach the sacraments of Penance and the Holy Eucharist at least once a year, especially in Easter time, you can scarcely find any among the newcomers who discharge this duty of religion, and there is every reason to fear that the example will be very pernicious especially in commercial towns. The abuses that have grown among Catholics are chiefly those that result with unavoidable intercourse with non-Catholics, and the examples thence derived: namely more free intercourse between young people of opposite sexes than is compatible with chastity in mind and body; too great fondness for dances and similar amusements; and an incredible eagerness, especially in girls, for reading love stories which are brought over in great quantities from Europe. Then among other things, a general lack of care in instructing their children and especially the negro slaves in their religion, as these people are kept constantly at work, so that they rarely hear any instructions from the priest, unless they can spend a short time with one; and most of them are consequently very dull in faith and depraved in morals. It can scarcely be believed how much trouble and care they give the pastors of souls.

3. Of the Numbers of Priests, Their Qualifications, Character, and Means of Support.

There are nineteen priests in Maryland and five in Pennsylvania. Of these two are more than seventy years old, and three others very near that age: and they are consequently almost entirely unfit to undergo the hardships without which the Vineyard of the Lord cannot be cultivated. Of the remaining priests some are in very bad health, and there is one recently approved by me for a few months only, that in the extreme want of priests I may give him a trial: for some things were reported of him which made me averse to employing him. I will watch him carefully, and if anything occurs unworthy of priestly gravity I will recall the faculties granted, whatever inconvenience this may bring to many Catholics. For I am convinced that the Catholic faith will suffer less harm if for a short time there is no priest in a place, than, if living as we do among fellow-citizens of another religion, we admit to the discharge of the sacred ministry—I do not say bad priests—but incautious and imprudent priests. All the other clergymen lead a life full of labour, as each one attends congregations far apart, and has to be riding constantly and with great fatigue, especially to sick calls. Priests are maintained chiefly from the proceeds of the estates; elsewhere by the liberality of Catholics. There is properly no ecclesiastical property here, for the property by which priests are supported is held in the names of individuals and transferred by will to devisees. This course was rendered necessary when the Catholic religion was cramped here by laws, and no remedy has yet been found for this difficulty, although we made an earnest effort last year.

John Carroll

10. John Carroll's Letter on Lay Trusteeism in New York City (1786)

The most serious organizational issue that confronted the U.S. Catholic Church in the two decades after the American Revolution was that of lay trusteeism. Many American Catholics sought to organize their parishes democratically on the congregational model of the Protestant churches around them, in which the congregation elected lay trustees to own the parish property, selected and paid the pastor, took charge of parish finances, etcetera. St. Peter's Church in New York City was the site of an especially acrimonious battle between the priest serving the congregation, Irish-born Charles Whelan, and the congregation. Leaders of the congregation wrote to John Carroll, the ecclesiastical superior of the young Catholic Church (and on the verge of being made its first bishop), asking him to replace Whelan with another Irish-born priest whom they preferred, Andrew Nugent. Carroll's reply [below] resulted in a schism within the congregation, resolved a year later with the coming of a third priest to restore order in the parish.

Gentlemen:

I was honored yesterday at the same time with your letters of Dec. 22, 1785 and January 11, 1786. You did me justice in supposing that the former was delayed on its way or had miscarried; for certainly I should not have failed in my duty of immediately answering so respectable a part of the congregation. You will however readily conceive, that this is not an easy nor, allow me to say, a very agreeable office in the present instance. One circumstance indeed gives me comfort: you profess to have no other views than for the service and credit of religion; and as I make it my endeavor to be influenced solely by the same motive, I trust that proposing to ourselves the same end we shall likewise agree in the means of obtaining it.

The first advices of any disturbances among you were transmitted to me in letters from Messrs. Whelan and Nugent which I answered on the 17th and 18th inst. Both these gentlemen represented the steps taken as extreme and improper. . . . Having now received a communication of your sentiments, I shall likewise deliver mine with the respect due to your representations, and with the freedom and plainness becoming the responsible and burdensome office, of which I feel myself every day more unworthy, in proportion as the duties and the weight of it grow upon me.

But I must first state to you the previous information I had received . . . 2d, that an opinion was formed and propagated of the congregation having a right not only to choose such parish priest as is agreeable to them, but discharging him at pleasure, and that after such election, the bishop or other ecclesiastical superior cannot hinder him from exercising the usual functions. 3dly, that two of the congregation (by whose orders I am not informed) on Sunday, December 18th, after Divine Service and in the face of all present in the chapel, seized in a tumultuary manner and kept possession of the collection then made. The first part of this intelligence shocked me very much. . . . If ever the principles then laid down should become predominant, the unity and catholicity of our Church would be at an end; and it would be formed into distinct and independent societies, nearly in the same manner as the congregational Presbyterians of our neighboring New England States. A zealous clergyman performing his duty courageously and without respect of persons would be always liable to be the victim of his earnest endeavors to stop the progress of vice and evil example, and others more complying with the passions of some principal persons of the congregation would be substituted in his room; and if the ecclesiastical superior has no control in these instances, I will refer to your own judgment what the consequences may be. The great source of misconception in this matter is that an idea appears to be taken both by you and Mr. Whelan that the officiating clergyman at New York is a parish priest, whereas there is yet no such office in the United States. The hierarchy of our American Church not yet being constituted, no parishes are formed, and the clergy coming to the assistance of the faithful are but voluntary laborers in the vineyard of Christ, not vested with ordinary jurisdiction annexed to their office, but receiving it as delegated and extra hierarchical commission. Wherever parishes are established no doubt, a proper regard (and such as is suitable to our government) will be had to rights of the congregation in the mode of election and representation; and even now I shall ever pay to their wishes every deference consistent with the general welfare of religion, of which I hope to give proof in the sequel of this letter. The third article of my information was particularly mortifying; for I could not but fear that a step so violent, at such a time and place, and probably in the presence of other religionists, would breed disunion among yourselves and make a very disadvantageous impression, to the prejudice of the Catholic cause, so soon after the first introduction of public worship into your city.

I now return to the contents of your letters, and observe that after stating some censurable instances of Mr. Whelan's conduct, you desire me to remove him, and imply a desire that Mr. Nugent, as being very acceptable, may succeed to his office. I can assure you, Gentlemen, that I have a very advantageous opinion of Mr. Nugent's abilities, and he shewed me very good testimonials of his zeal and virtue. I repeatedly told him, as I did to many of yourselves, that nothing but my own want of sufficient authority prevented me from giving him every power requisite for the exercise of his ministry. I hoped before this to have that restriction of my authority removed, but as it is not, it remains still out of my power to employ him agreeably to your and my desires. If I am ever able to do it, I will certainly remember my assurances to him. But in the meantime what can I do? Can I revoke Mr. Whelan's faculties and leave so great a congregation without assistance? Can I deprive him, when neither his morals, his orthodoxy, or his assiduity have been impeached, especially while I am uncertain whether his removal be desired by a majority of the congregation? . . .

[At the close] of your last letter you make some mention of eventually having recourse to legal means to rid yourselves of Mr. Whelan. The insinuation makes me very unhappy. I cannot tell what assistance the laws might give you; but allow me to say that you can take no step so fatal to that respectability, in which as a religious Society you wish to stand, or more prejudicial to the Catholic cause. I must therefore entreat you to decline a design so pernicious to all your prospects.

11. A Report on Catholic Life in New Orleans by Its First Bishop (1795)

In 1795, the Cuban-born Luis Ignatio de Penalver y Cardenas arrived in New Orleans as the first bishop of the Diocese of Louisiana and the Two Floridas. Cardenas's report to his European superiors outlined what he perceived to be a number of problems: the presence of Protestants and "others" in the diverse city of New Orleans; the lack of state enforcement of Catholic "holy days of obligation"; and so forth. The bishop's first letter thus embodies in a clear way the dilemma of European church officials encountering the North American cultural and religious context.

Since my arrival in this town on the 17th of July, I have been studying with the keenest attention the character of its inhabitants, in order to regulate by ecclesiastical government in accordance with the information which I may obtain on this important subject.

On the 2nd of August, I began the discharge of my pastoral functions. I took possession without any difficulty of all the buildings appertaining to the church, and examined all the books, accounts, and other matters thereto relating. But as to the re-establishing the purity of religion, and reforming the manners of the people, which are the chief objects El Tridentino [the reforms of the Council of Trent] has in view, I have encountered many obstacles.

The inhabitants do not listen to, or if they do they disregard, all exhortations to maintain in its orthodoxy the Catholic faith, and to preserve the innocence of life. But without ceasing to pray to the Father of all mercies to send his light into the darkness which surrounds these people, I am putting into operation human means to remedy these evils, and I will submit to your Excellency those which I deem conducive to the interests of religion and of the state.

Because his Majesty tolerates here the Protestants, for sound reasons of state, the bad Christians, who are in large numbers in this colony, think that they are authorized to live without any religion at all. Many adults die without having received the sacrament of communion. Out of the eleven thousand souls composing this parish, hardly three to four hundred comply with the precept of partaking at least once a year of the Lord's Supper. Of the regiment of Louisiana, there are not above thirty, including officers and soldiers, who have discharged this sacred duty for the last three years. No more than about the fourth part of the population of the town ever attends Mass, and on Sundays only, and on those great holydays which require it imperiously. To do so on the other holydays they consider as a superfluous act of devotion to which they are not bound. Most of the married and unmarried men live in a state of concubinage, and there are fathers who procure courtesans for the use of their sons, whom they thus intentionally prevent from getting lawful wives. The marriage contract is one which, from a universal custom, admitting only a few accidental exceptions, is never entered into among the slaves. Fasting on Fridays, in Lent, and during *vigilas y temporas* [vigils of feast days and on Ember Days] is a thing unknown; and there are other mal-practices which denote the little of religion existing here among the inhabitants, and which demonstrate that there remains in their bosoms but a slight spark of the faith instilled into them at the baptismal font.

I presume that a large portion of these people are vassals of the king, because they live in his domain, and accept his favors. But I must speak the truth. His Majesty possesses their bodies and not their souls. Rebellion is in their hearts, and their minds are imbued with the maxims of democracy; and had they not for their chief so active and energetic a man as the present governor, there would long since have been an eruption of the pent-up volcano; and should another less sagacious chief ever forget the fermenting elements which are at work under ground, there can be no doubt but that there would be an explosion.

Their houses are full of books written against religion and the state. They are permitted to read them with impunity and, at the dinner table, they make use of the most shameful, lascivious, and sacrilegious songs.

This melancholy sketch of the religious and moral customs and conditions of the flock that has fallen to my lot, will make you understand the cause of whatever act of scandal may suddenly break out which, however, I shall strive to prevent; and the better to do so, I have used and am still using some means, which I intend as remedies, and which I am going to communicate to your Excellency.

The Spanish school, which has been established here at the expense of the Crown, is kept as it ought to be; but as there are others which are French, and of which one alone is opened by authority and with the regular license, and as I was ignorant of the faith professed by the teachers and of their morality, I have prescribed for them such regulations as are in conformity with the provisions of our legislation.

Excellent results are obtained from the convent of the Ursulines, in which a good many girls are educated; but their inclinations are so decidedly French that they have even refused to admit among them Spanish women who wished to become nuns, so long as these applicants should remain ignorant of the French idiom, and they have shed many tears on account of their being obliged to read their spiritual exercises in Spanish books, and to comply with the other duties of their community in the manner prescribed to them.

This is the nursery of those future matrons who will inculcate in their children the principles which they here imbibe. The education which they receive in this institution is the cause of their being less vicious than the other sex. As to what the boys are taught in the Spanish school, it is soon forgotten. Should their education be continued in a college, they would be confirmed in their religious principles, in the good habits given to them, and in their loyalty as faithful vassals to the Crown. But they leave the school when still very young, and return to the houses of their parents mostly situated in the country, where they neither hear the name of God nor of the King, but daily witness the corrupt morals of their parents.

12. THE FIRST COUNCIL OF BALTIMORE (1829)

In 1820 Archbishop James Whitfield met with fellow American bishops in Baltimore to discuss issues affecting the 500,000 Catholics then residing in the United States. The decrees that issued from this first national meeting of American Catholic bishops reflected the concerns of the Catholic community in the early national period: the threat of Protestant encroachment on the Catholic community; the challenges of celebrating sacraments in a language most people—Catholics included—didn't understand, and so on. The very calling of this first council reflected a newfound awareness that Catholicism in the young American nation had to face challenges unknown in Europe.

IX. [On Scripture]

Since the faithful protection of the deposit of sacred scripture, committed to the Church by the Lord, requires from the bishops that they strive with all their powers that the Word of God not be presented to the faithful contaminated by the deceits or negligence of people, we exhort most strongly all the pastors of souls of this Province that at all times, they have always before their eyes what has been decreed by the Council of Trent, by the supreme pontiff, especially what is recommended in the encyclical letters of Leo XII and Pius VIII, and by the Most Illustrious and Reverend John Carroll, Archbishop of Baltimore, one with the other bishops of his province, gathered in a meeting in 1810. Let them guard their flock from bibles spoiled by non-Catholics and permit them to be nourished with the untainted food of the Word of God as found in approved versions and editions. Therefore, we decree that the Douay version, which is accepted in all the churches where English is spoken, and which has been properly prepared by our predecessors, must by all means be retained. Likewise, the bishops should take care that, according to the most approved exemplar designated by them, in the future all editions of both the new and old testaments of the Douay version be amended. Annotations may be chosen only from the Fathers of the Church or from learned Catholic teachers.

XVI. [On Baptism]

Since it is of great importance that a general law—Baptism in the Church —be immediately kept in the regions to which the law is contrary to regional custom, nevertheless we leave it to the judgments of Bishops and Missionaries, [and emphasize] that whenever possible they support [the custom] urging the Faithful to bring infants to the church in order that Baptism can be conferred on them.

XVII. [Baptism of Non-Catholics]

We believe infants of non-Catholics who are brought by their parents are to be baptized as long as there is a probable hope of their Catholic education. Moreover, they [the priests] must certainly be solicitous that the sponsors be Catholic. Let the priest remember that whenever there is danger of death all infants not only may but must be baptized.

XX. [On Burials]

We have decided, according to the prescribed Roman rituals, that in administering the sacraments, and in performing burials, the priests are obliged, at all times, to use the Latin language. If they think it appropriate for the sake of instruction to translate into English, only that version which has been approved by the ordinary may be used. Wherever some other custom has arisen contrary to this decree, we wish its immediate abrogation.

XXIII. [Location of Eucharistic Service]

We decree that no priest, by force of general faculties that will apply to him for celebrating Mass in "any decent place," may do so in private buildings, unless in private stations, and in those buildings which the Ordinary will have designated or where there is need to give attention to the Missions, which are far from some churches. But if, at another time, the Ordinaries grant permission to celebrate in private buildings because of special circumstances, we recommend to them to grant this for one time or another.

13. MOTHER BENEDICTA RIEPP DEFENDS
NUNS' AUTONOMY (1857, 1859)

Benedicta Riepp, a German Benedictine nun working with women religious on the American frontier, found herself embroiled with the superior of the male branch of the order, Abbot Boniface Wimmer. Wimmer [the "he" mentioned below] believed that Benedictine nuns should work at the service of the brothers of the Order [as they had in Europe]. Riepp, however, recognized that the frontier conditions of American life demanded both more freedom for the nuns, and a new model of nuns' relationship to each other—bonding with other Benedictine religious women rather than with the brothers. Riepp's battles with Wimmer eventually led to her appeal to Rome to disentangle the female branch of her order from the oversight of Abbot Wimmer.

He always wanted sisters from St. Mary's to be moved [to his new foundation] because we were in want and suffered from hunger. Every time he came to St. Mary's there was quarreling, especially in the brothers' house, over the fact that he could not support more people. In spite of this, every time he came, which was not seldom, he brought at least one or two postulants or students, who had neither money nor clothes. . . .

For a time the sisters, especially the teachers, had to work at night to prepare for a small fair to provide money for the traveling expenses of the sisters going to the West and to buy a few pounds of white flour, coffee, etc., for the convent in St. Mary's. Within the last year four very young sisters died as a result of the heavy diet. More than two-thirds of the others were ailing because for the entire year, day after day, we had nothing but cornbread, black soup and noodles made of rye flour, or salted and half-spoiled beef, and all of this very sparingly. . . .

When I wanted to arrange a proper parlor, which would have cost but little, he did not permit it. Instead we had to use a real woodshed where I was forced to bring respectable people—a room in the inner part of the house. He expected the brothers to be with the sisters and work with them; the sisters should wash, sew, bake, etc., for the brothers; the brothers, again, should work for the sisters and this in every place where he would put sisters. Often quarrels and disunity arose, and finally even scuffles happened among the brothers. . . . The Superior, therefore, especially during the last half year, could do nothing anymore, because not she, but the Rt. Reverend Abbot, ruled.

*

I do not regret having had recourse to the Sacred Congregation. I intend only the common good of the Order and that each sister be secure in this as a result of everything being put in order and confirmed by the Holy see. We could then also proceed with assurance, not only insofar as each individual convent is concerned, but also in what especially concerns the spread of the women's branch of our holy Order. . . .

I readily agree that the Reverend Prelate [Wimmer] in every respect understands better than I do how to direct our whole order. In respect to our sisters, however, Your Eminence will agree with me, I am sure, that much, and especially what concerns the internal direction of the convent, should not always be left to men.

It would be my consolation and joy if our new foundations in America, of which there are four at present, were to remain united and have a common novitiate so that one spirit and one life could be preserved in the hearts of all the sisters. I believe that in America especially, the unity of the Order, particularly in what pertains to the Holy rule and the Statutes, could by a common bonding together be more securely and more easily guaranteed, fostered and preserved. Then one way of life and one love would obtain among all.

Unfortunately, I already see only too soon and too clearly that in our whole Order this spirit is gradually disappearing. This happens because the convent judges itself even now to be strong enough to stand alone and there arises in our sisters, in general, a coldness and strangeness to each other. The life of unity in love will slowly dissolve and be completely destroyed unless the Holy See again restores it.

FURTHER SUGGESTED READING

Felix Almaraz, "Transplanting 'Deep, Living Roots': Franciscan Missionaries and the Colonization of New Mexico, 1598–1616," in *Seeds of Struggle/Seeds of Faith: The Papers of the Cuarto Centennial Conference on the History of the Church in New Mexico*, ed. Thomas Steele (Albuquerque, N.M.: LPD Press, 1998).

Henry Warner Bowden, *American Indians and Christian Missions: Studies in Cultural Conflict* (Chicago: University of Chicago Press, 1981).

Jay P. Dolan and Allan Figueroa Deck, eds., *Hispanic Catholic Culture in the U.S.: Issues and Concerns* (Notre Dame, Ind.: University of Notre Dame Press, 1994).

Virgilio Elizondo, *Guadalupe: Mother of the New Creation* (Maryknoll, N.Y.: Orbis Books, 1997).

Francis F. Guest, "An Examination of the Theses of S. F. Cook on the Forced Conversion of Indians in the California Missions," *Southern California Missions* 61 (1979): 1–77.

Harold Courlander, *The Fourth World of the Hopis* (New York: Crown, 1971).

Sam D. Gill, *Native American Religions: An Introduction* (Belmont, Calif.: Wadsworth, 1983).

James P. Rhonda, "'We Are as Well as We Are': An Indian Critique of Seventeenth Century Christian Missions," *William and Mary Quarterly* 34 (1977): 67ff.

Thomas J. Steele, *Santos and Saints* (Albuquerque, N.M.: Ancient City Press, 1974).

Francis X. Talbot, *Saint Among the Hurons: The Life of Jean de Brebeuf* (New York: Harper, 1949).

Reuben Gold Thwaites, ed., *The Jesuit Relations and Allied Documents* (Cleveland: The Burrows Brothers, 1896–1901).

Frederick Jackson Turner, *Rereading Frederick Jackson Turner: The Significance of the Frontier in American History and Other Essays* (New York: H. Holt, 1994).

Christopher Vecsey, *Imagine Ourselves Richly: Mythic Narratives of North American Indians* (New Yolk: Crossroad, 1988).

Part II

Inside/Outside

In the past few decades a number of scholars studying American intellectual and cultural history have focused on what is called "alterity"—from the Latin *alter,* meaning "other"—as a central category for interpreting U.S. history. That is, these scholars have argued that "otherness"—being an "outsider" or a "stranger"—represents a privileged category for being an American. These scholars point to the first English-speaking settlements (Puritans forced to leave their churches in old England to establish their "outsider" religion in New England), the literary canon of our "best authors" (Ralph Waldo Emerson, Henry David Thoreau, Edgar Allan Poe, and Walt Whitman all being religious, literary, or stylistic outsiders to then dominant establishments), and to twentieth-century popular culture (cowboys and the "good cop" being on the margins of their respective cultures) as examples of such alterity.

The "alterity" addressed in this section refers to American Catholicism's own sense of being outside the religious mainstream: the vast majority of American citizens, in 1700 as in 2006, were and are evangelical Protestants, anomalously making American Catholicism—the largest single religious body in the United States—an "outsider" group. American Catholics thus spent much time, energy, and money constructing a "Catholic mini-state" —a vast network of schools, colleges, hospitals, orphanages—within the culture precisely because they were not welcome (or because they did not feel welcomed) in "mainstream" cultural institutions.

But the "inside/outside" dichotomy in this section also refers to American Catholicism's own ambivalence on "arriving" in the verdant pastures of middle-class affluence and acceptance by the twentieth century: when U.S. Catholics achieved "insider" status in terms of wealth, education, and cultural prominence, many Catholic leaders feared that such acceptance would sap the strong group identity and distinctive value system that had served the community so well in the nineteenth century and the first half of the twentieth.

Selections in this section include documents witnessing to the construction of an "outsider" Catholic mini-state (Nos. 3, 4, 5, and 7), as well as Catholic critiques of the American cultural mainstream (Nos. 2, 9, and 11). But selections also include critiques of the hegemonic status of "Anglo" and Eurocentric forms of Catholicism by Hispanic, African American, and women Catholics on the margins of their own Church (Nos. 8, 10, 12, and 14). Two selections offer the counterintuitive argument that Catholicism's very countercultural value system will eventually make it the majority faith of Americans (Nos. 1 and 6).

14. ALEXIS DE TOCQUEVILLE ON AMERICAN CATHOLICS IN THE NEW REPUBLIC (1835)

No foreign visitor to the United States has published a more important—or more perceptive—study of its culture than Alexis de Tocqueville. In May 1831, de Tocqueville arrived in the United States from France on an investigative tour of the American prison system, and ended up touring a large portion of the eastern United States until his departure in February 1832. The publication of the first volume of his study four years later [De la democratie en Amerique] witnessed to a perceptive observer whose study of America's political, social, and religious customs has become part of the canon of American cultural studies. De Tocqueville's counterintuitive observations about the place of Catholics in the overwhelmingly Protestant culture of America surprised his French reading audience.

About fifty years ago Ireland began to pour a Catholic population into the United States; and on their part, the Catholics of America made proselytes, so that, at the present moment more than a million Christians professing the truths of the Church of Rome are to be found in the Union. These Catholics are faithful to the observances of their religion; they are fervent and zealous in the belief of their doctrines. Yet they constitute the most republican and the most democratic class in the United States. This fact may surprise the observer at first, but the cause of it may easily be discovered upon reflection.

I think that the Catholic religion has erroneously been regarded as the natural enemy of democracy. Among the various sects of Christians, Catholicism seems to me, on the contrary, to be one of the most favorable to equality of conditions among men. In the Catholic Church the religious community is composed of only two elements: the priest and the people. The priest alone rises above the rank of his flock, and all below him are equal.

On doctrinal points the Catholic faith places all human capacities on the same level; it subjects the wise and ignorant, the man of genius and the vulgar crowd, to the details of the same creed; it imposes the same observances upon the rich and the needy, it inflicts the same austerities upon the strong and the weak; it listens to no compromise with mortal man, but, reducing all the human race to the same standard, it confounds all the distinctions of society at the foot of the same altar, even as they are confounded in the sight of God. If Catholicism predisposes the faithful to obedience, it certainly does not prepare them for inequality; but the contrary may be said of Protestantism, which generally tends to make men independent more than to render them equal. Catholicism is like an absolute monarchy: if the sovereign be removed, all the other classes of society are more equal than in republics.

It has not infrequently occurred that the Catholic priest has left the service of the altar to mix with the governing powers of society and to take his place among the civil ranks of men. This religious influence has sometimes been used to secure the duration of that political state of things to which he belonged. Thus we have seen Catholics taking the side of aristocracy from a religious motive. But no sooner is the priesthood entirely separated from the government, as is the case in the United States, than it is found that no class of men is more naturally disposed than the Catholics to transfer the doctrine of the equality of condition into the political world.

If, then, the Catholic citizens of the United States are forcibly led by the nature of their tenets to adopt democratic and republican principles, at least they are not necessarily opposed to them, and their social position, as well as their limited number, obliges them to adopt these opinions. Most of the Catholics are poor, and they have no chance of taking a part in the government unless it is open to all citizens. They constitute a minority, and all rights must be respected in order to ensure to them the free exercise of their own privileges. These two causes induce them, even unconsciously, to adopt political doctrines which they would perhaps support with less zeal if they were rich and preponderant.

The Catholic clergy of the United States have never attempted to oppose this political tendency; but they seek rather to justify it. The Catholic priests in America have divided the intellectual world into two parts: in the one they place the doctrines of revealed religion, which they assent to without discussion; in the other they leave those political truths which they believe the Deity has left open to free inquiry. Thus the Catholics of the United States are at the same time the most submissive believers and the most independent citizens. . . .

I showed in the First Part of this work how the American clergy stand aloof from secular affairs. This is the most obvious but not the only example of their self-restraint. In America religion is a distinct sphere, in which the priest is sovereign, but out of which he takes care never to go. Within its limits he is master of the mind; beyond them he leaves men to themselves and surrenders them to the independence and instability that belong to their nature and their age. I have seen no country in which Christianity is clothed with fewer forms, figures, and observances than in the United States, or where it presents more distinct, simple, and general notions to the mind. Although the Christians of America are divided into a multitude of sects, they all look upon their religion in the same light. This applies to Roman Catholics as well as to other forms of belief. There are no Roman Catholic priests who show less taste for the minute individual observances, for extraordinary or peculiar means of salvation, or who cling more to the spirit and less to the letter of the law than the Roman Catholic priests of the United States. Nowhere is that doctrine of the church which prohibits the worship reserved to God alone from being offered to the saints more clearly inculcated or more generally followed. Yet the Roman Catholics of America are very submissive and very sincere. . . .

America is the most democratic country in the world, and it is at the same time (according to reports worthy of belief) the country in which the Roman Catholic religion makes the most progress. At first sight this is surprising.

Two things must here be accurately distinguished: equality makes men want to form their own opinions; but on the other hand, it imbues them with the taste and the idea of unity, simplicity, and impartiality in the power that governs society. Men living in democratic times are therefore very prone to shake off all religious authority; but if they consent to subject themselves to any authority of this kind, they choose at least that it should be single and uniform. Religious powers not radiating from a common center are naturally repugnant to their minds; and they almost as readily conceive that there should be no religion as that there should be several.

At the present time, more than in any preceding age, Roman Catholics are seen to lapse into infidelity, and Protestants to be converted to Roman Catholicism. If you consider Catholicism within its own organization, it seems to be losing; if you consider it from outside, it seems to be gaining. Nor is this difficult to explain. The men of our days are naturally little disposed to believe; but as soon as they have any religion, they immediately find in themselves a latent instinct that urges them unconsciously towards Catholicism. Many of the doctrines and practices of the Roman Catholic Church astonish them, but they feel a secret admiration for its discipline, and its great unity attracts them. If Catholicism could at length withdraw itself from the political animosities to which it has given rise, I have hardly any doubt but that the same spirit of the age which appears to be so opposed to it would become so favorable as to admit of its great and sudden advancement.

One of the most ordinary weaknesses of the human intellect is to seek to reconcile contrary principles and to purchase peace at the expense of logic. Thus there have ever been and ever will be men who, after having submitted some portion of their religious belief to the principle of authority, will seek to exempt several other parts of their faith from it and to keep their minds floating at random between liberty and obedience. But I am inclined to believe that the number of these thinkers will be less in democratic than in other ages, and that our posterity will tend more and more to a division into only two parts, some relinquishing Christianity entirely and others returning to the Church of Rome.

15. Archbishop John Hughes Condemns the Public School Society of New York and New York Politicians (1841)

The New York Public School Society was organized by several Protestant churches in New York City, receiving tax monies to educate children of all denominations. But from the point of view of Catholics like the city's pugnacious bishop, "Dagger John" Hughes, the Society's schools violated the rights of Catholic children by forcing them to read from the King James [Authorized] version of the Bible, and sometimes even from Protestant tracts which attacked the Catholic Church as the "Whore of Babylon." Hughes objected to this system of education well before the famous 1841 speech recorded below, but made no headway with either the Society or the New York legislature. In October 1841, Hughes gave the speech recorded below to a hall packed with angry Catholic parents, calling for a third party "Catholic" ticket of candidates to get the attention of New York City and state legislators. Archbishop Hughes succeeded in his effort.

A crowded and highly respectable meeting of citizens favorable to a just and equitable system of Common Schools in the city of New York, was held on the 29th of October at Carroll Hall, in this city, pursuant to public notice. . . . Mr. Carroll, one of the Secretaries, read the following requisition for the meeting from one of the public papers:

"SCHOOL QUESTION: A general meeting of citizens favorable to such a system of Common Schools in the city of New York, as will extend the benefits of public education to the children of all denominations, without trenching on the religious rights of any, will be held at Carroll Hall, this evening, 29th inst., at half past seven o'clock. By order of the General Committee."

Bishop Hughes then rose and said: "I am delighted, gentlemen, to find that the forlorn and neglected children of the city of New York have yet so many friends as I now see assembled around me. Amidst the passions and prejudices of public men, it is still consoling to observe that the rights of those children to the benefits of education are advocated by so many friends, and certainly if you were to abandon them in this emergency, their prospects for the future would be hopeless. When I speak of their forlorn condition with regard to education, I do not mean that there are not schools erected, but that those schools are conducted under such a system, and on such principles, as necessarily prevent those children from attending them. The consequence has been as you know, that for sixteen years past, that portion of our citizens represented by this meeting have been obliged to provide separate schools, while they were taxed for the support of those from whose existence they derived no benefit.

"Those facts determined the origin of this question. Some have supposed that the grievance had its origin only with the time when the agitation and explanation of it were publicly commenced; but let them look at your efforts for years past in providing in providing education for your children, and ask yourselves whether you would have gone to second expenditure to provide a defective and inefficient education for your children if you could have permitted them to attend the schools already provided.

"But first I must say a few words in explanation of my own position in this matter. I was in Europe when the question was first brought before the public, and when I first heard of its agitation, I believed that we had but to make a full, fair, and candid statement of our grievances to honorable men in order to produce an acknowledgment of the injustice of employing the funds raised by taxing all for the benefit of a portion of Society, and to the exclusion of an entire class. [Cheers.] I have attended in this place and elsewhere meeting after meeting, during which we have explained the grounds of our objection to the present system of education. We have uniformly avoided all questions of a political character, and I have more than once expressed publicly, as I do now, my determination to retire from such meetings the moment any political question was introduced. It is not my province to mingle in politics. . . . The object of this meeting is, after all previous measures have been adopted, to see what means yet remain in your power for attaining the end for which you are contending. . . .

"Our adversaries accuse us of acting with interested motives in this matter. They say that we want a portion of the school fund for sectarian purposes, to apply it to the support and advancement of our religion. This we deny now, as we have done heretofore. . . . There is no such thing as a predominant religion, and the small minority is entitled to the same protection as the greatest majority. No denomination, whether numerous or not, can impose its religious views on a minority at the common expense of that minority and itself. That was the principle from the unjust operation of which we desired to be released. . . .

"We do not ask for sectarian schools. We do not ask that any portion of the public money should be confided to us for purposes of education. We do not ask for the privilege of teaching our religion at the public expense —such a demand would be absurd and would richly merit the rebuke which it could not escape. [But] in the Public Schools which were established according to the system now in force, our children had to study books which we could not approve. Religious exercises were used which we did not recognize, and our children were compelled to take part in them. Then we withdrew them from the schools and taught them with our own means. We do not want money from the school funds—all we desire is that it be administered in such a way as to promote the education of all. Now the Public School Society has introduced just so much of religious and sectarian teaching as it pleased them, in the plentitude of their irresponsible character, to import. They professed to exclude religion, and yet they introduced so much in quantity as they thought proper, and of such a quality as violated our religious rights. If our children cannot receive education without having their religious faith and feelings modeled by the Public School Society, then they cannot receive it from under the auspices of that institution, and if for these reasons they cannot receive it from that institution, it is tyranny to tax them for its support. We do not ask the introduction of religious teachings in any public school, but we contend that if such religious influences be brought to bear on the business of education, it shall be, so far as our children are concerned, in accordance with the religious belief of their parents and families. . . .

"We first laid our case before the Common Council. They disposed of it in a manner with which you are familiar. We then applied to the Legislature. It is now, in the order of things, to be referred to yourselves. [Cheers.] . . . You are now to decide whether your children shall be educated as others shall prescribe—receive instruction from such books as are repugnant to your religious feelings, and whether you shall be constrained to give your voice in favor of those who would perpetuate such a state of things. And here we see the effect of our admirable system of laws. We have it in our own power to remedy the evils of which we complain. It may truly be said to be a government of the people—based as it is on just and adequate representations, founded on a principle in which there is an implied contract between the voter and the voted for. But in relation to the candidates who have been placed in nomination for your suffrage at the present time, mark the cunning of the gentlemen opposed to you. They have so managed it that those candidates, if elected, would go to the legislature pledged to oppose your claim, so that when the representatives are assembled in Albany, it may be said that if you voted at all you voted in favor of that to which to which it has been said you were opposed—that you were satisfied in favor of the Public Schools as they are—that in your judgment those schools inculcate the proper amount of moral precept, and religion as we were once told in the 'legal quantity.' [Cheering and laughter.] The time, then, has now arrived when the fathers and the brothers and the uncles of the children who are excluded from those public schools should pass judgment on the evils of the present system. . . .

"But I call upon you to resist this Public School System, whether you are sustained by public men or not. You are called upon to join with your oppression and they leave you no alternative in voting. It may appear uncommon—it may seem to be inconsistent with my character that I should thus take an interest in this matter; and I should not, were it not a subject of extraordinary import. But there has been an invasion of your religious rights, and as the spiritual guardian of those now before me, I am bound to help their cause. If you are taxed, you must be protected. [Cheers.] Were the tax so imposed that each denomination might receive the benefits of its own quota, the case would be fair enough. We are willing to have any system that operates *equally*; but we will never submit to a direct violation of our rights. . . .

"The representatives of the neglected portion of the children in the various parts of the city have met, and have all united for the purpose of arranging a plan by which they may escape the miserable alternative of voting for their enemies, and they have prepared a ticket bearing on it the names of men who are all known as favorable to your cause." [Great cheering.] The Secretary then read the following list [of names]. . . .

"You have now, gentlemen, heard the names of men who are willing to risk themselves in support of your cause. You now, for the first time, find yourselves in the position to vote at least for yourselves. You have often voted for others, and they did not vote for you, but now you are determined to uphold with your own votes, your own rights." [Thunders of applause, which lasted several minutes.]

16. The Launching of the American Protestant Association against Catholics (1842)

The rapid growth in membership of the U.S. Catholic Church during the 1830s and 1840s worried many Protestant Americans; still other Americans worried that the massive tides of Irish and German immigrants—most of them Catholic—would lead to "native born citizens" losing their jobs to cheaper foreign-born labor. These fears found a focus in November 1842, when the Catholic bishop of Philadelphia, Francis Kenrick, petitioned the city's public school board against Catholic children having to use the King James [Protestant] Bible during religious exercises in the public schools. A group of 94 ministers met that same month in Philadelphia, representing twelve Protestant denominations, to organize the American Protestant Association (the "A.P.A.") to raise public awareness of what they termed the "Catholic threat" in their midst. Many Philadelphia Catholics blamed the A.P.A. for the public riots that broke out in the city in May and June 1844, in which thirteen people were killed and two Catholic churches were burned.

Whereas, we believe the system of Popery to be, in its principles and tendency, subversive of civil and religious liberty, and destructive to the spiritual welfare of men, we unite for the purpose of defending our Protestant interests against the great exertions now making to propagate that system in the United States; and adopt the following constitution:

Article I. This Society shall be called the American Protestant Association.

Article II. The objects of its formation, and for the attainment of which its efforts shall be directed, are:

1. The union and encouragement of Protestant ministers of the gospel, to give to their several congregations instruction on the differences between Protestantism and Popery.

2. To call attention to the necessity of a more extensive distribution and thorough study of the Holy Scriptures.

3. The circulation of books and tracts adapted to give information on the various errors of Popery in their history, tendency, and design.

4. To awaken the attention of the community to the dangers which threaten the liberties, and the public and domestic institutions, of these United States from the assaults of Romanism.

Article III. This Association shall be composed of all such persons as agree in adopting the purposes and principles of this constitution and contribute to the funds by which it is supported.

Article IV. The officers of this Association shall be a President, three Vice-Presidents, a treasurer, a corresponding secretary, a recording secretary, and two lay directors from each denomination represented in the Association; to be elected annually; together with all the ministers belonging to it; who shall form a Board for the transaction of business of whom any seven, at a meeting duly convened, shall be a quorum. The stated meetings of the board to be quarterly.

Article V. The Board of managers shall, at the first meeting after their election, appoint an executive committee, consisting of a minister and layman from each of the denominations represented in the association, of which the secretaries and treasurer shall be ex-officio members. This committee to meet as often as they may find necessary for the transaction of the business committed to them, and to report quarterly to the Board of managers.

Article VI. The duties of the Board shall be, to carry out, in every way most expedient in their view, the ends and purposes for which this Association is organized; and to aid and encourage the formation of similar associations in the various parts of the United States; and to render an annual report of their proceedings to the Association, at their annual meeting on the second Tuesday in November.

Article VII. The Board of managers shall have power to enact such by-laws as may not be inconsistent with this constitution, and to fill all vacancies that may occur between the annual meetings.

Article VIII. This constitution shall be subject to amendments only at the annual meetings of the Association, by a vote of two thirds of the members present at such meeting.

17. Archbishop Hughes Explains American Liberty to Rome (1858)

American cultural values were puzzling—as often deeply suspicious—to Roman officials. The American cultural devotion to ideas of "freedom" and "liberty" were especially suspicious to the Vatican after the European Revolutions of 1848, one of the results of which led to Pope Pius IX's fleeing the city of Rome in November 1848 before advancing republican armies. Rome's deep suspicions about American republicanism were strengthened in 1854, when public riots greeted the visit of the pope's representative, Archbishop Gaetano Bedini. Thus, in his 1858 report to Roman officials on the state of his diocese, John Hughes felt it necessary to distinguish American ideas of "liberty" from the kind of European radicalism that had led to direct attacks on the Church in Europe. Indeed, Hughes implied that the most harmful ("Red") ideas to be found in the United States were not native to America, but were rather the result of European radicals immigrating into the country.

We come now to the Revolutions in Europe. [In the previous twenty years, the arrival of vast numbers of immigrants into] New York was most perilous to the faith and morals of the people committed to my charge. I cannot help regarding it as a singular protection of Almighty God and a singular evidence of the interposition of the Blessed Virgin Mary, under whose patronage this Diocese has been especially placed from its origin . . . that we have escaped the ordeal with so little injury to the principles of our Religion. In this Country, "Liberty" is the watch word, the boast, the pride of all men. The general tone of the country would seem to require that every man should touch his hat whenever the word "Liberty" is pronounced in his presence. This, you can easily imagine, applied especially to all aspirants for public office, and to the very numerous and ubiquitous class of professional politicians. . . .

Liberty, in this Country, has a very clear and specific meaning. It is not understood in Europe as it is here. Here, it means the vindication of personal rights; the fair support of public laws; the maintenance, at all hazards, of public order, according to those laws; the right to change them when they are found to be absurd or oppressive. Such, in brief, is the meaning of the word liberty, as understood by the people of the United States. Of course, you will think of the excesses that have been committed from time to time by mobs, "lynch laws" & etc., as marring the correctness of the foregoing statement. But I can assure you that these excesses are regarded here as outrages and violations of liberty, the same as they would be in Europe. But in Continental Europe Liberty is understood to mean the overthrow of all existing governments, recognizing the principle of Monarchy. It is the genius of destruction and bloodshed, ferociously bent on pulling down whatever exists, without the fore-sight or capacity to substitute any thing as good or better.

This distinction did not strike the American people at the outbreak of the late revolutions in Europe, as it does now. Their national pride, as a republic, was much flattered by the anticipation that their example was about to be imitated by all the civilized nations of the earth. There were to be no more Kings, or emperors, or Pope, or Princes; but in their stead, *"the people" "the people" "the people."* Experience, however, has taught them their mistake; and they have become quite satisfied that the specimens of patriotism, from the different nations of Western Europe, who by flight or expulsion have reached these shores, are to be ranked among the veriest wretches that ever disgraced humanity, or disturbed the well-being of Society.

This was not the case, however, fifteen years ago. About that time there was established in this City a paper called the *Echo d'Italia.* This journal was supported not by Italians but by the enemies of the Catholic church, who employed it to feed *their own papers* with the scandals and calumnies against Italy and its inhabitants, which might tend to damage the estimation of our holy religion throughout the world. Around this bad centre was congregated, as time went on, every renegade both to creed and country that Italy would allow to live in her bosom. Among these, I am sorry to say, that even some bad priests distinguished themselves by their atrocious assaults upon the Catholic Creed and its ministers. . . . The tyranny of the church, the wicked lives of the prelates, the dreadful bondage of the noble Italian people in their beautiful and classic land—were themes inexhaustible under the pens of native writers for that Journal. Hence, the hypocritical homage manifested in this Country, by the bitterest protestants, in favor of Our Illustrious Holy Father on his accession to the Papal Throne.

You will not be surprised if the Catholics were carried away in the enthusiasm of the Country at large—that they too were immensely flattered at having lived to see the Holy Father regarded with such universal admiration. Under such circumstances, *they* became also the blind idolators of what both Americans and Europeans designated as "Liberty"—the "progress of human freedom," &etc. &etc. I saw the impending danger of association, on this principle, which it was intended to bring about between the Catholics of New York and the "Red Republicans" of Europe. I began early to put my flock upon their guard—not by a direct assault upon liberty, but against its abuse, indirectly and to a measured extent, whenever an opportunity presented itself. I had most to apprehend from the spurious patriotism of "Young Irelanders." You know how fond is the attachment which Irishmen cherish for their native land, and this attachment seems to grow stronger the farther they are removed from its shores and the longer they have been absent. They had been wrought to a high pitch of expectation and hope for their country's freedom, by the bombastic rhetoric of the Dublin Nation and other journals of the same type. . . . This feeling was taken advantage of and turned into bitterness by some of the Irish Refugees, who, on reaching these shores, pretended to give a full account of the recent efforts in which they had been engaged. They charged the failure on the "Catholic Clergy" as enemies to the Irish people —denounced the hierarchy and priesthood of Ireland, proclaimed that if any of them should show his face on this side of the Atlantic he should be met with "hisses" instead of the ordinary signs of reverence and respect.

Our poor people were not in a frame of mind to discriminate, and to detect the malice of these cowardly and unjust accusations whilst the Refugee Patriots from France, Germany, and Italy did not hesitate to proclaim, openly, that there was no hope of freedom for the down trodden people of Europe until the Catholic Church and its clergy, from the Pope downwards, should be overthrown, and if necessary annihilated.

The first event which opened the eyes of the Catholics was the shout of joy which rang throughout the Country when it was announced that the Holy Father had been driven away from Rome. The jubilee of our enemies made the Catholics sad. They could not foresee the final result of the

measures which the usurpers in the Eternal City had put into execution
... I preached what might be called a political sermon in my Cathedral on
the Sunday next following the receipt of the news that the Holy Father had
been obliged to quit Rome. This became a turning point in the thoughts
of my own people, with the exception of a very few who were incurable,
but who ceased from that time to have any influence. . . .

You can easily understand that from the period [of that sermon] I became offensive to all those wild and unprincipled Republicans. They did
not spare me; but neither did they convert me: and the words which I uttered from time to time, and on various occasions, were published not
only here in New York, but throughout the Country—in some papers
out of enmity, in others to let their readers know what I thought in regard
to passing events. I have reason to know that these publications had a
great influence in keeping the Catholics steady, and little by little, bringing "Red Republicanism" into utter contempt among protestants as well as
Catholics.

18. "Instruction of the Propaganda Fide Concerning Catholic Children in American Public Schools" (1875)

The First and Second Plenary Councils of Baltimore—held in 1852 and 1866,
respectively—had passed legislation requiring Catholic parents to support
Catholic schools, to which they were expected to send their children. Because
of the failure of many U.S. parishes in fulfilling this requirement, a number of
American bishops asked the Holy See for a "directive" on this issue which they
might use. In November 1875, the Propaganda Fide—the missionary office of
the Vatican under whose authority the U.S. Catholic Church rested—send
this "Instruction" to the American bishops.

The Sacred Congregation of Propaganda has been many times assured
that for the Catholic children of the United States of America evils of the
gravest kind are likely to result from the so-called public schools.

The sad intelligence moved the Propaganda to propose to the illustrious prelates of that country a series of questions, with the object of ascer-
taining, first, why the faithful permit their children to attend non-catholic
schools, and, secondly, what may be the best means of keeping the young

away from schools of this description. The answers, as drawn up by the several prelates, were submitted, owing to the nature of the subject, to the Supreme Congregation of the Holy Office. The decision, reached by their Eminences, Wednesday, June 30, 1875, they saw fit to embody in the following *Instruction*, which the Holy Father graciously confirmed on Wednesday November 24, of the same year.

1. The first point to come under consideration was the system of education itself, quite peculiar to those schools. Now, that system seemed to the S. Congregation most dangerous and very much opposed to Catholicity. For the children in those schools, the very principles of which exclude all religious instruction, can neither learn the rudiments of the faith nor be taught the precepts of the Church; hence, they will lack that knowledge, of all else, necessary to man without which there is no leading a Christian life. For children are sent to these schools from their earliest years, almost from the cradle; at which age, it is admitted, the seeds sown of virtue or of vice take fast root. To allow this tender age to pass without religion is surely a great evil.

2. Again, these schools being under no control of the Church, the teachers are selected from every sect indiscriminately; and this, while no proper precaution is taken to prevent them injuring the children, so that there is nothing to stop them from infusing into the young minds the seeds of error and vice. Then evil results are certainly to be dreaded from the fact that in these schools, or at least in very many of them, children of both sexes must be in the same class and class-room and must sit side by side at the same desk. Every circumstance mentioned goes to show that the children are fearfully exposed to the danger of losing their faith and that their morals are not properly safeguarded.

3. Unless this danger of perversion can be rendered remote, instead of proximate, such schools cannot in conscience be used. This is the dictate of natural as well as of divine law. It was enunciated in unmistakable terms by the Sovereign Pontiff, in a letter addressed to a former Archbishop of Freiburg, July 14, 1864. He thus writes: "There can be no hesitation; wherever the purpose is afoot or carried out of shutting the Church out from all authority over the schools, there the children will be sadly exposed to loss of their faith. Consequently the Church should, in such circumstances, not only put forth every effort and spare no pains to get for the children the necessary Christian training and education, but would be further compelled to remind the faithful and publicly declare that schools hostile to Catholicity cannot in conscience be attended." These words only

express a general principle of natural and divine law and are consequently of universal application wherever that most dangerous system of training youth has been unhappily introduced.

4. It only remains, then, for the prelates to use every means in their power to keep the flocks committed to their care from all contact with the public schools. All are agreed that there is nothing so needful to this end as the establishment of Catholic schools in every place—and schools no whit inferior to the public ones. Every effort, then, must be directed towards starting Catholic schools where they are not, and where they are, towards enlarging them and providing them with better accommodations and equipment until they have nothing to suffer, as regards teachers and equipment, by comparison with the public schools. And to carry out so holy and necessary a work, the aid of religious brotherhoods and of sister-hoods will be found advantageous where the bishop sees fit to introduce them. In order that the faithful may the more freely contribute the necessary expenses, the bishops themselves should not fail to impress on them, at every suitable occasion, whether by pastoral letter, sermon, or private conversation, that as bishops they would be recreant to their duty if they failed to do their utmost to provide Catholic schools. This point should be especially brought to the attention of the more wealthy and influential Catholics and members of the legislature.

5. In that country there is no law to prevent Catholics having their own schools and instructing and educating their youth in every branch of knowledge. It is therefore in the power of Catholics themselves to avert, with God's help, the dangers with which Catholicity is threatened from the public school system. Not to have religion and piety banished from the school-room is a matter of the very highest interest, not only to certain individuals and families, but to the entire country—a country now so prosperous and of which the Church has had reason to conceive such high hopes.

6. However, the S. Congregation is not unaware that circumstances may be sometimes such as to permit parents conscientiously to send their children to the public schools. Of course they cannot do so without having sufficient cause. Whether there be sufficient cause in any particular case is to be left to the conscience and judgment of the bishop. Generally speaking, such cause will exist when there is no Catholic school in the place, or the one that is there cannot be considered suitable to the condition and circumstances in life of the pupils. But even in these cases, before the children can conscientiously attend the public school, the danger, greater or

less, of perversion, which is inseparable from the system, must be rendered remote by proper precaution and safeguards. The first thing to see to, then, is whether the danger of perversion, as regards the school in question, is such as cannot possibly be rendered remote; as, for instance, whether the teaching there is such, or the doings of a nature so repugnant to Catholic belief and morals, that ear cannot be given to the one, nor part taken in the other without grievous sin. It is self-evident that danger of this character must be shunned at whatever cost, even life itself.

7. Further, before a child can be conscientiously placed at a public school, provision must be made for giving it the necessary Christian training and instruction, at least out of school hours. Hence parish priests and missionaries in the United States should take seriously to heart the earnest admonitions of the [Second Plenary] Council of Baltimore, and spare no labor to give children thorough catechetical instructions, dwelling particularly on those truths of faith and morals which are called most in question by Protestants and unbelievers: children beset with so many dangers they should guard with tireless vigilance, induce them to frequent the sacraments, excite in them devotion to the Blessed Virgin and on all occasions animate them to hold firmly by their religion. The parents or guardians must look carefully after those children. They must examine them in their lessons, or if not able themselves, get others to do it. They must see what books they use and, if the books contain passages likely to injure the child's mind, explain the matter. They must keep them from freedom and familiarity with those of the other school children whose company might be dangerous to their faith or morals, and absolutely away from the corrupt.

8. Parents who neglect to give this necessary Christian training and instruction to their children, or who permit them to go to schools in which the ruin of their souls is inevitable, or finally, who send them to the public school without sufficient cause and without taking the necessary precautions to render the danger of perversion remote, and so while there is a good and well-equipped Catholic school in the place, or the parents have the means to send them elsewhere to be educated—that such parents, if obstinate, cannot be absolved [in confession] is evident from the moral teaching of the Church.

19. Isaac Hecker on Catholic Scholasticism and the Scientific Tendencies of the Age (1887)

Founder of the Paulist Fathers, Isaac Hecker believed that the Catholic Church —far from being fated as a permanent outsider to mainstream American culture—offered the kind of "scientific" theology which most Americans at the end of the nineteenth century were looking for. Thus, in Hecker's estimation, the kind of scholastic theology done by the "Schoolmen" of the Middle Ages represented a perfect "fit" for hard-nosed, scientifically inclined educated Americans, portending great things for the growth of the Catholic Church in America among the educated classes.

It is an obvious fact that a considerable number of minds in our day have been trained in scientific studies and are devoted to intellectual pursuits. It is equally evident that the general diffusion of education will enlarge the circle of this class of persons and extend their influence. And it is quite natural that minds so trained, when their attention is turned to the study of religion, should look for its presentation under scientific forms. This expectation is not to be censured or thwarted; on the contrary, it should be met with due consideration and fairly satisfied. For the claim which Christianity lays upon man is that of "reasonable service," and, unless it can make this demand good in the court of reason, it must lose its hold upon his intelligence, cease to exert its influence upon society, and give up the ideal of ever winning the homage of the whole human race.

And it was precisely this scientific presentation of Christianity with the aid of philosophy that was aimed at, and in great part achieved, by the Schoolmen. "For it is due to the service of philosophy that sacred theology take up and enrich itself with the nature, habit, and genius of a true science" (Leo XIII, Encyclical *Aeterni Patris*). Before their day positive theology, which consisted in proving the divinity of Christianity by the authority of the inspired Scriptures and the words of Christ delivered to His apostles and handed down from generation to generation in His Church with the testimony of the Fathers, had received its completion. This prepared the way of the Schoolmen, who added to the arguments of positive theology those drawn from philosophy. Philosophy, as held by them, consisted in those truths which had been "discovered with the sole light of natural reason by the eminent thinkers of the past," especially by their

Prince, Aristotle, who reduced these truths into a system, but not unmixed with most serious, not to say appalling, errors. St. Thomas [Aquinas], the prince of the Schoolmen, with the aid derived from the writings of his precursors . . . and above all from the light of his own incomparable and sanctified genius, eliminated these errors, and at the same time modified, enlarged, and enriched with his own ideas the boundaries and scope of philosophy.

The aim of the Schoolmen was to produce, by the full play of the light of natural reason on the intellectual side of Christianity, aided by philosophy and consistently with positive theology, a strictly logical demonstration of Christianity. The great task which they had before them was that of the synthesis of natural and revealed truth, of science and faith. But there came a halt in the march of this intellectual progress.

In the early part of the sixteenth century earnest and zealous efforts were made by sincere churchmen to reform the evils and expiate the abuses existing in the Church, more especially in Germany. By certain leaders whose passions swayed their judgments, combined with temporal princes who made use of these to gain their despotic power, this most praiseworthy movement was turned from that of reform into one of heresy, schism, and revolution. Seized with the insane idea of destroying the Church which Christ had built, they conspired together and organized a systematic opposition, protesting defiantly against her doctrines, and rudely overturning, wherever they succeeded in gaining the power, what she had with great difficulty reared and with greater sacrifices sustained.

Consistently with the fundamental principle of their system of confining the attention exclusively to the Bible, and the interpretation of its texts by the sole light of the internal illumination of the Holy Spirit, they denied the value of human reason, contemned philosophy, opposed the spread of education and the study of the liberal arts and sciences, burnt up or sold as waste paper precious manuscripts, depopulated the schools and universities, and shattered to pieces, wherever they came within their reach, all works of art. . . .

It has taken the greater part of three centuries for the body of those who have been infected by [this] contagion to throw off its effects, and to regain their intellectual and moral health sufficiently to walk again erect. This state of convalescence upon which the better part of the descendants of original Protestantism have entered has taken place by the intellect slowly assimilating those truths which the leaders of this secession from the Church denied, and in rejecting their principal errors. For the intellect, according to its own laws, as St. Thomas teaches, seeks truth, assimilates it when found, and has a natural abhorrence of error, and when once detects it, rejects it. Thus the Protestantism of the nineteenth century, or what goes now pretty much by that name, is the reverse of the Protestantism of the sixteenth century.

The process of this transformation has been somewhat as follows: The truths of divine revelation and of human reason against which a protest was made in the beginning have been placed in such a clear light by long and frequent discussion that further controversy about them in our day is hardly possible. Where will you find an intelligent man among Protestants who could be induced to repeat Martin Luther's diatribes against human reason? Or against man's free will? Or against human nature? How many Presbyterians of this generation hold and believe the five points of Calvinism pure and simple? . . . Very few among Protestants of this century take the pains to read their creeds, and those who do and get an idea of their contents, either clamor for their change or would smile at the simplicity of one who seriously asked whether they believed in them. Even the human sciences appear to have had for their mission, especially since their revival in our times, to undermine the position assumed by Protestantism in its attacks on the Catholic Church, and the drift of their real discoveries harmonizes with Catholic philosophy and theology. . . . Every forward step in the sciences is a conquest of truth, and as the supernatural finds its confirmation in the natural, so every advance in the natural sciences is a new conquest of Catholicity over heresy. . . .

Assuming, then, the fact, which many among themselves frankly acknowledge, that Protestantism as an organized opposition to the Catholic Church has spent its main strength, and as an adequate representation of Christianity is an utter failure, is doomed to disappear, and is disappearing rapidly; assuming that in the eyes of intelligent men the efforts to invent or construct a new religion are unworthy of a moment of serious thought . . . the question then immediately before us is this: What prospect is there that the Catholic religion will solve [the intellectual demands of the age]?

This is the question with which we started out, and insisted on being frankly met and fairly answered. Religion, Christianity, the Catholic Church—which is Christianity in its unity and totality in a concrete form —has for its actual task to answer satisfactorily the intellectual demands of the age, and to perceive its opportunities in modern civilization and its onward tendencies.

The Catholic Church, so far from shrinking from this precise problem and those imperative demands, hails them with inmost delight. She is not only ready to face them fearlessly, but, conscious of the indwelling divinity and the possession of divine truth, she looks upon this problem and these demands as the very opportunities prepared by her Divine Spouse to secure, by her satisfactory solution and answers, a new and glorious triumph. . . .

Let him, therefore, who would serve the Catholic Church in this generation, show her in her true light, in her unity and universality, in all her beauty and majesty. It is this true vision of her divinity that will captivate man's intelligence, secure the unbidden homage of his will, and elicit his most heroic devotedness. Herein lies the mysterious force of her duration for so many centuries, the secret of the power of her sway over more than two hundred millions of souls, and the reason for the never-broken stream of her converts and the capture of the ablest minds of our century.

20. JOHN IRELAND, INTRODUCTION TO THE *LIFE OF FATHER HECKER* (1891)

Isaac Thomas Hecker, one of the most influential American Catholic intellectuals of the nineteenth century, converted to the Church under the influence of Orestes Brownson. Having become a priest, he founded the Paulist order, with the double missionary charge of explaining Catholics to Protestant America, and explaining America to the new waves of European Catholic immigrants. The Paulist Walter Elliott wrote a Life *of Hecker in 1891, with an introduction by the so-called "Americanist" bishop of St. Paul, John Ireland. Elliott and Ireland's work, translated into French, became celebrated throughout Europe, and the Roman interpretation of these ideas caused alarm at the Vatican, resulting in Leo XIII's encyclical* Testem Benevolentiae *(No. 21).*

Father Hecker was the typical American priest; his were the gifts of mind and heart that go to do great work for God and for souls in America at the present time. Those qualities, assuredly, were not lacking in him which are the necessary elements of character of the good priest and the great man in any time and place. Those are the subsoil of priestly culture, and with the absence of them no one will succeed in America any more than elsewhere. But suffice they do not. There must be added, over and above, the

practical intelligence and pliability of will to understand one's surroundings, the ground upon which he is to deploy his forces, and to adapt himself to circumstances and opportunities as Providence appoints. . . . It is as
clear to me as noon-day light that countries and peoples have each their
peculiar needs and aspirations as they have their particular environments,
and that, if we would enter into souls and control them, we must deal with
them according to their conditions. The ideal line of conduct for the priest
in Assyria will be out of all measure in Mexico or Minnesota. . . . The Saviour prescribed timeliness in pastoral caring. . . .

The circumstances of Catholics have been peculiar in the United States,
and we have unavoidably suffered on this account. Catholics in the largest
numbers were Europeans, and so were their priests, many of whom—by
no means all—remained in heart and mind and mode of action as alien to
America as if they had never been removed from the Shannon, the Loire,
or the Rhine. . . .

Father Hecker understood and loved the country and its institutions.
. . . His favorite topic in book and lecture was, that the Constitution of
the United States requires, as its necessary basis, the truths of Catholic
teaching regarding man's natural state, as opposed to the errors of Luther
and Calvin. The republic, he taught, presupposes the Church's doctrine,
and the Church ought to love a polity which is the offspring of her own
spirit. . . .

[Hecker] laid stress on the natural and social virtues. The American
people hold these in the highest esteem. They are the virtues that are most
apparent, and are seemingly the most needed for the building up and the
preservation of an earthly commonwealth. Truthfulness, honesty in business dealings, loyalty to law and social order, temperance, respect for the
rights of others, and the like virtues are prescribed by reason before the
voice of revelation is heard, and the absence of specifically supernatural
virtues has led the non-Catholic to place paramount importance upon
them. . . . It is a fact, however, that in other times and other countries the
Church has been impeded in her social work, and certain things or customs of those times and countries, transplanted upon American soil and
allowed to grow here under a Catholic name, will do her no honor among
Americans. The human mind, among the best of us, inclines to narrow
limitations, and certain Catholics, aware of the comparatively greater importance of the supernatural, partially overlook the natural. . . .

The Church is nowadays called upon to emphasize her power in the
natural order. God forbid that I entertain, as some may be tempted to sus-

pect me of doing, the slightest notion that vigilance may be turned off one single moment from the guard of the supernatural. For the sake of the supernatural I speak. And natural virtues, practised in the proper frame of mind and heart, become supernatural. Each century calls for its type of Christian perfection. At one time it was martyrdom; at another it was the humility of the cloister. To-day we need the Christian gentleman and the Christian citizen. An honest ballot and social decorum among Catholics will do more for God's glory and the salvation of souls than midnight flagellations or Compostellan pilgrimages. . . .

I once heard a good old priest, who said his beads well and made a desert around his pulpit by miserable preaching, criticise Father Hecker, who, he imagined, put too much reliance in man, and not enough in God. . . . My old priest—and he has in the church to-day, both in America and Europe, tens of thousands of counterparts—was more than half willing to see in all outputtings of human energy a lack of confidence in God. We sometimes rely far more on God than God desires us to do, and there are occasions when a novena is the refuge of laziness or cowardice. . . . We must work as if all depended on us, and pray as if all depended on God. . . .

[Hecker's] was the profound conviction that, in the present age at any rate, the order of the day should be individual action—every man doing his full duty, and waiting for no one else to prompt him. This, I take it, was largely the meaning of Father Hecker's oft-repeated teaching on the work of the Holy Ghost in souls. There have been epochs in history where the Church . . . put the brakes . . . upon individual activity, and moved her soldiers in serried masses; and then it was the part and the glory of each one to move with the column. The need of repression has passed away. . . . There is work for individual priests, and individual laymen, and so soon as it is discovered let it be done. The responsibility is upon each one; the indifference of others is no excuse. Said Father Hecker one day to a friend: "There is too much waiting upon the action of others. The layman waits for the priest, the priest for the bishop, and the bishop for the pope, while the Holy Ghost sends down to all the reproof that He is prompting each one, and no one moves for Him." Father Hecker was original in his ideas, as well as in his methods; there was no routine in him, mental or practical. . . .

The work of evangelizing America demands new methods. It is time to draw forth from our treasury the "new things" of the Gospel; we have been long enough offering "old things." . . .

21. TESTEM BENEVOLENTIAE AND THE
CONDEMNATION OF AMERICANISM (1899)

In January 1899, Pope Leo XIII wrote to Cardinal Gibbons of Baltimore re-garding certain "tendencies" among some American Catholics about which rumors had reached Rome. That letter, "Testem benevolentiae," represents one of the most famous documents in American Catholic history. Gibbons (the "Beloved Son" in this letter) is warned about the tendency of American culture to believe itself superior to other cultures, and more specifically the (supposed) belief among some American Catholics that the U.S. Catholic Church should be different from other national Catholic churches. The spe-cific event that generated the letter was the French translation of Walter El-liott's "Life of Fr. Hecker" in 1891, the introduction to which presented Hecker (and, by extension, American Catholicism itself) as representing a new, more "modern" form of Catholicism (see No. 20).

We send you this letter as a testimony of that devoted affection in your re-gard, which during the long course of Our Pontificate, We have never ceased to profess for you, for your colleagues in the Episcopate, and for the whole American people, willingly availing Ourselves of every occasion to do so, whether it was the happy increase of your church, or the works which you have done so wisely and well in furthering and protecting the interests of Catholicity. The opportunity also often presented itself of re-garding with admiration that exceptional disposition of your nation, so eager for what is great, and so ready to pursue whatever might be con-ducive to social progress and the splendor of the State. But although the object of this letter is not to repeat the praise so often accorded, but rather to point out certain things which are to be avoided and corrected, yet be-cause it is written with that same apostolic charity which We have always shown you, and in which We have often addressed you, We trust that you will regard it likewise as a proof of Our love; and all the more so as it is conceived and intended to put an end to certain contentions which have arisen lately among you, and which disturb the minds, if not of all, at least of many, to the no slight detriment of peace.

You are aware, Beloved Son, that the book entitled, "The Life of Isaac Thomas Hecker," chiefly through the actions of those who have under-taken to publish and interpret it in a foreign language, has excited no small controversy on account of certain opinions which are introduced concerning the manner of leading a Christian life. We, therefore, on account of Our apostolic office, in order to provide for the integrity of the faith, and to guard the security of the faithful, desire to write to you more at length upon the whole matter.

The principles on which the new opinions We have mentioned are based may be reduced to this: that, in order the more easily to bring over to Catholic doctrine those who dissent from it, the Church ought to adapt herself somewhat to our advanced civilization, and relaxing her ancient rigor, show some indulgence to modern popular theories and methods. Many think that this is to be understood not only with regard to the rule of life, but also to the doctrines in which the deposit of faith is contained. For they contend that it is opportune, in order to work in a more attractive way upon the wills of those who are not in accord with us, to pass over certain heads of doctrines, as if of lesser moment, or to so soften them that they may not have the same meaning which the Church has invariably held. Now, Beloved Son, few words are needed to show how reprehensible is the plan that is thus conceived, if we but consider the character and origin of the doctrine which the Church hands down to us. On that point the [First] Vatican Council says: "The doctrine of faith which God has revealed is not proposed like a theory of philosophy which is to be elaborated by the human understanding, but as a divine deposit delivered to the Spouse of Christ to be faithfully guarded and infallibly declared. . . .That sense of sacred dogma is to be faithfully kept which Holy Mother Church has once declared, and is not to be departed from under the specious pretext of a more profound understanding." (*Const. De Fid. Cath.,* c, iv).

Nor is the suppression to be considered altogether free of blame, which designedly omits certain principles of Catholic doctrine and buries them, as it were, in oblivion. . . . Far be it, then, for any one to diminish or for any reason whatever to pass over anything of this divinely delivered doctrine. . . .

The rule of life which is laid down for Catholics is not of such a nature as not to admit modifications, according to the diversity of time and place. The Church, indeed, possesses what her Author has bestowed on her, a kind and merciful disposition; for which reason from the very beginning she willingly showed herself to be what Paul proclaimed in his own regard: "I became all things to all men, that I might save all" (Corinthians ix, 22). The history of all past ages is witness that the Apostolic See, to which not only the office of teaching but also the supreme governance of the whole

Church was committed, has constantly adhered "to the same doctrine. In the same sense and in the same mind" (Vatican Council [1]): but it has always been accustomed to so modify the rule of life that, while keeping the divine right inviolate, it has never disregarded the manners and customs of the various nations which it embraces. If required for the salvation of souls, who will doubt that it is ready to do so at the present time? But this is not to be determined by the will of private individuals, who are mostly deceived by the appearance of right, but ought to be left to the judgment of the Church. . . .

But in the matter of which we are now speaking, Beloved Son, the project involves a greater danger and is more hostile to Catholic doctrine and discipline, inasmuch as the followers of these novelties judge that a certain liberty ought to be introduced into the Church, so that, limiting the exercise and vigilance of its powers, each of the faithful may act more freely in pursuance of his own natural bent and capacity. They affirm, namely, that this is called for in order to imitate that liberty which, though quite recently introduced, is now the law and the foundation of almost every civil community. On that point We have spoken very much at length in the Letter written to all the bishops [*Immortale Dei*, 1885] about the constitution of States; where we have also shown the difference between the Church, which is of divine right, and all other associations which subsist by the free will of men. It is of importance, therefore, to note particularly an opinion which is adduced as a sort of argument to urge the granting of such liberty to Catholics. For they say, in speaking of the infallible teaching of the Roman Pontiff, that after the solemn decision formulated in the [First] Vatican Council, there is no more need of solicitude in that regard, and, because of its being now out of dispute, a wider field of thought and action is thrown open to individuals. A preposterous method of arguing, surely. . . . The license which is commonly confounded with liberty; the passion for saying and reviling everything; the habit of thinking and of expressing everything in print, have cast such deep shadows on men's minds, that there is now greater utility and necessity for this office of teaching than ever before, lest men should be drawn away from conscience and duty. . . .

We come now in due course to what are adduced as consequences from the opinions which We have touched upon: in which if the intention seem not wrong, as We believe, the things themselves assuredly will not appear by any means free from suspicion. For, in the first place, all external guidance is rejected as superfluous, nay even as somewhat of a disadvantage, for those who desire to the acquisition of Christian perfection; for the Holy Spirit, they say, pours greater and richer gifts into the hearts of the faithful now than in times past; and by a certain hidden instinct teaches and moves them with no one as an intermediary. . . . For who, when going over the history of the apostles, the faith of the rising church, the struggles and slaughter of the valiant martyrs, and finally most of the ages past so abundantly rich in holy men, will presume to compare the past with the present times and to assert that they received a lesser outpouring of the Holy Ghost? . . .

We gather from certain pronouncements of theirs about the vows which religious orders pronounce. For, they say, such vows are altogether out of keeping with the spirit of our age, inasmuch as they narrow the limits of human liberty; are better adapted to weak minds than to strong ones; avail little for Christian perfection and the good of human society, and rather obstruct and interfere with it. But how false these assertions are is evident from the usage and doctrine of the Church, which has always given the highest approval to religious life. And surely not undeservedly. . . . What they add to this—namely, that religious life helps the Church not at all or very little—apart from being injurious to religious orders, will be admitted by no one who has read the history of the Church. Did not your own United States receive from the members of religious orders the beginning of its faith and civilization? . . . And at this very time, with what alacrity and success are these religious orders doing their work wherever we find them. . . .

Hence, from all that We have hitherto said, it is clear, Beloved Son, that We cannot approve the opinions which some comprise under the head of Americanism. If, indeed, by that name be designated the characteristic qualities which reflect honor on the people of America, just as other nations have what is special to them; or if it implies the condition of your commonwealths, or the laws and customs which prevail in them, there is surely no reason why We should deem that it ought to be discarded. But if it is to be used not only to signify, but even to commend the above doctrines, there can be no doubt but that our Venerable Brethren the bishops of America would be the first to repudiate and condemn it, as being especially unjust to them and to the entire nation as well. For it raises the suspicion that there are some among you who conceive of and desire a church in America different from that which is in the rest of the world. One in the unity of doctrine as in the unity of government, such is the Catholic Church, and since God has established its center and foundation in the Chair of Peter, one which is rightly called Roman, for where Peter is there is the Church. . . . What We write, Beloved Son, to you in particular, by reason of Our office, we shall take care to have communicated to the rest of the bishops of the United States, expressing again that love in which we include your whole nation, which as in times past has done much for religion and bids fair with God's good grace to do still more in the future.

22. "Report on the Religious Conditions of Puerto Ricans in New York City" (1951)

In 1951 Encarnacion Padilla de Armas, herself a Puerto Rican immigrant and a lawyer in the recently formed Puerto Rican governmental affairs office in New York City, met Fordham University Jesuit Joseph Fitzpatrick. Fitzpatrick asked if she was willing to write a report about the New York Archdiocese's neglect of the Puerto Rican community in the city, promising that, if she agreed, he would deliver the report personally to New York's archbishop, Francis Cardinal Spellman. The resulting report, prepared by a group of Puerto Rican women convened by Mrs. Padilla de Armas, led to the formation of the archdiocese's Spanish Catholic Action Office in 1953. Mrs. Padilla de Armas's subsequent career led to a number of distinguished leadership roles in Hispanic ministry, including work at the Secretariat for Hispanic Affairs at the National Conference of Catholic Bishops.

As a group of Catholic women, we have been deeply concerned, as many other Catholics have been, about the religious condition of the many Spanish-speaking people who are coming into the city of New York. We are aware of the wonderful efforts that are being made by a number of pastors in the city to provide these people with adequate religious care, and to enable their children to attend parochial schools. However, like everyone familiar with the situation, we are amazed at the immensity of this problem, and we realize how inadequate are the existing efforts of Catholics to meet this task. At the same time, Protestant groups seem to have no end of energy and resources to do the work that we as Catholics should be doing.

In order to bring to the attention of our Catholic authorities some of the facts of this situation which they may not be aware of, we have compiled the following information gathered in our ordinary, everyday lives, about the Spanish-speaking people. It may serve as a help to a more organized, coordinated effort to bring these people the religious help they desperately need.

Lower East Side: This has been a predominantly Jewish and Italian neighborhood and is probably still considered such by most people in the city. However, the Puerto Ricans have been crowding into the area, some of them newly arrived from the island, others forced to leave their homes in other sections where new housing projects are being built. It is estimated that in the area from South Street up to East Houston, there are 80,000 Puerto Ricans. There are more than 8,000 families, many of which have more than 5 children. In this entire area there is only one Catholic church that provides spiritual care by Spanish-speaking people for the Puerto Ricans. This church is on 6th Street and Houston. Actually it is the mission of Nativity parish, is staffed during the week by a Spanish-speaking sister, and has the services of a Spanish-speaking priest on Saturdays and Sundays. This church, actually a little chapel, accommodates 75 persons, although the sister says she knows 246 families in the immediate vicinity alone. . . . Unfortunately, there is no parochial school in the area for any of these children.

At the same time in the area there are twelve (12) Puerto Rican Protestant churches with fourteen Puerto Rican Protestant ministers. Each minister has at least his wife helping him to do community and house-to-house work. In that same area the community centers, Manhattan House, Livingstone House, and the New Era Club are doing tremendous community work with after school programs for Spanish-speaking people of the area. The Puerto Rican children attend these clubs and are influenced by the Protestant religion and views.

There is also a hospital in the area, Governor's Hospital, where it is estimated that 75% of the patients are Puerto Rican. There seem to be no Spanish-speaking priests who visit the Catholic patients here. However, a Protestant minister is available every single day in this area and the Puerto Rican ladies serve in the hospital as volunteer interpreters. . . .

Activity of Protestants: Undoubtedly the most striking aspect of the Puerto Rican situation is the constant and energetic activity of Protestants among these people.

This is the mainland counterpart to the situation on the island itself. Since the American occupation of Puerto Rico and the departure of the Spanish clergy, there were never sufficient priests to provide spiritual care for the people. The American influence was followed by a large influx of Protestant missionaries. For instance, at present there are only 800 priests on the island compared to 3,200 Protestant missionaries, many of whom are of Puerto Rican origin. In New York, there are about 800 Puerto Rican Protestant ministers but not a single Catholic priest of Puerto Rican origin.

The number of Protestant churches is enormous. In an appendix at the end of this report is a list of [more than 100] Protestant churches for Puerto Ricans in New York. What is more, these Puerto Rican ministers follow the same external rites and customs that are characteristic of the Catholic Church in Puerto Rico. Thus the people are confused, believing that they are practicing their religion even when they attend the Protestant church.

Perhaps not a little of the success of the Protestant ministers is the fact that they come from the Spanish tradition, understand the psychology of the people, and can work effectively with them. This may indicate that, in the transition to American ways, it will not be sufficient to depend entirely on the zeal of English-speaking priests. Rather, a blend of spiritual care given both by English-speaking priests together with assistance from priests of Spanish or Puerto Rican background may be most effective. However, the most important thing is zealous concern for these people on the part of any Priest who can reach them. If this could equal the zeal and effort of Protestants, the difficulties could soon begin to be met. . . . If Puerto Ricans have the proper leadership, they will respond to it generously. . . .

Community centers: The importance of community centers as a means of helping the P.R.s and of influencing them cannot be stressed enough. It is through this medium that Protestant influence is often strongest. In view of this, it was doubly unfortunate that the Community center on 106th Street opposite Saint Cecilia's was allowed to fall into Protestant hands. . . .

Mixed congregations: It has apparently been the policy of the New York Archdiocese not to set up separate "national" parishes for the Puerto Ricans. In view of the speed with which they are moving through the city, this seems to be a wise policy. But it must be accompanied by clear instructions to all churches that Puerto Ricans must be received as regular parishioners. There are doubts about this on the minds of some pastors who do not know whether they would be encroaching on specialized jurisdictions if they went all out to attract the Puerto Ricans to their parish. Similarly, Catholics already in the parish should be instructed of this policy and should be instructed also of their obligation of receiving these new people as brothers in Christ. Unfortunately, this last has not always been so, since there are a number of parishes where the Puerto Ricans are given to understand that they are not wanted, that they should go to some "Spanish" church.

Marriage: The difficulties of Puerto Rican family life are well known. Thousands of these families exist only through common law arrangement. This is a carry over from a practice on the island, where priests reach them too seldom, and where they begin to live together as husband and wife. This leads to serious problems when they come to the mainland. Thousands cannot get into public housing projects because they cannot prove the legality of their marriage. Some of them are common law marriages because they have never been taught differently, others because they do not have the money for a civil or religious marriage. . . .

Protestants are able to handle this much more easily than Catholics because they avoid most of the complicating details of Catholic marriage. Similarly in burials. Thus some attention must be given to facilitating both these rites in order to make the return of the Puerto Rican to the church that much easier. . . .

In view of all this, it appears that much information is needed about the spread of Puerto Ricans throughout the city, of the care they need, the care they actually receive. This would have to be followed by some coordinated approach to the entire problem. It cannot be solved by a single parish nor a single pastor. It requires the coordinated effort and understanding of the entire Catholic population.

23. John LaFarge, S.J., *The Catholic Viewpoint on Race Relations* (1956)

John LaFarge, profoundly influenced by the Catholic Church's growing body of teaching on social questions, was the founder of the Catholic Interracial Council in New York City in 1934. Building on the [French-based] Catholic Action Movement's model of "observe-judge-act," LaFarge was instrumental in making American Catholics aware of the growing body of Church teaching that defined racism as a moral—as well as a political—problem that violated Catholic teaching. In his 1956 book, LaFarge combined biographical memories as one of the earliest American Catholics involved in interracial causes with lucid expositions of the Church's condemnation of racial discrimination.

The Church holds that fundamental human rights are not something conferred by the State or by any other human institution. They are not the result of mere social conventions or current folkways. Basic human rights, as such, are equal in all human beings, even though in other matters—personal merit, culture, native or acquired ability—people are usually unequal. This equality of rights derives from the essential dignity and destiny of the human being as such, a being created by an all-wise and infinitely loving God in order to enjoy, by his own deliberate choice, eternal happiness in union with his creator and origin. Hence, in the Christian concept, man's essential dignity does not arise from anything apart from his relationship with his Creator and last end. Man does not create his own sublime worth out of his own littleness, but enjoys it by his very nature as a creature of God and—through the gift of divine grace—an heir of heaven. . . .

The Church is likewise deeply solicitous for those whose spiritual, social, or cultural position has been retarded because they have been deprived of the exercise of human rights. Pope Pius XII expressed this solicitude in his letter to the American hierarchy: "We confess that we feel a special paternal affection, which is certainly inspired by heaven, for the Negro people dwelling among you; for in the field of religion and education we know they need special care and comfort and are very deserving of it. We pray fruitful success for those whose generous zeal is devoted to their welfare."

Hence, the Catholic Church does not look upon the race problem as a mere problem of social adjustment: how can we best figure out from experience ways and means for people to get along together? As Chester Bowles says: "It is not a question primarily to be solved by laws and law courts, even though these are both useful and necessary in guaranteeing our rights. It is essentially a *moral* problem," a question of right and wrong, of sin and justice. Since the Catholic Church believes that men can and do sin against their Creator, and can be held accountable for their sins, she will not excuse violations of basic human rights as mere matters of unkindness or lack of delicacy. Race prejudice, discrimination, and compulsory racial segregation are morally sinful.

There are two approaches to Catholic teaching on racial problems: one of reason and one of faith. Reason and faith are not opposed; they complement one another. The Church respects reason and the scientific research developed by reasoning. Our natural reasoning powers are impaired, but they are not destroyed, as a consequence of the sin of our first parents. Weakened as they are by passion and greed, particularly in matter of human relations, those powers can be strengthened and rehabilitated by the grace of God. Jesus Christ, our supreme Teacher and Founder of our faith, frequently calls on ordinary human reason and good sense, in order to enforce His sublime lessons. He nevertheless asks us to study and weigh the considerations that stem from ordinary human experience.

A cold, purely intellectual approach to the problems of living, suffering, and aspiring human beings is doomed to ultimate sterility. Simon-pure social science or simon-pure political science is not the effective answer. Nevertheless, genuine science—documented knowledge, armed with the techniques of modern methodology—is not only a powerful but an indispensable aid in the service of the higher charity. The divinely-inspired Good Samaritan used very practical means in dealing with the wounded victim on the road to Jericho. . . .

The genuinely Catholic viewpoint on race relations takes into account the body of sound, reasoned knowledge which intelligent study of this question has accumulated, particularly in the United States, over a period of nearly one hundred years. . . .

The Church Condemns Racism

As Cardinal Spellman says, there can be no doubt about Catholic teaching in this matter. In the last few decades, the exaltation of pride of race by nazis and fascists, and their contempt and scorn for "inferior races," drew stern rebuke from both Pius XI and our present Holy Father, Pius XII. . . .

These principles are widely recognized today, even though many do not follow them in practice. Very few in this country today, and practically no one in any position of responsibility, would be willing to make public profession of a doctrine of racial superiority or of "white supremacy."

Even the politicians who have most strongly opposed the Supreme Court's decision outlawing segregation in schools have been careful to avoid any imputation that Negroes are "inferior." And the espousals of such a doctrine by Calvinist theologians in South Africa who support the dominant National Party's racial policies have evoked widespread condemnation in non-Catholic as well as Catholic circles.

Against the background of recent events in Mississippi and elsewhere, the National Council of Churches of Christ (Protestant) declared on October 5, 1955: "The National Council of Churches defends the rights and liberties of cultural, racial, and religious minorities. Christians must be especially sensitive to the oppression of minorities."

24. Patty Crowley Addresses the Papal Birth Control Commission (1965)

Patty Crowley, with her husband, Pat, were among the founders of the Christian Family Movement in 1949, chairing its national committee until 1970 (see No. 63). In 1964 the Vatican appointed them to the Papal Birth Control Commission, one of four couples invited to represent the laity. The primary issue was whether or not the use of "the pill" and other forms of birth control was a violation of the natural law (see Nos. 43, 46, 50). The Crowleys testified, on the basis of data they had compiled internationally on Catholic married couples in the CFM, that couples found the "rhythm method" neither natural nor an aid to intimacy, love, or unity in married life.

We have been blessed with only 5 children of our own but have housed more than a dozen foster children during the past 20 years under the supervision of the Catholic Charities. In addition to an active professional life as a lawyer and the duties of a housewife, together during the past 20 years we have devoted much of our spare time to organizing and activating couples in the Christian Family Movement. This experience brought us into close contact with thousands of apostolic, intelligent young families who by their lives have demonstrated a great love for the Church. . . .

CFM is known to be a sympathetic setting for large families. Since being told of our appointment and being authorized to consult our contemporaries, we have been shocked into a realization that even the most dedicated, committed Catholic couples are deeply troubled by this problem. We have gathered hundreds of statements from many parts of the United States and Canada and have been overwhelmed by the strong consensus in favor of some change. Most expressed a hope that the positive values in love and marriage need to be stressed and that an expanded theology of marriage needs to be developed.

Most say they think there must be a change in the teaching on birth control. Very few know what this change should be; they are puzzled but hopeful.

We understand that when the Church was considering the problem of what to do about reviewing the teaching on usury, the testimony of business people was heard and considered. If there is any parallel between the teaching of usury and the teaching on family limitation, then possibly there is a precedent for the testimony of those most affected by the doctrine. Our long identification with Christian families gives our report on how family people feel on this subject some evidentiary value.

In response to our inquiries we received a number of interesting letters, copies of which we make available to all who wish to read them. We have attempted to classify in some order those against change, those in favor of change. Most of the statements were made in response to questions about the subject outlined by Dr. John Marshall. Almost all feel there must be a reconsideration of the Church's stand. The solution is not clear to most but the need to be concerned is. Many of the couples have large families— 6 to 13 children—most are able to educate and support the children. Some have had intermittent financial, physical, and in a few cases, psychological problems. Many expressed the hope that the Church will change; a very few have given up and practiced some form of birth control. Most expressed dissatisfaction over the Rhythm method for a variety of reasons, running from the fact that it was ineffective, hard to follow; and some had psychological and physiological objections. We suspect that many are not too familiar with the science of practicing Rhythm.

People are puzzled by statements they have heard or seen in print that the old arguments based on natural law are being questioned. One report came from a couple; the wife was an obstetrical nurse; the husband, a successful management engineer; who have had wide experience in the Christian Family Movement in five states. They have no personal involvement because they could not have more than three children and have adopted one. They expressed the hope that there would be some change. They think pills are medical problems for medical research rather than theological speculation at this stage. They were horrified at the thought of the Church possibly approving of pills and later the medical profession rejecting them.

One very articulate group of six couples, all of whom are engaged in Catholic Social Action submitted a statement on the subject which we think deserves to be incorporated in this report:

"They believe the end of marriage, considered in its natural as well as sacramental aspects, is both personal and social—the fulfillment of the individual partners as Christians and human beings and the perfection of society."

"The bearing and raising of children are normally the means by which this end is reached; the intention of fruitfulness is normally part of the marriage union."

"The number of children by which a couple can best reach this end can be determined—*should* be determined—by the couple alone; if the decision is made to limit the number of children, this should be done on the basis of Christian charity; i.e., unselfishly, out of a love that sees some larger good to be accomplished by the limitation."

Discussions of the morality of sex in marriage should be based on considerations such as these, not on analysis of the isolated act of intercourse.

For these reasons they urged among other things that the Church state that regulation of conception is a decision to be left to the informed conscience of the couple."

Our impression is that this enormous problem deserves extensive investigation. The Church must convince its devoted followers that she is willing to re-open and re-examine this subject with all of the new insights of theological, as well as biological, physiological, psychological; sociological, demographic and historic background, etc., currently available to facilitate this important search for truth.

A Woman's Viewpoint

As a woman, I am grateful for the chance to address this Commission. Neither Pat nor I consider ourselves as "experts." Rather we look upon ourselves as "communication channels." As much as possible, we hope to pass on to you our interpretation of how married people that we know feel about this subject that is so overwhelmingly important to them.

During our adult lives we have worked with married people. We have talked with them, argued with them, perhaps preached to them more than we like to recognize, worked with them, and, most important, we have listened to them. Our work in the Christian Family Movement, which is now active in sixty-one countries, has taken us around the world several times. Just last month we visited CFM people in Australia, New Zealand, South Africa, Nigeria, Uganda, Tanzania. Since our appointment to this Commission we have asked people how they feel about these momentous questions. We have asked them informally, in casual conversation—where so much can be said in so few words—and we have asked them in three formal, scientific surveys. So we think that we can speak with some authority on how the married people we know and work with feel. . . .

For more than a year we have gathered data, written and oral. Our first questionnaire went to thousands of couples. They were tabulated in a report compiled by Professor Donald Barrett of the University of Notre Dame.

To confirm the findings in this study, we made still another survey, a course of action suggested by Dr. Andre Helligers. We asked CFM "contact couples" throughout the world to fill out a questionnaire dealing with rhythm. "Contact Couples" are leaders within their CFM geographical area. Ordinarily they have worked within CFM for a number of years. They are specially devoted to its aims. To do their CFM work and to succeed at it, they must be a husband and wife who communicate well with each other and are devoted to making their marriage a success. They strive to be, in short, a happy, successful family unit, and our observations would indicate they have succeeded. We stress this point, quite obviously, to indicate that these questionnaires were not filled out by disaffected Catholics, those who may be discouraged, disillusioned, or disenchanted, or whose personal problems within marriage may have caused them to drift apart from each other and from the Church.

Naturally, we do not presume to judge the success or happiness of a marriage or the quality of a person's Christianity. Yet if one were to ask us to select on the basis of outward appearances men and women who are indeed happy, who are committed to pursuing Christ's work on earth, who love the Church and look to her for guidance, these are precisely the couples we would select. For the details of the surveys themselves—the facts, figures, percentage of replies, and the like—I refer you to the reports themselves. Let me summarize a few of the conclusions.

Is there a bad psychological effect in the use of rhythm?

Almost without exception, the responses were that, yes, there is.

Does rhythm serve any useful purpose at all?

A few say it may be useful for developing discipline. Nobody says that it fosters married love.

Does it contribute to married unity?

No. That is the inescapable conclusion of the reports we have received.

In marriage a husband and wife pledge themselves to become one in mind, heart, and affection. They are no longer two, but one flesh—and they must find mutual help and serve each other through intimate union of their persons and their actions; through this union an experience of their oneness and attain to it with growing affection day by day.

Some wonder whether God would have us cultivate such unity by using what seems to them an unnatural system.

I must add that the best place children learn the importance of love is from the example of their parents. Yet these reports seem to indicate that instead of unity and love, rhythm tends to substitute tension, dissatisfaction, frustration, and disunity.

I feel that I would be disloyal to women if I didn't also emphasize one other point: We have heard some men, married and celibate, argue that rhythm is a way to develop love. But we have heard few women who agree with them.

Is rhythm unnatural?

Yes—that's the conclusion of these reports. Over and over, directly and indirectly, men and women—and perhaps especially women—voice the conviction that the physical and psychological implications of rhythm are not adequately understood by the male Church.

Very shortly I will quote at length from some of the responses we have received. Many of them point out a very simple physical and psychological fact, best expressed in those simple but sad words, "It's the wrong time." Over and over, respondents pointed out that nature prepares a woman at the time of ovulation to have the greatest urge to mate with her husband. Similarly at that time, her husband wants to respond to his wife. She craves his love. Yet month after month she must say no to her husband because it is the wrong date on the calendar or the thermometer reading isn't right.

No amount of theory by man will convince women that this way of making and expressing love is natural.

Listen, for example, to a couple that has been married 17 years. They have seven children and have had two miscarriages. They are both 38:

"This method of family planning is very harmful to our marriage and to many others. There has been many bad times and tears over this unreasonable law in this family. My husband is away on long business trips and unfortunately his company doesn't take our calendar into consideration when he has to be gone all over this country and now all over the world. He has left on trips at the wrong time of the month and arrived, all in the same month, at the wrong time of the month. Sometimes he's been gone weeks and arrived home at the wrong time of the month, too. This problem is detrimental to family rapport, since Mother and Father are very upset and edgy with one another since they cannot reaffirm their love at this time. One cannot make love by a calendar, since illness, fatigue and emotions are involved. More often than not, strangely, there is not a desire at this time, but you go through with it because it's safe, maybe, and there may not be another time. One or the other probably doesn't really prefer that particular time, but feels at least it is a release. This isn't a true expression of love! It must be free! It must be spontaneous as much as is possible."

A very dedicated couple who have worked for years in Marriage Preparation with women writes this:

"We have always been taught by the Church to strive for the ideal—the true Christian life, the best kind of marriage. However, it is psychologically sound that even a limited marriage, let alone really sound one is best achieved by two people with a good interpersonal relationship—one that is least hampered by fear, guilt and tension. No marriage will be without these tensions, just by virtue of two people living together, and then, the children entering into the relationship. This is why it is so important for a couple to be able to maintain as loving a relationship between themselves as possible. Therefore, I feel that we must do all in our power to help the Christian couple to foster their love. Certainly the best parents are 'whole' people psychologically and it is most difficult to be whole when you are constantly 'separated' from the loved one where sometimes you most need him or her in the vital emotional relationship which gets at feelings. Those who are torn by emotional upsets are not going to be able to fulfill the aim of marriage of 'responsible parenthood.' Certainly birth control is not going to solve all marriage problems, but it is another one that is constant and causes turmoil and agony in the lives of so many couples—couples who must be 'whole' in order to raise 'whole' people. Rhythm certainly can be the answer for some, but I would suggest that this is a very limited few. What is to be done for the millions of underprivileged who can't even count—or for the millions who are irregular—or for those in change of life. Is their emotional life supposed to shrivel up and die—really the worst kind of psychology! Actually rhythm fulfills a need because for many who absolutely cannot take the risk of more children without dire consequences to the marriage, rhythm could be combined with a contraceptive in order to give the greatest kind of assurance. With this kind of assurance many can be warm loving persons once again instead of fearful and tense. In the realm of psychology, any simple psychology book tells us that people who are in a constant stricture in an area that should be open and free and loving are damaging themselves and consequently, others.

Any emotions that are bottled up when one does not want them to be bottled up are dangerous. And how many millions of couples live in this situation daily—certainly far more than those who sublimate their desires or who are taught control. Finally, is our Church for a select few or are we trying to find solutions for the millions who need this kind of help."

The second psychological phenomena that was seen in many of the responses is that of *fear*. Once again, several quotes:

From a couple married 3 years, 2 children, 2 miscarriages: "Abstinence puts a strain on marriage. Each full-term pregnancy has meant a major operation (Caesarean)—miscarriages—and pregnant again and health has taken a beating. As a result, I cannot care for husband, children, or house as I should. The *fear* of another unwanted pregnancy puts such a fear in sex as to make it almost prohibitive."

A couple who has been very active in CFM since their marriage 11 years ago, both 35, 7 living children, tell us:

"Rhythm causes a lot of tension end preoccupation with the calendar. Some women can't take that monthly anxiety period (commonly called 'safe period') of waiting to find out if they made it through another month. For me it is difficult to rely on a 'safe period,' as I am always fearful that the cycle might have been thrown off by the frequent upsets of a 9-person household. The marriage act becomes less an expression of love and more a reminder of possible pregnancy and a duty grudgingly fulfilled. Many times I have gone through this turmoil, feeling reluctant, even resentful, and at the same time feeling guilty because my mind and heart are worrying about such things rather than thinking of my love for my husband. Add to this the anxiety of some of my friends whose husbands travel. If his weekend at home comes at the wrong time, then what? The wife always says, 'I trust my husband, but. . . .' The lunch hour hotel room affair is common enough in our society that even a woman whose husband does not travel wonders how much temptation she puts in his way by denying him at home. My point here is not that the husbands are not able to withstand the temptation, but the wives, being women who want, to be generous, feel guilty and sometimes worried by this aspect of rhythm. Another burden put on the wife is the fact that she, or rather her menstrual cycle, controls the exercise of the marriage act. 'You may not' or 'You may' or 'I don't know' says the calendar, thermometer, or fertility tape. It must be checked every day. It is a constant reminder that love may be expressed, or must be channeled elsewhere, depending upon the impersonal schedule of the cycle. What do I mean by 'channelled elsewhere?'

Aren't there other expressions of love besides the marriage act? Yes, but for me this creates another problem. I 'bend over backwards' to avoid raising false hopes on my husband's part. This sounds ridiculous, but I stiffen at a kiss on the cheek, instantly reminded that I must be discreet. I withdraw in other ways, too, afraid to be an interesting companion, gay or witty, or charming; hesitant about being sympathetic or understanding, almost wishing I could be invisible. At the same time I ask myself if my husband resents being dominated by a calendar, or if he misunderstands my cool behavior. And I wonder why I can't shake off the fear and uncertainty during the rest of the month.

Even though we have discussed these problems together they still bother me. I have limited this opinion strictly to rhythm and its effect upon me in regard to the marriage act. Much more could be said about the effects of this tension upon the children, about my husband's feelings in regard to rhythm, and about the early years of our marriage when we were taught that we had no reason or even right to limit or space our children." . . .

Thus we see the anguish expressed by some faithful Catholics. They are not alone. Some of them have suffered terribly and are only now asking themselves if their travail was really necessary. Others, expressing their love for each other and their families, nevertheless insist that they should have done it otherwise had they been free to choose their course of action. We can only admire the courage and honesty of a woman who looks at her family of seven (or more), loving her children, and yet admitting that she wishes she had the time to do something more than "act as a referee."

Notice how these reactions contradict what in the past has been the stereotyped, conventional way of looking at the Catholic husband and wife and their large family. These fathers and mothers, surveying their children, do not sit back with pride and satisfaction. Instead, they reflect a hardly muted bitterness as a condition in their lives that has forced them to stay apart from each other when their natures cried out for each other.

What shall we do?

Thirty years ago the Church introduced rhythm with the understanding that it was to be used only with permission of the confessor. Today the Church permits its use and even extends its blessings to those who use rhythm for good reason and in good conscience.

Our observation and experience confirms the fact that couples the world over are consciously or unconsciously asking a question:

"Why, then, cannot the Church permit Catholics with good reason and in good conscience to select their own methods in limiting births?"

Is not the sex drive instilled by God a normal one?

Should not husbands and wives be encouraged to express their love without adding a series of do's and don'ts?

Is it a sign of man's dignity that he must study the calendar to express the love he feels for his wife by an action that will deepen and intensify that love?

We think it is time for a change. We think it is time that this Commission recommend that the sacredness of conjugal love not be violated by thermometers and calendars. Marital union does lead to fruitfulness, psychologically as well as physically. Couples want children and will have them generously and love them and cherish them—we do not need the impetus of legislation to procreate—it is the very instinct of life, love and sexuality. It is in fact largely our very love for children as persons and our desire for their full development as committed Christians that leads us to realize that numbers alone and the large size of a family is by no means a Christian ideal unless parents can truly be concerned about and capable of nurturing a high *quality* of Christian life.

We express these thoughts, as nearly as we can reflect them, of thousands of couples.

We sincerely hope and do respectfully recommend that this Commission redefine the moral imperatives of fertility regulation with a view toward bringing them in conformity with our new and improved understanding of men and women in today's world.

We realize that some may be scandalized? [sic] Those who have no awareness of the meaning of renewal—those who disagree with the Conciliar emphasis on personhood and those who do not understand that the Church is the living People of God guided by the Holy Spirit.

Respectfully submitted,

Patty Crowley

25. THE U.S. CATHOLIC BISHOPS, "THE CHALLENGE OF PEACE" (1983)

In May 1983 the National Conference of Catholic Bishops issued one of the most important letters in its history of pastoral pronouncements: "The Challenge of Peace: God's Promise and Our Response." The American bishops took up the call of the second Vatican Council to position the Church squarely at the center of the public debate on important social and political issues; but it also issued its call for more focused efforts on peace-keeping during an especially tense period at the end of the Cold War, when the United States was building up its nuclear arsenal to help bring about the collapse of the Soviet Union. This letter provoked one of the most heated debates within the American Catholic community in the twentieth century.

2. As bishops and pastors ministering in one of the major nuclear nations . . . we write this letter because we agree that the world is at a moment of crisis, the effects of which are evident in people's lives. It is not our intent to play on fears, however, but to speak words of hope and encouragement in time of fear. Faith does not insulate us from the challenges of life; rather, it intensifies our desire to help solve them precisely in light of the Good News which has come to us in the person of Jesus, the Lord of history. From the resources of our faith we wish to provide hope and strength to all who seek a world free of the nuclear threat. Hope sustains one's capacity to live with danger without being overwhelmed by it; hope is the will to struggle against obstacles even when they appear insuperable. Ultimately our hope rests in the God who gave us life, sustains the world by his power, and has called us to revere the lives of every person and all peoples.

3. The crisis of which we speak arises from this fact: nuclear war threatens the existence of our planet; this is a more menacing threat than any the world has known. It is neither tolerable nor necessary that human beings live under this threat. But removing it will require a major effort of intelligence, courage, and faith. As Pope John Paul II said at Hiroshima: "From now on it is only through a conscious choice and through a deliberate policy that humanity can survive."[1]

4. As Americans, citizens of the nation which was first to produce atomic weapons, which has been the only one to use them, and which today is one of the handful of nations capable of decisively influencing the course of the nuclear age, we have grave human, moral, and political responsibilities to see that a "conscious choice" is made to save humanity. This letter is therefore both an invitation and a challenge to Catholics in the United States to join with others in shaping the conscious choices and deliberate policies required in this "moment of supreme crisis."

5. The global threat of nuclear war is a central concern of the universal Church, as the words and deeds of recent popes and the Second Vatican Council vividly demonstrate. In this pastoral letter we speak as bishops of

the universal Church, heirs of the religious and moral teaching on modern warfare of the last four decades. We also speak as bishops of the United States, who have both the obligation and the opportunity to share and interpret the moral and religious wisdom of the Catholic tradition by applying it to the problems of war and peace today.

6. The nuclear threat transcends religious, cultural, and national boundaries. To confront its danger requires all the resources reason and faith can muster. This letter is a contribution to a wider common effort, meant to call Catholics and all members of our political community to dialogue and specific decisions about this awesome question.

7. The Catholic tradition on war and peace is a long and complex one, reaching from the Sermon on the Mount to the statements of Pope John Paul II. Its development cannot be sketched in a straight line and it seldom gives a simple answer to complex questions. It speaks through many voices and has produced multiple forms of religious witness. . . .

9. In this pastoral letter, too, we address many concrete questions concerning the arms race, contemporary warfare, weapons systems, and negotiating strategies. We do not intend that our treatment of each of these issues carry the same moral authority as our statement of universal moral principles and formal Church teaching. Indeed, we stress here at the beginning that not every statement in this letter has the same moral authority. At times we reassert universally binding moral principles (e.g., noncombatant immunity and proportionality). At still other times we reaffirm statements of recent popes and the teaching of Vatican II. Again, at other times we apply moral principles to specific cases. . . .

12. On some complex social questions, the Church expects a certain diversity of views even though all hold the same universal moral principles. The experience of preparing this pastoral letter has shown us the range of strongly held opinion in the Catholic community on questions of war and peace. Obviously, as bishops we believe that such differences should be expressed within the framework of Catholic moral teaching. We urge mutual respect among different groups in the Church as they analyze this letter and the issues it addresses. Not only conviction and commitment are needed in the Church, but also civility and charity. . . .

16. Catholic teaching on peace and war had two purposes: to help Catholics form their consciences and to contribute to the public policy debate about the morality of war. These two purposes have led Catholic teaching to address two distinct but overlapping audiences. The first is the Catholic faithful, formed by the premises of the Gospel and the principles of Cath-

olic moral teaching. The second is the wider civil community, a more pluralistic audience, in which our brothers and sisters with whom we share the name Christian, Jews, Moslems, and other religious communities, and all people of good will also make up our polity. Since Catholic teaching has traditionally sought to address both audiences, we intend to speak to both in this letter, recognizing that Catholics are also members of the wider political community.

17. The conviction, rooted in Catholic ecclesiology, that both the community of the faithful and the civil community should be addressed on peace and war has produced two complementary but distinctive styles of teaching. The religious community shares a specific perspective of faith and can be called to live out its implications. The wider civil community, although it does not share the same vision of faith, is equally bound by certain key moral principles. For all men and women find in the depth of their consciences a law written on the human heart by God.[2] From this law reason draws moral norms. These norms do not exhaust the Gospel vision, but they speak to critical questions affecting the welfare of the human community, the role of states in international relations, and the limits of acceptable action by individuals and nations on issues of war and peace. . . .

19. As bishops we believe that the nature of Catholic moral teaching, the principles of Catholic ecclesiology, and the demands of our pastoral ministry require that this letter speak both to Catholics in a specific way and to the wider political community regarding public policy. Neither audience and neither mode of address can be neglected when the issue has the cosmic dimensions of the nuclear arms race. . . .

22. The distinctive contribution of the Church flows from her religious nature and ministry. The Church is called to be, in a unique way, the instrument of the Kingdom of God in history. Since peace is one of the signs of that Kingdom present in the world, the Church fulfills part of her essential mission by making the peace of the Kingdom more visible in our time.

23. Because peace, like the Kingdom of God, is both a divine gift and a human work, the Church should continually pray for the gift and share in the work. We are called to be a Church at the service of peace, precisely because peace is one manifestation of God's word and work in our midst. Recognition of the Church's responsibility to join with others in the work of peace is a major force behind the call today to develop a theology of peace. Much of the history of Catholic theology on war and peace has

focused on limiting the resort to force in human affairs; this task is still necessary. . . .

73. The Christian has no choice but to defend peace, properly understood, against aggression. This is an inalienable obligation. It is the *how* of defending peace which offers moral options. We stress this principle again because we observe so much misunderstanding about both those who resist bearing arms and those who bear them. Great numbers from both traditions provide examples of exceptional courage, examples the world continues to need. Of the millions of men and women who have served with integrity in the armed forces, many have laid down their lives. Many others serve today throughout the world in the difficult and demanding task of helping to preserve that "peace of a sort" of which the [Second Vatican] Council speaks. We see many deeply sincere individuals who, far from being indifferent or apathetic to world evils, believe strongly in conscience that they are best defending true peace by refusing to bear arms. In some cases they are motivated by their understanding of the Gospel and the life and death of Jesus as forbidding all violence. In others, their motivation is simply to give personal example of Christian forbearance as a positive, constructive approach toward loving reconciliation with enemies. In still other cases, they propose or engage in "active nonviolence" as programmed resistance to thwart aggression, or to render ineffective any oppression attempted by force of arms. No government, and certainly no Christian, may simply assume that such individuals are mere pawns of conspiratorial forces or guilty of cowardice.

74. Catholic teaching sees these two distinct moral responses as having a complementary relationship, in the sense that both seek to serve the common good. They differ in their perception of how the common good is to be defended most effectively, but both responses testify to the Christian conviction that peace must be pursued and rights defended within moral restraints and in the context of defining other basic human values. . . .

80. The moral theory of the "just-war" or the "limited-war" doctrine begins with the presumption which binds all Christians: we should do no harm to our neighbors; how we treat our enemy is the key test of whether we love our neighbor; and the possibility of taking even one human life is a prospect we should consider in fear and trembling. . . .

85. Why and when recourse to war is permissible.

86. War is permissible only to confront "a real and certain danger," i.e., to protect innocent human life, to preserve conditions necessary for decent human existence, and to secure basic human rights. As both Pope

Pius XIII and Pope John XXIII made clear, if war of retribution was ever justifiable, the risks of modern war negate such a claim today.

87. In the Catholic tradition the right to use force has always been joined to the common good; war must be declared by those with responsibility for public order, not by private groups or individuals. . . .

96. For resort to war to be justified, all peaceful alternatives must have been exhausted. There are formidable problems in this requirement. No international organization currently in existence has exercised sufficient internationally recognized authority to be able either to mediate effectively in most cases or to prevent conflict by the intervention of the United Nations or other peace-keeping forces. Furthermore, there is a tendency for nations or peoples which perceive conflict between or among other nations as advantageous to themselves to attempt to prevent a peaceful settlement rather than advance it. . . .

99. In terms of [just war] criteria, proportionality means that the damage to be inflicted and the costs incurred by war must be proportionate to the good expected by taking up arms. Nor should judgments concerning proportionality be limited to the temporal order without regard to a spiritual dimension in terms of "damage," "cost," and even "the good expected." In today's interdependent world even a local conflict can affect people everywhere; this is particularly the case when the nuclear powers are involved. Hence a nation cannot justly go to war today without considering the effect of its action on others and on the international community.

100. This principle of proportionality applies throughout the conduct of the war as well as to the decision to begin warfare. During the Vietnam war our bishops' conference ultimately concluded that the conflict had reached such a level of devastation to the adversary and damage to our own country that continuing it could not be justified. ["Resolution on Southeast Asia," 1971]

101. Even when the stringent conditions which justify resort to war are met, the conduct of war (i.e., strategy, tactics, and individual actions) remains subject to continuous scrutiny in light of two principles which have special significance today precisely because of the destructive capability of modern technological warfare. These principles are proportionality and discrimination . . . for today it becomes increasingly difficult to make a decision to use any kind of armed force, however limited initially in intention and in the destructive power of the weapons employed, without facing at least the possibility of escalation to broader, or even total, war and to the use of weapons of horrendous destructive potential. . . .

26. HISPANIC DEACONS' STATEMENT TO CARDINAL O'CONNOR (1988)

In 1988, John Cardinal O'Connor, the Archbishop of New York, abolished the tradition of training Hispanic deacons in their native language and stated that all diaconate training would be conducted in English. The Confraternidad de Hispanos de la Arquidioceis de Nueva York—the Confraternity of Hispanic Deacons of the Archdiocese of New York—sent this letter of concern to the Archbishop in August 1988, protesting not only the change of language in diaconal training, but also other new directives the Cardinal mandated: prohibiting the deacons from wearing the Roman collar, cutting back the ceremonies in which the deacons could appear on the altar with priests, and prohibiting their participation in a number of celebrations held by Hispanic Catholics. Cardinal O'Connor eventually re-established the Spanish-language training program for Hispanic deacons, although mandating that it reflect the program used in training English-speaking deacons.

Your Eminence:

We, the Hispanic deacons of the Archdiocese of New York, wish to share with Your Eminence the concerns that at present we have regarding our identity and purpose both as ordained ministers in the Church of New York and specifically as Hispanic deacons of that Church. . . .

I. Liturgical Functions

As you probably know by now, most Hispanics under your pastoral care come from simple, humble backgrounds. Our Church does not largely reach the many educated and wealthy Hispanics. Our Hispanic faithful are not intellectuals, not professionals, for the most part. For *all* Hispanics, however, signs and symbols, context more than content, play a major role in their expression, experience, celebration of faith. . . .

Hispanic deacons in their great majority come from this humble base [of society]. All of them identify themselves as true neighbors and friends of the laity. It is needless to mention the joy experienced by our Hispanic community as they saw some of their own being called to orders leading to a much desired *native* Hispanic clergy. At last the Hispanic community could provide its own ordained ministers. What a disappointment as they saw their own "ordained" deacons reduced to function as altar boys in many parishes as preference was given to extraordinary ministers of the Eucharist and other lay ministers or as priests took over diaconal functions in the presence of deacons.

To make things worse, by recent mandate, we have now been ordered out of the sanctuary, out of our liturgical vesture, and physically removed from the body of the clergy. We are indeed clerics incardinated in this archdiocese (canon 266). The symbols removed and others substituted, change the reality, our being; as Hispanics they effectively remove us from the native clergy in the eyes of our people. . . .

For us Hispanics the symbol of attending as a body is an essential one. Hispanics view life in symbolic rather than abstract terms, and the ordination of neighbors and fellow workers to the ministry of the Word and Sacrament is a powerful symbol of our own worth and validity "in medio Ecclesiae" [in the midst of the Church]. When these ordained ministers are ejected from the sanctuary and told to dress like the laity and sit among the laity, this too is a powerful symbol—but a powerful *negative* symbol. It may not mean to tell them, but it *does* tell them that "you do not belong with us," and to the Hispanic deacons in particular, "you are not *really* clergy but only glorified lay ministers." No amount of *verbal* explanation will undo the damage of this negative symbol, because Hispanics do not take words seriously when behavior, and especially symbolic behavior, goes counter to the words being said.

II. Ecclesiastical Attire

. . . The Hispanic faithful, which we so much love and among which we live, are being effectively deprived of the Church's Hispanic ministry as orders have now been received which in fact divest us deacons of our identity as Roman Catholic clergymen. The reason for this phenomenon is as stated above: for Hispanics at large, and particularly for ours, context, signs and symbols "constitute" reality. The scholastic axiom "quid quid recipitur ad modum recipientis recipitur" [what is received is received according to the mode of the recipient] is superbly illustrated here. The fact is that a Hispanic deacon, out of the sanctuary and out of the Roman collar, what is generally considered as ecclesiastical dress in the United States, does not convey the presence of the Catholic clergyman to our people. . . .

In the United States, the Roman collar is a powerful sign of the assuring presence of the Roman Catholic clergyman. This sign is not an end in itself. The sign is the "enabler," not the man—kind and loving as he might be. . . . This [lack of collar] opens our people to Pentecostals and other sectarians who, wearing the Roman collar, appear to them as "Catholic." . . . Need we remember how Fundamentalist proselytism prey on Hispanics: 5% of our Catholic Hispanics are attracted annually to sects, about 400 daily. . . . For God "the habit does not make the monk" but, in a most real sense, in our people's minds, "the habit" *does* "make the monk." We have changed, in our people's eyes we have reverted to the laity. . . . Our effectivity has been *reduced* to that of a dedicated lay minister which is what most Hispanic deacons appear to be in the dioceses where the collar is not worn. . . . In the end we ask ourselves why commit ourselves for life through sacramental consecration for something that is *needlessly ineffective,* as inffective as Hispanic deacons are in other dioceses where they appear as "lay" ministers. . . .

III. Formation Program

Another area of grave concern lies with the changes in the formation program for Hispanic permanent deacons. At the precise time when other dioceses are establishing diaconate programs in the Spanish language and have requested from the New York Hispanic deacons copies of their Spanish program, our Hispanic candidates to the diaconate are now asked to be literate in English so that they may study in English with the native speakers, as the Spanish program has now been absorbed by the English program. Unless these candidates come from the more advanced and academically oriented Hispanic classes, which our church hardly reaches, the good candidates that come from our parishes will never be able to get through the program. One thing is to be able to communicate in English and another is to read books and attend classes, much less write papers and take examinations in English. Classes in English have been tried before, ending in failure.

As the tides of immigration continue to arrive, Spanish is here to stay; it cannot be wished away. It is a fact that demands action from our part for, as younger generations learn English, the adults remain monolingual in Spanish and the new arrivals are overwhelmingly Spanish speakers: their spiritual needs must be met in Spanish. The diaconate, coming from the same social strata, can minister to them even in ways the priests cannot. But in order to do so we need Spanish-speaking, Spanish-trained deacons.

The new program does not take into account our culture, our liturgy, and tradition and values; it can only produce infertile and confused hybrids with serious identity problems. This program does not take into account that our deacons have to counteract sectarian proselytism where trinitarian, christological, and ecclesiological issues are central. While an English-speaking deacon may not need to know what Arianism is, a Hispanic confronts it on a daily basis in the Jehovah's Witnesses. Need we say anything about the divine maternity of the Blessed Virgin Mary? How are our deacons going to preach without the facile use of theological, biblical, and ecclesial vocabulary in Spanish? This vocabulary cannot be given through a program in English. In fact, the burden of having to study in English spells the end of the Hispanic diaconate in the church of New York. We are sure Your Eminence does not wish this to happen.

27. Michael Novak on the Spirit of Capitalism (1993)

In 1991 Pope John Paul II issued an encyclical, Centesimus Annus—*Latin for "On the Hundredth Year"—to celebrate the anniversary of Pope Leo XIII's landmark encyclical on Catholic social teaching,* Rerum Novarum. *But while marking the collapse of communism two years previously, John Paul's encyclical also set off a debate within the American Catholic community about whether it actually condemned or praised the kind of "market capitalism" exemplified by the U.S. economy. Catholic neoconservative Michael Novak thus published an extended commentary on the Pope's encyclical, arguing that America's type of limited capitalism actually made the best sense of the moral and theological "ends" of society proposed by the Pope in 1991.*

[Pope John Paul II] particularly worries about the elderly, the young who cannot find jobs, and "in general those who are weakest." He refers to the vulnerable in advanced societies as "the Fourth World." Meeting their needs is the unfinished work of *Rerum Novarum,* including a "sufficient wage for the support of the family, social insurance for old age and employment, and adequate protections for the conditions of unemployment." (*Centesimus Annus,* #34) All such deficiencies of a market system need to be redressed with practical wisdom. In some cases government will have to take a leading role, in other cases various sectors of civil society. The Pope is no libertarian—but neither is he a statist. Christian ends leave a great deal of room within these boundaries for rival approaches to means, programs, policies. . . .

The Pope repeats three times that "it is unacceptable to say that the defeat of so-called 'real socialism' leaves capitalism as the only model of economic organization." (*Centesimus Annus*, #35) But here as elsewhere his cure for unbridled capitalism is capitalism of a more balanced, well-ordered kind. . . . In #42, after having introduced capitalism rightly understood, the Pope again attacks "a radical capitalistic ideology. . . ." By "radical capitalistic ideology," the Pope seems to mean total reliance on market mechanisms and economic reasoning alone. In the United States, we usually call such a view "libertarianism"; it is the view of a small (but influential) minority. United States libertarians do not "refuse to consider" the poverty of multitudes; they offer their own sustained analyses and practical remedies, and with some success. . . .

Ironically, nonetheless, the Pope prefers to call the capitalism of which he approves the "*business economy, market economy,* or simply *free economy.*" This is probably because of European emotional resistance to the word "capitalism." My own reasoning in preferring to speak of "democratic capitalism," rather than the "market economy," is to avoid sounding libertarian—that is, narrowly focusing on the market system alone. For in reality, in advanced societies the institution of both the juridical order and the cultural order do impinge greatly on, modify, and "control" the economic system. Indeed, any religious leftist or traditionalist who still believes that the United States is an example of unrestrained capitalism has not inspected the whole thirty-foot-long shelf of volumes containing the Federal Register of legally binding commercial regulations. One might more plausibly argue that the economies of the capitalist nations today are too heavily regulated (and too unwisely) than too lightly.

In the real world of fact, the business economy is restrained by law, custom, moral codes, and public opinion, as anyone can see who counts the socially imposed costs they are obliged to meet—and the number of employees they must hire (lawyers, affirmative-action officers, public affairs officers, inspectors, community relations specialists, pension-plan supervisors, health-plan specialists, child-care custodians, etc.). The term "democratic capitalism" is an attempt to capture these political and cultural restraints upon any humane economic system. It is defined in a way broad enough to include political parties from the conservative to the social democratic, and systems as diverse as Sweden and the United States.

In a similar vein, the Pope notes three clear moral limits to the writ of the free market: (1) many human needs are not met by the market but lie beyond it; (2) some goods "cannot and must not be bought and sold"; and (3) whole groups of people are without the resources to enter the market and need nonmarket assistance. The market principle is a good one, but it is neither universal in its competence nor perfectly unconditional. It is not an idol.

In addition, the Pope thinks in terms of international solidarity. The whole world is his parish. The Pope's frequent travels by jet to the Third World are meant to dramatize the primary human (and Christian) responsibility to attend to the needs of the poor everywhere. Economic interdependence and the communications revolution have brought the Catholic people (and indeed all people) closer together than ever. This fact brings to his attention many moral and social imperatives surrounding and suffusing economic activities. For example, care must be taken not to injure the environment. (#37) States and societies need to establish a framework favorable to creativity, full employment, a decent family wage, and social insurance for various contingencies. (#34) The common good of all should be served, not violated by a few. Individuals should be treated as ends, not as means—and their dignity should be respected. (#34)

The tasks to be met by the good society are many. No system is as likely to achieve all these goods as is the market system, (#34) but in order to be counted as fully good, the market system must in fact achieve them. The Pope explicitly commends the successes registered in these respects by mixed economies after World War II. (#19) But he also stresses how much needs yet to be done. *Finding* good systems is a step forward; but *after* that comes the hard part.

On matters of population growth, the Pope's claim that human capital is the chief resource of nations may lead to a new approach to population control. Those who say dogmatically that a large population causes poverty have not thought carefully about highly successful societies of dense population such as Japan, Hong Kong, and the Netherlands. . . .The pope's emphasis on the creative capacity of every human being offers one reason why densely populated countries can become wealthy. *The principle behind economic progress is the fact that most people can create more in one lifetime than they can consume.* The cause of poverty is not "overpopulation." It is, on the contrary, a system of political economy that represses the economic creativity that God has endowed in every woman and man. Nations ought not to repress that creative capacity.

NOTES TO 25. THE U.S. CATHOLIC BISHOPS

1. John Paul II, "Address to Scientists and Scholars," 4, *Origins* 10 (1981): 621.
2. Vatican II, *The Pastoral Constitution on the Church in the Modern World,* 16.

FURTHER SUGGESTED READING

R. Scott Appleby, Patricia Byrne, and William Portier, eds., *Creative Fidelity: American Catholic Intellectual Traditions* (Maryknoll, N.Y.: Orbis Books, 2004).

Patrick Carey, *People, Priests, and Prelates: Ecclesiastical Democracy and the Tensions of Trusteeism* (Notre Dame, Ind.: University of Notre Dame Press, 1987).

Jay P. Dolan and Jaime R. Vidal, eds., *Puerto Rican and Cuban Catholics in the U.S., 1900–1965* (Notre Dame, Ind.: University of Notre Dame Press, 1994).

Gerald Fogarty, S.J., ed., *Patterns of Episcopal Leadership* (New York: Macmillan Publishing Company, 1989).

William M. Halsey, *The Survival of American Innocence: Catholicism in the Era of Disillusionment, 1920–1940* (Notre Dame, Ind.: University of Notre Dame Press, 1980).

Paula Kane, James Kenneally, and Karen Kennelly, eds., *Gender Identities in American Catholicism* (Maryknoll, N.Y.: Orbis Books, 2001).

Timothy Matovina and Gerald Poyo, eds., *Presente! U.S. Latino Catholics from Colonial Origins to the Present* (Maryknoll, N.Y.: Orbis Books, 2000).

Joseph M. McShane, S.J., *"Sufficiently Radical": Catholic Progressivism and the Bishops' Program of 1919* (Washington, D.C.: Catholic University of America Press, 1986).

Sandra Yocum Mize and William Portier, eds., *American Catholic Traditions: Resources for Renewal* (Maryknoll, N.Y.: Orbis Books, 1997).

R. Lawrence Moore, *Religious Outsiders and the Making of Americans* (New York: Oxford University Press, 1986).

Charles R. Morris, *American Catholic: The Saints and Sinners Who Built America's Most Powerful Church* (New York: Random House, 1997).

David O'Brien, *American Catholics and Social Reform: The New Deal Years* (New York: Oxford University Press, 1968).

Part III

Catholicism and the Intellectual Life

This section offers examples of the variety of intellectual styles that have influenced American Catholic thought in the twentieth century. The scholastic tradition of natural law, as classically embodied in John Courtney Murray's famous "Catholic Reflections on the American Proposition" (No. 29), profoundly influenced American Catholic political theory until well into the twentieth century. Several distinctive American voices have critiqued or revised that older scholastic tradition, as evidenced in Elizabeth Johnson's groundbreaking critique of scholastic male metaphors for God (No. 34).

John Tracy Ellis offered what is arguably the most searing—and far-reaching—internal critique of American Catholic intellectual timidity and problematic commitment to higher education (No. 28), while the famous "Land O' Lakes Statement" sought to establish academic freedom and a serious commitment to advanced research as the cornerstones of Catholic higher education (No. 31). Madeleva Wolff, one of the most forceful and prophetic voices for educating Catholic women (No. 30), stands in marked contrast to Flannery O'Connor's quite distinctive reflection on being a "Catholic" woman writer in the American South (No. 32). All of these voices are genuinely—and distinctively—"Catholic," although in the diverse ways one would expect in a national Church the sociologist Andrew Greeley has described as a "tribe of tribes" (No. 33).

28. JOHN TRACY ELLIS, "AMERICAN CATHOLICS AND THE INTELLECTUAL LIFE" (1955)

In 1955 John Tracy Ellis, a famed scholar of American Catholicism teaching at the Catholic University of America, published one of the most important and far-reaching essays in twentieth-century U.S. Catholicism. Ellis's essay, published in Fordham University's Thought *magazine, elicited what John McGreevey has termed a "spectacular eruption of cultural self-criticism" among Catholics in the decade following its publication. Responding to criticisms both inside and outside the U.S. Catholic community, Ellis accused American Catholics of betraying their proud intellectual heritage to sponsor colleges and universities known more for their football ("athleticism") teams than for their Nobel laureates, schools marked more by their concern for training students for "vocational placement" ("vocationalism") than for love of learning for its own sake.*

I . . . instituted an investigation among the students of my seminar on the subject of Catholic leadership in the three fields of business, politics, and scholarship during the 1940s. Their findings were, of course, quite tentative in nature, but they did indicate that, relatively speaking, Catholic business leadership on a national scale in those years ran ahead of leadership in national politics, and it made the showing by Catholics who had attained national recognition through productive scholarship seem insignificant by comparison. There is, then, warrant for saying that Catholics have not only shown an increasing participation in the native penchant for making money, but that, all things considered, they have probably attained more distinction in the business world than they have in any other section of American life.

But has the arrival of a fairly large number of American Catholic businessmen at the status of millionaires—many of whom are college graduates—occasioned any notable change in their attitude toward or increase in their support of the intellectual pursuits of their coreligionists? That question brings us to the sixth major point which I would like to make, namely the failure of Catholics in posts of leadership, both clerical and lay, to understand fully, or to appreciate in a practical way, the value of the vocation of the intellectual. First, to return to the question of the laity, the answer is not, I believe, a clear Yes or an unqualified No. About the only norm of judgment that one can apply to their attitude, unless one knows them personally, is their outward action in the form of endowments of the things of the mind. In that respect one can say that the situation at present reveals a higher appreciation of intellectual values on the part of Catholics of wealth than it did two generations ago when, to be sure, the number possessing large fortunes was much smaller. To cite once more the history of our own [Catholic] University, with which I am best acquainted, I think it was somewhat significant that when the committee of the hierarchy sought funds for the institution in the 1880s they received only two gifts of really large size, the sum of $300,000 from Miss Mary Gwendolyn Caldwell and $100,000 from Eugene Kelly of New York. Moreover, in the sixty years that the University has been in existence there have not been more than about ten instances where bequests of $100,000 or more have been received from individual American Catholics of wealth. . . .

That brings us to the role played by the clerical leaders of the American Church. In anything that is said or written on the subject of either the clerical or lay leaders in the Church of the United States it should be kept in mind that, *mutatis mutandis,* the vast majority of them have been men of their own generation, reflecting—apart from the dogmatic and moral views which they held as Catholics—the predominant attitudes and prevailing tendencies of their time. Thus the solemn dignity and stately bearing of Archbishop [John] Carroll suggested the eighteenth-century gentleman of Washington's generation in a way that might even seem a trifle stuffy to a twentieth-century prelate. . . . In the same sense the bishops and major superiors of the religious orders of this generation reveal, it seems to me, the characteristics of their time, for among them one will find men whose executive and administrative talents are of a very high order. It is fortunate that this is so, for it is no exaggeration to say that the Catholic Church of the United States has become "big business" in the typically American meaning of that term. And, we may add, woe to Catholic interests if the bishops and the heads of the principal religious orders were not men who possessed the ability to cope with the problems that the far-flung commitments of the American Church now daily impose upon them!

Yet it is to be regretted that the pressing tasks of administration leave so little time and leisure to these spiritual superiors for a more active participation and effective encouragement to intellectual concerns. Their backgrounds do not account for the lack of it, for they are basically the same as that of the Catholic intellectuals themselves. That point was made clear by Archbishop Cushing in 1947 when he stated to the ninth annual convention of the CIO meeting in his see city:

> I have said this before, but it is important to repeat it here: in all the American hierarchy resident in the United States, there is not known to me one Bishop, Archbishop or Cardinal whose father or mother was a college graduate. Every one of our Bishops and Archbishops is the son of a working man and a working man's wife.

Many of these prelates of whom the Archbishop of Boston spoke are, of course, themselves college graduates, and a considerable number of them are the products of graduate training in fields like theology, philosophy, canon law, education, and social work. . . . [But] relatively few of the higher clergy have taken graduate work in the humanities and liberal arts. As a consequence one will find among them, I believe, a far greater emphasis on what are the professional and vocational aspects of higher education, since they serve a practical end in their diocesan chanceries, charities, and offices of superintendents of schools, than might otherwise be the case. In this, I submit, they faithfully mirror the intense preoccupation of American leaders in all walks of life with the practical. That the practical order of things is of vital importance to the Church, no one with any understanding of its mission would attempt to deny. But by the same token the Church has a mission to the intellectual elite and this, I fear, has been allowed to suffer neglect by reason of the prevalence of the practical. . . .

[Another] part of the reason why American Catholics have not made a notable impression on the intellectual life of their country is due, I am convinced, to what might be called a betrayal of that which is peculiarly their own. The nature of that betrayal has been highlighted during the last quarter of a century by such movements as the scholastic revival in philosophy which found its most enthusiastic and hard-working friends on the campuses of the University of Chicago, the University of Virginia, Princeton University, and St. John's College, Annapolis. Meanwhile the Catholic universities were engrossed in their mad pursuit of every passing fancy that crossed the American educational scene, and found relatively little time for distinguished contributions to scholastic philosophy. Woefully lacking in the endowment, training, and equipment to make them successful competitors of the secular universities in fields like engineering, business administration, nursing education, and the like, the Catholic universities, nonetheless, went on multiplying these units and spreading their budgets so thin—in an attempt to include everything—that the subjects in which they could, and should, make a unique contribution were sorely neglected.

That American educators expect Catholic institutions to be strong in the humanities and the liberal arts—to say nothing of theology and philosophy—is not surprising. Eighteen years ago Robert M. Hutchins, then President of the University of Chicago, in an address before the Middle West regional unit of the National Catholic Educational Association made that point in a very forceful way. Speaking of the Catholic Church as having what he called "the longest intellectual tradition of any institution in the contemporary world," Hutchins criticized the Catholic institutions for failing to emphasize that tradition in a way that would make it come alive in American intellectual circles. He thought the ideals of Catholic educators were satisfactory, but as far as actual practice was concerned, he said, "I find it necessary to level against you a scandalous accusation." He then went on:

> In my opinion you have imitated the worst features of secular education and ignored most of the good ones. There are some good ones, relatively speaking—high academic standards, development of habits of work and research. . . .

Hutchins listed the bad features he had in mind as athleticism, collegialism, vocationalism, and anti-intellectualism. In regard to the first two we can claim, I think, that in recent years Catholic institutions have shown improvement, just as all other educational groups have done. As for the second two, vocationalism and anti-intellectualism, I find no striking evidence of reform in the Church's colleges and universities since 1937. Regarding the three good features of secular institutions which Hutchins named, high academic standards, development of habits of work, and the ideal of research, I would say that a better showing has been made here and there on the first, but on the development of habits of work and a cherished ideal of research, I cannot personally see much by way of a fundamental change. . . .

An additional point which should find place in an investigation of this kind is the absence of a love of scholarship for its own sake among American Catholics, and that even among too large a number of Catholics who are engaged in higher education. It might be described as the absence of a sense of dedication to the intellectual apostolate. This defect, in turn, tends to deprive many of those who spend their lives in the universities of the American Church of the admirable industry and unremitting labor in research and publication which characterize a far greater proportion of their colleagues on the faculties of secular universities. . . .

Closely connected with the question of the prevailing Catholic attitudes in education is the overemphasis which some authorities of the Church's educational system in the United States have given to the school as an agency for moral development, with an insufficient stress on the role of the school as an instrument for fostering intellectual excellence. That fact has at times led to a confusion of aims and to a neglect of the school as a training ground for the intellectual virtues. No sensible person will for a moment question that the inculcation of moral virtue is one of the principal reasons for having Catholic schools in any circumstances. But that goal should never be permitted to overshadow the fact that the school, at whatever level one may consider it, must maintain a strong emphasis on the cultivation of intellectual excellence. Given superior minds, out of the striving for intellectual virtues there will flow, with its attendant religious instruction, the formation of a type of student who will not only be able to withstand the strains which life will inevitably force upon his religious faith, but one who will have been so intellectually fortified that he will reflect distinction upon the system of which he is a product. . . .

In conclusion, then, one may say that it has been a combination of all the major points made in this paper, along with others which I may have failed to consider, that has produced in American Catholics generally, as well as in the intellectuals, a pervading spirit of separatism from their fellow citizens of other religious faiths. They have suffered from the timidity that characterizes minority groups, from the effects of a ghetto they have themselves fostered, and, too, from a sense of inferiority induced by their consciousness of the inadequacy of Catholic scholarship. But who, one may rightly ask, has been responsible in the main for its inadequacy? Certainly not the Church's enemies, for if one were to reason on that basis St. Augustine would never have written the *City of God*, St. Robert Bellarmine the *Tractatus de potestate summi pontificis*, nor would Cardinal Baronius have produced the *Annales ecclesiastici*. In fact, it has been enmity and opposition that have called forth some of the greatest monuments of Catholic scholarship. The major defect, therefore, lies elsewhere than with the unfriendly attitude of some of those outside the Church. The chief blame, I firmly believe, lies with Catholics themselves. It lies in their frequently self-imposed ghetto mentality which prevents them from mingling as they should with their non-Catholic colleagues, and in their lack of industry and the habits of work, to which Hutchins alluded in 1937. It lies in their failure to have measured up to their responsibilities to the incomparable tradition of Catholic learning of which they are the direct heirs, a failure which Peter Viereck noted, and which suggested to him the caustic question, "Is the honorable adjective 'Roman Catholic' truly merited by America's middleclass-Jansenist Catholicism, puritanized, Calvinized, and dehydrated . . . ?"

There is not a man of discernment anywhere today who is unaware that the intellectual climate of the United States is undergoing a radical change from the moribund philosophy of materialism and discredited liberalism that have ruled a good portion of the American mind for the better part of a century. Clinton Rossiter spoke of this in a thoughtful article published some months ago. He foresees a new day dawning for our country when religious and moral values will again be found in the honored place they once occupied. Concerning that ray of hope upon the horizon, he concluded: "And it will rest its own strong faith in liberty and constitutional democracy on the bedrock of these traditional, indeed eternal, values: religion, justice, morality." If this prediction should prove true, and there is increasing support for the view that it will, to whom, one may ask, may the leaders of the coming generation turn with more rightful expectance in their search for enlightenment and guidance in the realm of religion and morality than to the American Catholic intellectuals? For it is they who are in possession of the oldest, wisest, and most sublime tradition of learning that the world has ever known. There has, indeed, been considerable improvement among American Catholics in the realm of intellectual affairs in the last half-century, but the need for far more energetic strides is urgent if the receptive attitude of contemporary thought is to be capitalized upon as it should be. It is, therefore, a unique opportunity that lies before the Catholic scholars of the United States which, if approached and executed with the deep conviction of its vital importance for the future of the American Church, may inspire them to do great things and, at the end, to feel that they have in some small measure lived up to the ideal. . . .

29. John Courtney Murray, S.J., *We Hold These Truths: Catholic Reflections on the American Proposition* (1960)

Published in the year during which John F. Kennedy was running for President, Murray's collection of natural law articles represents one of the high points of Catholic intellectual endeavor in the twentieth century. Murray, himself a theology professor at the Jesuit order's seminary in Woodstock, Maryland, sought to provide an answer to those critics of Kennedy who argued that a Catholic could not (and should not) be elected president because the American Constitution presented the democratic principle as the source of ultimate authority for all free institutions in the United States. That is, Murray sought to answer those critics who argued that all true authority—in every genuinely American institution—flowed from the people to those in authority. Given this understanding, Kennedy as a Catholic held a profoundly un-American understanding of authority, and should be kept out of presidential office. But Murray argued that, ironically enough, those very critics of Kennedy who sought to assure his defeat because of the fear of bringing in an un-American and authoritarian understanding of religion were themselves guilty of effecting an "establishment of religion"!

Theologies of the First Amendment

The question here is one of theory, the theory of the First Amendment in itself and in its relation to Catholic theories of freedom of religion and the church-state relation. It is customary to put to Catholics what is supposed to be an embarrassing question: Do you really believe in the first two provisions of the First Amendment? The question calls to mind one of the more famous among the multitudinous queries put by Boswell to Dr. Johnson, "whether it is necessary to believe in all the Thirty-Nine Articles." And the doctor's answer has an applicable point: "Why, sir, that is a question which has been much agitated. Some have held it necessary that all be believed. Others have considered them to be only articles of peace, that is to say, you are not to preach against them."

An analogous difference of interpretation seems to exist with regard to the first articles of the First Amendment.

On the one hand, there are those who read into them certain ultimate beliefs, certain specifically sectarian tenets with regard to the nature of religion, religious truth, the church, faith, conscience, divine revelation, human freedom, etc. In this view these articles are invested with a genuine sanctity that derives from their supposed religious content. They are dogmas, norms of orthodoxy, to which one must conform on pain of some manner of excommunication. They are true articles of faith. Hence it is necessary to believe them, to give them a religiously motivated assent.

On the other hand, there are those who see in these articles only a law, not a dogma. These constitutional clauses have no religious content. They answer none of the eternal human questions with regard to the nature of truth and freedom or the manner in which the spiritual order of man's life is to be organized or not organized. Therefore they are not invested with the sanctity that attaches to dogma, but only with the rationality that attaches to law. Rationality is the highest value of law. In further consequence, it is not necessary to give them a religious assent but only a rational civil obedience. In a word, they are not articles of faith but articles of peace, that is to say, you may not act against them, because they are law and good law.

Those who dogmatize about these articles do not usually do so with all clarity that dogmas require. Nor are they in agreement with one another. The main difference is between those who see in these articles certain Protestant religious tenets and those who see in them certain ultimate suppositions of secular liberalism. The differences between those two groups tend to disappear in a third group, the secularizing Protestants, so called, who effect an identification of their Protestantism with American secular culture, consider the church to be true in proportion as its organization is commanded by the norms of secular democratic society, and bring about a coincidence of religious and secular-liberal concepts of freedom.

All three of these currents of thought have lengthy historical roots; the first, predominantly in the modified Puritan Protestantism of the "free church" variety; the second, in early American deism and rationalism; the third, in less specific sources, but importantly in the type of Protestantism, peculiar to America, whose character was specified during the Great Awakening, when the American climate did as much to influence Protestantism as Protestantism did to influence the American climate. This more radical secularizing Protestantism has in common with the later Puritan tradition the notion that American democratic institutions are the necessary secular reflection of Protestant anti-authoritarian religious individualism and its concept of the "gathered" church. Protestantism and Americanism, it is held, are indissolubly wedded as respectively the religious and the secular aspects of the one manner of belief, the one way of life. . . .

Do these clauses [of the First Amendment] assert or imply that the nature of the church is such that it inherently demands the most absolute separation from the state? Do they assert or imply that the institutional church is simply a voluntary association of like-minded men; that its origins are only in the will of men to associate freely for purposes of religion and worship; that all churches, since their several origins are in equally valid religious inspirations, stand on a footing of equality in the face of the divine and evangelical law; that all ought by the same token to stand on an equal footing in the face of the civil law? In a word, does separation of church and state in the American sense assert or imply a particular sectarian concept of the church?

Further, does the free-exercise clause assert or imply that the individual conscience is the ultimate norm of religious belief in such wise that an external religious authority is inimical to Christian freedom? Does it hold that religion is a purely private matter in such wise that an ecclesiastical religion is inherently a corruption of the Christian Gospel? Does it maintain that true religion is religion-in-general. . . . Does it pronounce that religious truth to be simply a matter of personal experience, and religious faith to be simply a matter of subjective impulse, not related to any objective order of truth or to any structured economy of salvation whose consistence is not dependent on the human will?

The questions could be multiplied, but they all reduce themselves to two. Is the no-establishment clause a piece of ecclesiology, and is the free-exercise clause a piece of religious philosophy? The general Protestant tendency, visible in its extreme in the free-church tradition, especially among the Baptists, is to answer affirmatively to these questions. Freedom of religion and separation of church and state are to be, in the customary phrase, "rooted in religion itself." Their substance is to be conceived in terms of sectarian Protestant doctrine. They are therefore articles of faith; not to give them a religious assent is to fall into heterodoxy.

The secularist dissents from the Protestant theological and philosophical exegesis. . . . But it is to him likewise an article of faith (he might prefer to discard the word "faith," and speak rather of ultimate presuppositions). . . . These men commit themselves singly to the method of scientific empiricism. There is therefore no eternal order of truth and justice; there are no universal verities that require man's assent, no universal moral law that commands his obedience. Such an order of universals is not empirically demonstrable. Truth therefore is to be understood in a positivistic sense; its criteria are either those of science or those of practical life, i.e., the success of an opinion in getting itself accepted in the market place. With this view of truth there goes a corresponding view of freedom. The essence of freedom is "non-committalism. . . ." The mind or will that is committed, absolutely and finally, is by definition not free. It has fallen from grace by violating its own free nature. In the intellectual enterprise the search for truth, not truth itself or its possession, is the highest value. . . .

This school of thought, which is of relatively recent growth in America, thrusts into the First Amendment its own ultimate views of truth, freedom and religion. Religion itself is not a value, except insofar as its ambiguous reassurances may have the emotional effect of conveying reassurance. Roman Catholicism is a dis-value. Nevertheless, religious freedom, as a form of freedom, is a value. It has at least the negative value of an added emancipation, another sheer release. It may also have the positive value of another blow struck at the principle of authority in any of its forms, for in this school authority is regarded as absolutely antonymous to freedom.

Furthermore, this school usually reads into the First Amendment a more or less articulated political theory. Civil society is the highest societal form of life; even the values that are called spiritual and moral are values by reason of their reference to society. Civil law is the highest form of law and it is not subject to judgment by prior ethical canons. Civil rights are the highest form of rights; for the dignity of the person, which grounds these rights, is only his civil dignity. The state is purely the instrument of the popular will, than which there is no higher sovereignty. Government is to the citizen what the cab-driver is to the passenger. And since the rule of the majority is the method whereby the popular will expresses itself, it is the highest governing principle of statecraft, from which there is no appeal. Finally, the ultimate value within society and state does not consist in any substantive ends that these societal forms may pursue; rather it consists in the process of their pursuit. That is to say, the ultimate value resides in the forms of the democratic process itself, because these forms embody the most ultimate of all values, freedom. . . .

Given this political theory, the churches are inevitably englobed within the state, as private organizations for particular purposes. Their right to freedom is a civil right, and it is respected as long as it is not understood to include any claim to independently sovereign authority. Such a claim must be disallowed on grounds of the final and indivisible sovereignty of the democratic process over all the associational aspects of human life. The notion that any church should acquire status in public life as a society in its own right is per se absurd; for there is only one society, civil society, which may so exist. In this view, separation of church and state, as ultimately implying a subordination of church to state, follows from the very nature of the state and its law. . . .

If these clauses are made articles of faith . . . there are immediately in this country some 35,000,000 dissenters, the Catholic community. Not being either a Protestant or a secularist, the Catholic rejects the religious position of Protestants with regard to the nature of the church, the meaning of faith, the absolute primacy of conscience, etc.; just as he rejects secularist views with regard to the nature of truth, freedom, and civil society as man's last end. He rejects these positions as demonstrably erroneous in themselves. What is more to the point here, he rejects the notion that any of these sectarian theses enter into the content or implications of the First Amendment in such wise as to demand the assent of all American citizens. If this were the case the very article that bars any establishment of religion would somehow establish one. . . .

From the standpoint both of history and of contemporary reality the only tenable position is that the first two articles of the First Amendment are not articles of faith but articles of peace. Like the rest of the Constitution these provisions are the work of lawyers, not of theologians or even of political theorists. They are not true dogma but only good law. That is praise enough. This, I take it, is the Catholic view. But in thus qualifying it I am not marking it out as just another "sectarian" view. It is in fact the only view that a citizen with both historical sense and common sense can take.

30. Sr. Madeleva Wolff, C.S.C., "Educating Our Daughters as Women" (1961)

Sister Madeleva Wolff, president of St. Mary's College in South Bend, Indiana, was one of the most forceful and compelling voices in American Catholicism for the rigorous education of Catholic women. Her work at St. Mary's— crafting it into one of the premier women's colleges in the United States—lent her great credibility as a spokeswoman calling for more resources from the Catholic community in educating young women. Her essay here witnesses to both her advocacy for a (then) progressive cause and to the time-conditioned nature of some of her ideas, like "essential womanhood."

A college board of trustees is an excellent tribunal before which to test our theories and practices in the education of our daughters. Individually, these trustees have academic interests as wide and as varied as their professions, their industries, their immediate occupations. Within their own localities, they may be working on a hospital project, a new elementary school or a high school. They may be concerned with programs in nursing, in education. We can lead them down all the paths and bypaths of academic specialization with varying responses of interest or inquiry. For the most part they have moved away from the worlds of educational theory to the stern realities of practice. One question is common to all of them. This they ask: "Does anyone think of educating a woman as a woman?"

The question pulls us up sharply. Basically we face a double problem in education. "Should the college educate a woman as a woman? If so, how?" These are two questions that suggest a third equally important one: Do all types of college educate our daughters equally well in their proper vocation of being women?

Running the gauntlet of semantics, we may say that we always educate a woman as a woman. The quantity and quality of her womanhood depend very much, first upon herself; then upon the school she attends, the school that is her Alma Mater. She will probably resemble her intellectual mother. Our trustees may have in mind a quintessence of womanliness as a quality to be preserved, if not indeed to be developed in the education of our daughters. We believe in the quintessence of womanliness as the very flower and fruit of the education of women.

These daughters of ours have had two choices in the kind of college training they wished: coeducation or education in the private college for women. If they chose the latter, they elected to be educated as women with an existential major and minor in womanhood. Their academic choices became effective in this environment, in this their essential existence. Their entire life, their worlds, their unused futures have already received certain determinations, certain directions by this choice.

They may go to coeducational schools. Why not? Coeducational universities and colleges educate women in exactly the same way as they educate men. In fact all of our coeducational schools, on the college level, until within the past decade perhaps, began as schools for men. Women were admitted at first cautiously and by exception. Once matriculated, they proved, by and large, their ability to be educated in the same way as men or in curricula set up for men. Gradually departments in home economics and nursing were provided specifically for women. Today they constitute a large percentage of the enrollment in the coeducational schools. Tens of thousands of our American girls are in college with hundreds of thousands of our American boys, and love it. They emerge as educated women, but not quite the same type of women as they might have been if they had been educated as women.

These are merely statements of fact. They are neither a measure of the value of coeducation to our daughters, or of our daughters to coeducation. The value of girls on the coeducational campus is pervasive, subtle.

It has something to do with ties, with grooming in general, with the gentle arts of courtesy. Recently a newspaper published the picture of a student carrying his girl friend's books. This was front-page news. Upon a time one of our best American universities reported the registration of two pretty young women in the graduate school as effecting a palpable return to the fine arts and courtesies of living among these high-grade men students.

Girls do not go to coeducational schools for these reasons, but they do affect coeducation in these ways. Reciprocally, their coeducational colleges affect them. A girl educated with, and as, boys, will be a different woman from the girl educated as girls are and with them.

This does not imply that they are, or should be educated exclusively by women. The better the college for women, the healthier ballast of scholarly men it will invite to its faculty. The mind of a growing girl realizes its capacities more perfectly under the tutelage of both scholarly men and scholarly women. This is true for boys as well. Men are quick and proud to recognize this.

But as boys, they do not clamor to go to colleges for women; they do not stampede our private schools and insist on being educated as girls are educated. We women have reversed the story of the Sabine women; we have put ourselves in a somewhat unintellectual position in our very endeavor to prove our intellectual equality with men.

For more than a century and a quarter our girls have had excellent colleges for women from which to choose. They select this type of school because they want this experience of the intellectual life as and with young women. Most of them do not change their minds on this score during their four undergraduate years.

Just how might a college educate young women as women? It might recognize the great fields of knowledge, the sciences, the liberal arts, the fine arts. Since theology is the queen of the sciences it might make it the core, the central and integrating subject in the curriculum. The student's entire experience can become significant in terms of its relation to God. The student herself will grow in the knowledge of her own supernatural stature in consequence, and of the supernatural world itself in which we all live and move. Her womanhood will be measured by, and uplifted to the womanhood of Mary. This in itself educates her as woman.

Around the science of theology, the profane sciences range themselves in orders and potencies which atomic energies and electronics merely shadow. Women can move among these as freely as men, with the authentic freedom of truth. Such fields as cancer research and care of premature babies are being successfully investigated by teachers and students in colleges for women. They are living in their Father's house, working with His tools, playing at times perhaps with the fascinating toys He has provided for them. This is far from fancy. The greatest scientists know it to be a divine fact.

The liberal arts are the most liberal, most liberating when they rest on complete rather than on partial truth. Here the Catholic college was the authentic exponent for the first sixteen centuries of Christian arts and sciences. One may say the same of the fine arts. Also, girls study, learn, and respond to teaching differently from the way boys do, and differently in classes with boys from the way they do in groups of girls only. Whatever the reasons for the delicate psychology governing these facts, they are facts. Girls achieve a type of womanhood when educated with girls which differs from the results of coeducation. We believe that this difference is a more refined, a more perfect womanhood, the quintessential womanliness.

Perfection is not achieved without costs. The women's colleges in the United States are monuments to the enterprise, the sacrifice, the fortitude of women. They are the most expensive to maintain, the last to benefit by philanthropy. Present educational crises are being met by colossal gifts from corporations, foundations, individuals.

At a recent meeting of the American Council on Education, the question was asked: "Where in the order of these gifts do colleges for women stand?" This is the answer which was given, not without embarrassment: "Gifts for education go first, to schools with big names; second, to big schools; third, to coeducational schools; fourth, to women's colleges." Considering that half the parents of the world, all of the mothers, the wives, the daughters, and the sisters are women, this does not reflect gloriously to the generosity, the chivalry, the gratitude, or even the justice of the manhood of our country.

We come back to the question with which we began: "Are we educating our daughters as women?" We have put before our hypothetical tribunal of college trustees our two general answers. Coeducation does not educate our daughters essentially as women. The women's private college does. Its survival is precarious, since it is the last and the least supported of all the colleges in our educational structure. We can continue to educate our daughters as women only with adequate help. Our men who have been educated as men know the answer. The education of our daughters as women depends upon them.

31. The "Land O' Lakes" Statement on American Catholic Universities (1967)

In 1967 Fr. Theodore Hesburgh, C.S.C., president of the University of Notre Dame, hosted twenty-six representatives from nine Catholic universities at Land O' Lakes, Wisconsin, to draw up a statement on American Catholic higher education in light of the Second Vatican Council, which had ended two years earlier. Especially important in influencing their statement was the text of Vatican II's document "Gaudium et Spes" (the "Constitution on the Church in the Modern World"), which had called Catholic Christians to a greater engagement with the world around them. The resulting "Statement" had a profound influence on all 300 Catholic colleges and universities in the United States, effecting changes which some Catholic educators would later criticize as offering "secular" models of higher education as normative for Catholic institutions in problematic ways.

1. The Catholic University: A True University with Distinctive Characteristics

The Catholic university today must be university in the full modern sense of the word, with a strong commitment to and concern for academic excellence. To perform its teaching and research functions effectively the Catholic university must have a true autonomy and academic freedom in the face of authority of whatever kind, lay or clerical, external to the academic community itself. To say this is simply to assert that institutional autonomy and academic freedom are essential conditions of life and growth and indeed of survival for Catholic universities as for all universities.

2. The Theological Disciplines

In the Catholic university this operative presence is achieved first of all and distinctively by the presence of a group of scholars in all branches of theology. The disciplines represented by this theological group are recognized in the Catholic university, not only as legitimate intellectual disciplines, but as ones essential to the integrity of a university. Since the pursuit of the theological sciences is therefore a priority for a Catholic university, academic excellence in these disciplines becomes a double obligation in a Catholic university.

3. The Primary Task of the Theological Faculty

The theological faculty must engage directly in exploring the depths of Christian tradition and the total religious heritage of the world, in order to come to the best possible intellectual understanding of religion and revelation, of man in all his varied relationships with God. Particularly important today is the theological exploration of all human relations and the elaboration of a Christian anthropology. Furthermore, the theological investigation today must serve the ecumenical goals of collaboration and unity.

4. Interdisciplinary Dialogue in the Catholic University

To carry out this primary task properly there must be a constant discussion within the university community in which theology confronts all the rest of modern culture and all the areas of intellectual study which it includes. Theology needs this dialogue in order:

a) to enrich itself from the other disciplines;

b) to bring its own insights to bear upon the problems of modern culture;

c) to stimulate the internal development of the disciplines themselves.

In a Catholic university all recognized university areas of study are frankly and fully accepted and their internal autonomy affirmed and guaranteed. There must be no theological or philosophical imperialism; all scientific and disciplinary methods, and methodologies, must be given due honor and respect. However, there will necessarily result from the interdisciplinary discussions an awareness that there is a philosophical and theological dimension to most intellectual subjects when they are pursued far enough. Hence in a Catholic university there will be a special interest in interdisciplinary problems and relationships. This total dialogue can be eminently successful:

a) if the Catholic university has a broad range of basic university disciplines;

b) if the university has achieved considerable strength in these disciplines;

c) if there are present in many or most of the non-theological areas Christian scholars who are not only interested in and competent in their own fields, but also have a personal interest in the cross-disciplinary confrontation.

This creative dialogue will involve the entire university community, will inevitably influence and enliven classroom activities, and will be reflected in curriculum and academic programs.

5. The Catholic University as the Critical Reflective Intelligence of the Church

Every university, Catholic or not, serves as the critical reflective intelligence of its society. In keeping with this general function, the Catholic university has the added obligation of performing this same function for the church. Hence, the university should carry on a continual examination of all aspects and all activities of the church and should objectively evaluate them. The church would thus have the benefit of continual counsel from Catholic universities. Catholic universities in the recent past have hardly played this role at all. It may well be one of the most important functions of the Catholic university of the future.

6. The Catholic University and Research

The Catholic university will, of course, maintain and support broad programs of research. It will promote basic research in all university fields, but, in addition, it will be prepared to undertake by preference, though not exclusively, such research as will deal with problems of greater human urgency or of greater Christian concern.

7. The Catholic University and Public Service

In common with other universities, and in accordance with given circumstances, the Catholic university is prepared to serve society and all its parts, e.g., the Federal Government, the inner city, etc. However, it will have an added special obligation to carry on similar activities, appropriate to a university, to serve the Church and its component parts.

8. Some Characteristics of Undergraduate Education

The effective intellectual presence of the theological disciplines will affect the education and life of the students in ways distinctive of a Catholic university.

With regard to the undergraduate—the university should endeavor to present a collegiate education that is truly geared to modern society. The student must come to basic understanding of the actual world in which he lives today. This means that the intellectual campus of a Catholic university has no boundaries and no barriers. It draws knowledge and understanding from all the traditions of mankind; it explores the insights and achievements of the great men of every age; it looks to the current frontiers of advancing knowledge and brings all the results to bear relevantly on man's life today. The whole world of knowledge and ideas must be open to the student; there must be no outlawed books or subjects. Thus the student will be able to develop his own capabilities and to fulfill himself by using the intellectual resources presented to him.

Along with this and integrated into it should be a competent presentation of relevant, living, Catholic thought. This dual presentation is characterized by the following emphases:

a) a concern with ultimate questions; hence a concern with theological and philosophical questions;

b) a concern for the full human and spiritual development of the student; hence a humanistic and personalistic orientation with special emphasis on the interpersonal relationships within the community of learners;

c) A concern with the particularly pressing problems of our era, e.g., civil rights, international development and peace, poverty, etc.

9. Some Special Characteristics of the Catholic Community of Learners

As a community of learners, the Catholic university has a social existence and an organizational form.

Within the university community the student should be able not simply to study theology and Christianity, but should find himself in a social situation in which he can express his Christianity in a variety of ways and live it experientially and experimentally. The students and faculty can explore together new forms of Christian living, of Christian witness, and of Christian service.

The students will be able to participate in and contribute to a variety of liturgical functions, at best creatively contemporary and experimental. They will find the meaning of the sacraments for themselves by joining theoretical understanding to the lived experience of them. Thus the students will find and indeed create extraordinary opportunities for a full, meaningful liturgical and sacramental life.

The students will individually and in small groups carry on a warm personal dialogue with themselves and with faculty, both priests and laymen.

The students will experiment further in Christian service by undertaking activities embodying the Christian interest in all human problems— inner city, social action, personal aid to the educationally disadvantaged, and so forth.

Thus will arise with the Catholic university a self-developing and self-deepening society of students and faculty in which the consequences of Christian truth are taken seriously in person-to-person relationships, where the importance of religious commitments is accepted and constantly witnessed to, and where the students can learn by personal experience to consecrate their talent and learning to worthy and social purposes.

All of this will display itself on the Catholic campus as a distinctive style of living, a perceptible quality in the university's life.

10. Characteristics of Organization and Administration

The total organization should reflect this same Christian spirit. The social organization should be such as to emphasize the university's concern for persons as individuals and for appropriate participation by all members of the community of learners in university decisions. University decisions and administrative actions should be appropriately guided by Christian ideas and ideals and should eminently display the respect and concern for persons.

The evolving nature of the Catholic university will necessitate basic re-organizations of structure in order not only to achieve a greater internal cooperation and participation, but also to share the responsibility of direction more broadly and to enlist wider support. A great deal of study and experimentation will be necessary to carry out these changes, but changes of this kind are essential for the future of the Catholic university.

In fine, the Catholic university of the future will be a true modern university but specifically Catholic in profound and creative ways for the service of society and the people of God.

32. FLANNERY O'CONNOR ON BEING A "CATHOLIC" WRITER (1969)

The Southern Catholic writer Flannery O'Connor achieved national promi-nence as the author of vivid and violent short stories like "The Violent Bear It Away," "The River," and "The Displaced Person." Some of the characters in her stories, set in the Southern "Bible Belt," were so bizarre and eccentric, and so many of her plot lines were about violent death, injustice, and misunder-standing the "signs" of grace, that O'Connor was often asked about how these stories engaged her faith.

The very term "Catholic novel" is, of course, suspect, and people who are conscious of its complications don't use it except in quotation marks. If I had to say what a "Catholic novel" is, I could only say that it is one that represents reality adequately as we see it manifested in this world of things and human relationships. Only in and by these sense experiences does the fiction writer approach the contemplative knowledge of the mystery they embody.

To be concerned with these things means not only to be concerned with the good in them, but with the evil, and not only with the evil, but also with that aspect which appears neither good nor evil, which is not yet Christianized. The Church we see, even the universal Church, is a small segment of the whole of creation. If many are called and few are chosen, fewer still perhaps choose, even unconsciously, to be Christian, and yet all of reality is the potential kingdom of Christ, and the face of the earth is waiting to be recreated by his spirit. This all means that what we roughly call the Catholic novel is not necessarily about a Christianized or Catholic world, but simply that it is one in which the truth as Christians know it has been used as a light to see the world by. This may or may not be a Catholic world, and it may or may not have been seen by a Catholic.

Catholic life as seen by a Catholic doesn't always make comfortable reading for Catholics, for that matter. In this country we have J. F. Powers, for example, a very fine writer and a born Catholic who writes about Catholics. The Catholics that Mr. Powers writes about are seen by him with a terrible accuracy. They are vulgar, ignorant, greedy, and fearfully drab, and all these qualities have an unmistakable Catholic social flavor. Mr. Powers doesn't write about such Catholics because he wants to embarrass the Church; he writes about them because, by the grace of God, he can't write about any other kind. A writer writes about what he is able to make believable. . . .

Poorly written novels—no matter how pious and edifying the behavior of the characters—are not good in themselves and are therefore not really edifying. Now a statement like this creates problems. An individual may be highly edified by a sorry novel because he doesn't know any better. We have plenty of examples in this world of poor things being used for good purposes. God can make any indifferent thing, as well as evil itself, an instrument for good; but I submit that to do this is the business of God and not of any human being. . . .

I have found the people outside the Church like to suppose that the Church acts as a restraint on the creativity of the Catholic writer and that she keeps him from reaching his full development. These people point to the fact that there are not many Catholic artists and writers, at least in this country, and that those who do achieve anything in a creative way are usually converts. This is a criticism that we can't shy away from. I feel that it is a valid criticism of the way Catholicism is often applied by our Catholic educational system, or from the pulpit, or ignorantly practiced by ourselves; but that it is, of course, no valid criticism of the religion itself.

There is no reason why fixed dogma should fix anything that the writer sees in the world. On the contrary, dogma is an instrument for penetrating reality. Christian dogma is about the only thing left in the world that surely guards and respects mystery. The fiction writer is an observer, first, last, and always, but he cannot be an adequate observer unless he is free from uncertainty about what he sees. Those who have no absolute values cannot let the relative remain merely relative; they are always raising it to the level of the absolute. The Catholic fiction writer is entirely free to observe. He feels no call to take on the duties of God or to create a new universe. He feels perfectly free to look at the one we already have and to show exactly what he sees. He feels no need to apologize for the ways of God to man or to avoid looking at the ways of man to God. For him, to "tidy up reality" is certainly to succumb to the sin of pride. Open and free observation is founded on our ultimate faith that the universe is meaningful, as the Church teaches.

And when we look at the serious fiction written by Catholics in these times, we do find a striking preoccupation with what is seedy and evil and violent. The pious argument against such novels goes something like this: if you believe in the Redemption, your ultimate vision is one of hope, so in what you see must be true to this ultimate vision; you must pass over the evil you see and look for the good because the good is there; the good is the ultimate reality.

The beginning of an answer to this is that though the good is the ultimate reality, the ultimate reality has been weakened in human beings as a result of the Fall, and it is this weakened life that we see. And it is wrong, moreover, to assume that the writer chooses what he will see and what he will not. What one sees is given by circumstances and by the nature of one's particular kind of perception.

The fiction writer should be characterized by his kind of vision. His kind of vision is prophetic vision. Prophecy, which is dependent on the imaginative and not the moral faculty, need not be a matter of predicting the future. The prophet is a realist of distances, and it is this kind of realism that goes into great novels. It is the realism which does not hesitate to distort appearances in order to show a hidden truth.

For the Catholic novelist, the prophetic vision is not simply a matter of his personal imaginative gift; it is also a matter of the Church's gift, which, unlike his own, is safeguarded and deals with greater matters. It is one of the functions of the Church to transmit the prophetic vision that is good for all time, and when the novelist has this as a part of his own vision, he has a powerful extension of sight.

It is, unfortunately, a means of extension which we constantly abuse by thinking that we can close our own eyes and that the eyes of the Church will do the seeing. They will not. We forget that what is to us an extension of sight is to the rest of the world a peculiar and arrogant blindness, and that no one today is prepared to recognize the truth of what we show unless our purely individual vision is in full operation. When the Catholic novelist closes his own eyes and tries to see with the eyes of the Church, the result is another addition to that large body of pious trash for which we have so long been famous.

It would be foolish to say that there is no conflict between these two sets of eyes. There is a conflict, and it is a conflict which we escape at our peril, one which cannot be settled beforehand by theory or fiat or faith. We think that faith entitles us to avoid it, when in fact, faith prompts us to begin it, and to continue it until, like Jacob, we are marked.

For some Catholic writers the combat will seem to be with their own eyes, and for others it will seem to be with the eyes of the Church. The writer may feel that in order to use his own eyes freely, he must disconnect them from the eyes of the Church and see as nearly as possible in the fashion of a camera. Unfortunately, to try to disconnect faith from vision is to do violence to the whole personality, and the whole personality participates in the act of writing. The tensions of being a Catholic novelist are probably never balanced for the writer until the Church becomes so much a part of his personality that he can forget about her—in the same sense that when he writes, he forgets about himself.

This is the condition we aim for, but one which is seldom achieved in this life, particularly by the novelists. The Lord doesn't speak to the novelist as he did to servant, Moses, mouth to mouth. He speaks to him as he did to those two complainers, Aaron and Aaron's sister, Mary: through dreams and visions, in fits and starts, and by all the lesser and limited ways of the imagination.

I would like to think that in the future there will be Catholic writers who will be able to use these two sets of eyes with consummate skill and daring; but I wouldn't be so reckless as to predict it. It takes readers as well as writers to make literature. One of the most disheartening circumstances that the Catholic novelist has to contend with is that he has no large audience he can count on to understand his work. The general intelligent reader today is not a believer. He likes to read novels about priests and nuns because these persons are a curiosity to him, but he does not really understand the character motivated by faith. The Catholic reader, on the other hand, is so busy looking for something that fits his needs, and shows him in the best possible light, that he will find suspect anything that doesn't serve such purposes.

33. ANDREW GREELEY, "MODELS FOR VIEWING AMERICAN CATHOLICISM" (1977)

The sociologist Andrew Greeley argued in his 1977 book, The American Catholic: A Social Portrait, *that one can come to a much better understanding of American Catholicism by imaging the various "models" people have of the relationship of Catholics to American culture. One privileged older model —the so-called "Melting Pot" model—presumed that different groups would eventually assimilate so completely into American culture that they would eventually lose all of their distinctive traits. Religiously, this would mean that Catholic Americans would, in time, lose all of their distinctive characteristics and that American Catholicism would (eventually) look much like other religious faiths. Greeley argued that this model is deeply flawed, primarily because it did not describe the actual history of Catholicism in the United States. The "mosaic model," on the other hand, posited a much more pluralistic state of things: different parts of the "mosaic" would retain their distinctive characteristics while also allowing for "permeable boundaries"—that is, while allowing for rich exchange and movement between groups.*

The two principal models for viewing the phenomenon of ethnicity and acculturation in the United States are the melting pot model of the assimilationists and the mosaic model of the cultural pluralists. Both have their uses, at least as descriptions; neither have been effective as prescriptions. In fact, I would suggest that the most useful model available to us is a mosaic with permeable boundaries. There are boundaries among the various nationality groups in the United States, there are boundaries among the religious denominations, there are boundaries between Catholics and non-Catholics; but these boundaries are not fixed or impermeable. One can choose which collectivity to affiliate with, and one can also choose the degree of affiliation. For example, one can be a "devout" Catholic, an "active" Catholic, a "practicing" Catholic, a "marginal" Catholic, or a "disaffected" Catholic, and one can move back and forth among the various positions along the affiliation continuum. One can be angry at one's Catholic past, ignore it, be militant about it, be fascinated by it, or endeavor to forget it completely (although Catholicism as a world view and Catholicism as a means of ethnic identification are both acquired very early in the childhood experience, and hence, both are very difficult to dispose of). American society does not force you to be or not to be a Catholic; it leaves

Catholicism open to you as a world view and also open as a means of self-definition. Catholicism is a collectivity, an ethnic group which is available for your use if you want to use it. It can be important to you in choosing friends, fellow workers, a professional career, and especially a marriage partner. Given the pluralistic nature of American society and the importance of religion and ethnicity in defining one's place within the society, most people tend, more or less, to identify with the religious or the religio-ethnic collectivity. There is no evidence that such a tendency is diminishing appreciably, but it is not nearly so rigid as the model of the mosaic society presents it. Precisely because it is such a flexible tool, the permeable boundary has a much better chance of surviving in a dynamic, mobile society.

The Catholic collectivity, then, as it exists in America, is to some considerable extent an American creation. It is a religious group which provides both world view and self-definition, and which passes on certain behavioral traits, values, and personality characteristics in a process which is normally quite unself-conscious. The Catholic collectivity is much more tightly defined here than it is in a country like Italy, where virtually everyone is Catholic in some fashion. But it is also much more loosely defined, in the sense that its boundaries are much more easily crossed than would be the case in countries like Holland or northern Ireland, where religio-ethnic boundaries are very sharp and rigid. In virtually all Western societies, denominational groupings have some sort of boundaries which make them at least quasi-ethnic groups; only the United States has the curious mixture of a high degree of religious or religio-ethnic self-consciousness and relatively flexible and permeable boundaries. To be a Catholic means to be different. Catholicism offers you a potentially important form of self-definition, a social location in which you define yourself by those very differences as being separate from the rest of society, but the separateness need not and usually does not imply hostility or major conflict; it is rather a way of carving out a piece of social turf for yourself. It is ground on which to stand, but not a fortified area to defend. It is ground around which one can wander more or less as one pleases, so there is no reason for yielding this useful means of social location and self-definition as a price for participating in the larger society. On the contrary, it is viewed as a means of participating in the larger society.

The theoretical perspective for viewing American pluralism laid out [here] calls into question the notion that with the passage of time the differences between Catholics and other Americans will go away. Ethnic groups develop a momentum and a life history of their own, sometimes veering more toward assimilation, other times leaning toward more highly conscious differentiation. Simple unilinear models of the relationships among ethnic groups and between ethnic groups and the host culture are usually not very helpful. Indeed, as I shall argue . . . the American Catholic collectivity is presently going through a period when much of its former organizational loyalty to the Catholic church as an institution is waning (largely because of the incredibly inept leadership of this institution). But at the same time, its loyalty to certain "ethnic" manifestations of Catholicism, such as parochial schools, is not changing in the slightest, and a much more self-conscious and reflective approach to those aspects of the Catholic heritage, which hitherto had been a largely unself-conscious process, seems to be increasing. . . .

The model for considering American Catholics and the various subgroups within Catholicism that has been presented . . . is not a simple one. The melting pot and the mosaic models are easy ways to conceptualize American society; they do not require complex, nuanced, and dynamic pictures. They are therefore easy to use, and just as easily deceptive. The mosaic with permeable boundaries approach is more difficult to use but subsumes more evidence. Minimally it prepares one to encounter surprising empirical evidence, which is perhaps the best criterion one can find for a useful social science model.

34. ELIZABETH JOHNSON, C.S.J., "TO SPEAK RIGHTLY OF GOD" (1992)

Elizabeth Johnson's prize-winning book, She Who Is, *took St. Thomas Aquinas's famous Latin definition of God (*quid est, *usually translated as "He who is") and pointed out that the Latin word* quid *was a neuter form that could be translated as "she" as well as "he." Thus building on the work of Catholicism's most famous medieval theologian, Johnson argued that exclusive use of male pronouns in talking of the Holy One was not only idolatrous (and therefore very bad Catholic theology) but also socially oppressive to the vast majority of Catholicism's faithful, who were and are women.*

What is the right way to speak about God? This is a question of unsurpassed importance, for speech to and about the mystery that surrounds human lives and the universe itself is a key activity of a community of faith. In that speech the symbol of God functions as the primary symbol of the whole religious system, the ultimate point of reference for understanding experience, life, and the world. Hence the way in which a faith community shapes language about God implicitly represents what it takes to be the highest good, the profoundest truth, the most appealing beauty. Such speaking, in turn, powerfully molds the corporate identity of the community and directs its praxis. A religion, for example, that would speak about a warlike god and extol the way he smashes his enemies to bits would promote aggressive group behavior. A community that would acclaim God as an arbitrary tyrant would inspire its members to acts of impatience and disrespect toward their fellow creatures. On the other hand, speech about a beneficent and loving God who forgives offenses would turn the faith community toward care for the neighbor and mutual forgiveness. . . .

In our day interest in right speech about God is exceptionally alive in a new way thanks to the discourse of a sizable company of bakers, women who historically have borne primary responsibility for lighting the cooking fires and feeding the world. The women's movement in civil rights and the church has shed a bright light on the pervasive exclusion of women from the realm of public symbol formation and decision making, and women's consequent, strongly enforced subordination to the imagination and needs of a world designed chiefly by men. In the church this exclusion has been effective virtually everywhere: in ecclesial creeds, doctrines, prayers, theological systems, liturgical worship, patterns of spirituality, visions of mission, church order, leadership and discipline. It has been stunningly effective in speech about God. While officially it is rightly and consistently said that God is spirit and so beyond identification with either male or female sex, yet the daily language of preaching, worship, catechesis, and instruction conveys a different message: God is male, or at least more like a man than a woman, or at least more fittingly addressed as male than female. The symbol of God functions. Upon examination it becomes clear that this exclusive speech about God serves in manifold ways to support an imaginative and structural world that excludes or subordinates women. Wittingly or not, it undermines women's human dignity as equally created in the image of God. . . .

What is the right way to speak about God? The presenting issue in debates about inclusive language is ostensibly whether the reality of women can provide suitable metaphor for speech about God. The intensity with which the question is engaged from the local to the international level, however, makes clear that more is at stake than simply naming toward God with women-identified words such as mother. The symbol of God functions. Language about God in female images not only challenges the literal-mindedness that has clung to male images in inherited God-talk; it not only questions their dominance in discourse about holy mystery. But insofar as the "symbol gives rise to thought," such speech calls into question prevailing structures of patriarchy. It gives rise to a different vision of community, one in which the last shall be first, the excluded shall be included, the mighty put down from their thrones and the humble exalted —the words of Mary of Nazareth's song of praise (Lk 1:52), creating conditions for the formation of community characterized by relationships of mutuality and reciprocity, of love and justice. Introducing this mode of speech signals a shift, among those who use it, in their sense of the divine, a shift in total world view, in highest ideals and values, in personal and corporate identity. Such usage is urged upon the whole community of faith in the conviction that it bears a fruitful and blessed promise. What is the right way to speak about God in the face of women's newly cherished human dignity and equality? This is a crucial theological question. What is at stake is the truth about God, inseparable from the situation of human beings, and the identity and mission of the faith community itself. . . .

The historical open-endedness of talk about God is due not only to its location in time, place, and culture, which is the case with all human speech, but to the very nature of what we are talking about. The reality of God is mystery beyond all imagining. So transcendent, so immanent is the holy mystery of God that we can never wrap our minds completely around this mystery and exhaust divine reality in words or concepts. The history of theology is replete with this truth: recall Augustine's insight that if we have understood, then what we have understood is not God; Anselm's argument that God is that than which nothing greater can be conceived; Hildegard's vision of God's glory as Living Light that blinded her sight; Aquinas's working rule that we can know that God is and what God is not, but not what God is; Luther's stress on the hiddenness of God's glory in the shame of the cross; Simone Weil's conviction that there is nothing that resembles what she can conceive of when she says the word God; Sallie McFague's insistence on imaginative leaps into metaphor since no language about God is adequate and all of it is improper. It is a matter of the livingness of God. Given the inexhaustible mystery inherent in what the word God points to, historically new attempts at articulation are to be expected and even welcomed. . . .

My aim is to speak a good word about the mystery of God recognizable within the contours of Christian faith that will serve the emancipatory praxis of men and women, to the benefit of all creation, both human beings and the earth. In so doing I draw on the new language of Christian feminist theology as well as on the traditional language of scripture and classical theology, all of which codify religious insights.

By Christian feminist theology I mean a reflection on God and all things in the light of God that stands consciously in the company of all the world's women, explicitly prizing their genuine humanity while uncovering and criticizing its persistent violation in sexism, itself an omnipresent paradigm of unjust relationships. In terms of Christian doctrine, this perspective claims the fullness of religious heritage for women precisely as human, in their own right and independent from personal identification with men. Women are equally created in the image and likeness of God, equally welcomed by Christ, equally sanctified by the Holy Spirit: women are equally involved in the on-going tragedy of sin and the mystery of grace, equally called to mission in this world, equally destined for life with God in glory. . . .

Theology done from this perspective [of Christian feminist theology] presses a strong critique against traditional speech about God. It judges it to be both humanly oppressive and religiously idolatrous. Oppressive: by drawing imagery and concepts for God almost exclusively from the world of ruling men, inherited speech functions effectively to legitimate structures and theories that grant a theomorphic character to men who rule but that relegate women, children, and other men to the deficient margins. Whether consciously or not, sexist God language undermines the human equality of women made in the divine image and likeness. The result is broken community, human beings shaped by patterns of dominance and subordination with attendant violence and suffering. Idolatrous: insofar as male-dominant language is honored as the only or the supremely fitting way of speaking about God, it absolutizes a single set of metaphors and obscures the height and depth and length and breadth of divine mystery. Thus it does damage to the very truth of God that theology is supposed to cherish and promote.

A superficial notion of this critique judges it to be narrowly concerned with what is bemusedly labeled "a women's issue." The issue of the right way to speak about God, however, is central to the whole faith tradition, nor does its pivotal role diminish because the speakers are coming anew into their own voice. The charges of oppression and idolatry cannot be so lightly dismissed. What is ultimately at stake in this question is profoundly substantive, being simultaneously the quest for a more just and peaceful order among human beings and the truth, however darkly glimpsed, of the holy mystery of God. Nor can the two be separated.

Feminist theology's critique of traditional God language enters the history of theology at a critical juncture. Under the impact of modernity and postmodernity for the last two centuries, Christian speech about God has suffered a series of shocks that have rendered it more and more problematic. In response, theology has been generating new language by a creative combination of hermeneutical retrieval of ancient texts and appropriation of contemporary experience. Women's search for less inadequate ways of speaking about God today intersects with other theological efforts to re-think the inherited doctrine of God, which itself has already been in a crisis of reformulation for some time. . . .

To even the casual observer it is obvious that the Christian community ordinarily speaks about God on the model of the ruling male human being. Both the images that are used and the concepts accompanying them reflect the experience of men in charge within a patriarchal system. The difficulty does not lie in the fact that male metaphors are used, for men too are made in the image of God and may suitably serve as finite beginning points for reference to God. Rather, the problem consists in the fact that these male terms are used exclusively, literally, and patriarchally.

Exclusively. In spite of the multitude of designations for divine mystery in the Bible, and later, lesser-known sources, prevailing Christian language names God solely with male designations, causing the rest to be forgotten or marginalized. Thus speech about God in female metaphors or in images taken from the natural world lies fallow, and can even appear deviant. To give one outstanding example, liturgical prayer is directed to the Father, through the Son, in the unity of the Holy Spirit, with even the latter being masculinized through the use of grammatically male pronouns.

Literally. In spite of ample testimony in the Scriptures and later tradition that the mystery of God is beyond all human comprehension, the exclusively male symbol of God is spoken in an uncritically literal way. Such speech signifies, if not in explicit theory at least effectively in the subliminal power of the imagination, that maleness is an essential character of divine being. We have forgotten what was clear to early Christian thinkers, namely, that the Father and Son are names that designate relationships rather than an essence in itself, and that as applied to God they, like all human names, are subject to the negation of the rule of analogy. It is true that sophisticated thinkers deny that the maleness of the symbol of God is meant to be taken literally, for divine being transcends sexual bodiliness. Yet the literal association of God with maleness perdures even in highly abstract discussions. . . .

Patriarchally. The precise ideal from the world of men that has provided the paradigm for the symbol of God is the ruling man within a patriarchal system. Divine mystery is cast in the role of a monarch, absolute ruler, King of Kings, Lord of Lords, one whose will none can escape, to whom is owed total and unquestioning obedience. This powerful monarch is sometimes spoken of as just and harsh, threatening hell to sinners who do not measure up. . . .

Feminist theological analysis makes clear that exclusive, literal, patriarchal speech about God has a twofold negative effect. It fails both human beings and divine mystery. In stereotyping and then banning female reality as suitable metaphor for God, such speech justifies the dominance of men while denigrating the human dignity of women. Simultaneously this discourse so reduces divine mystery to the single, reified metaphor of the ruling male that the symbol itself loses its religious significance and ability to point to ultimate truth. It becomes, in a word, an idol. These two effects are inseparable, for damage to the *imago Dei* in the creature inevitably shortchanges knowledge of the Creator in whose image she is made. Inauthentic ways of treating other human beings go hand-in-glove with falsifications of the idea of God.

FURTHER SUGGESTED READING

William Lynch, *Christ and Apollo: The Dimensions of the Literary Imagination* (New York: New American Library, 1963).

Thomas McAvoy, *The Great Crisis in American Catholic History, 1895–1900* (Chicago: University of Chicago Press, 1957).

Thomas F. O'Dea, *American Catholic Dilemma: An Inquiry into the Intellectual Life* (Milwaukee, Wisc.: Sheed & Ward, 1958).

Donald Pellotte, *John Courtney Murray: Theologian in Conflict* (Mahwah, N.J.: Paulist Press, 1976).

Margaret Mary Reher, *Catholic Intellectual Life in America: A Study of Persons and Movements* (New York: Macmillan Publishing Company, 1989).

David Tracy, *The Analogical Imagination* (New York: Crossroad, 1981).

Part IV

Politics

At the time when John England (No. 35) wrote, American Catholics were a tiny and often persecuted minority in the United States. But during the late nineteenth and early twentieth centuries Catholic numbers skyrocketed, mostly through immigration from Ireland, Germany, and eastern and southern Europe. Through sheer weight of numbers they were a political force from the start in the big eastern and midwestern cities where they soon made up the bulk of the population; but it was years before their education and organization matched their numbers.

This section contains documents covering some of the hottest issues in several kinds of "politics" over the last two centuries. In very different ways, Cardinal Gibbons (No. 36) and John F. Kennedy (No. 41) address the issue of dual loyalties to the Church and the state. Nos. 35, 37, 39, 42, and 48, again from a wide variety of angles, discuss the issue of how we, as Catholics, should treat society's most vulnerable members. Is legislation or personal service and conversion the answer?

But perhaps the bitterest political fights for American Catholics have been internal, as even the documents mentioned above often suggest. Most obviously, this means the long-running battle over sexual politics, which encompasses everything from the proper roles of men and women (Nos. 40, 44, 47) to the struggle over birth control and, more recently, abortion (Nos. 38, 43, 46, 47, 48, and 27). In the 1920s, when Joseph Nevins (No. 38) wrote his advice to confessors, anxiety over this issue was just beginning to develop and there was still widespread agreement among lay Catholics that the Church's teaching on birth control was correct. Today, up to 95 percent of married American Catholics use some kind of artificial birth control. Many see the widespread and in many ways unprecedented rejection of the papal teaching in *Humanae Vitae* as a key moment in the history of the church; some, including the late Pope John Paul II (who helped to develop the encyclical while still a bishop), characterize the document as a prophetic bulwark against the destructive tendencies of modern society, which are indeed demonstrated by the seduction of Catholics into rebellion against the Church. Others mourn it as a kind of sexual Maginot Line, a line in the sand drawn so far forward that it has forced many otherwise loyal Catholics to live in dissent from their church.

Taken as a whole, the documents in this section display the writers' sense of themselves as distinctly American and distinctly Catholic, and also suggest the limitations of such descriptive words. Their identities as Americans have been formed by dialogue with the global Catholic Church, and their identity as Catholics has been challenged and reshaped by their encounters with the particular forms that the human politics of gender, race, class, and sexual behavior have taken in this country.

35. Bishop John England on Slavery (1840)

John England (1786–1842) was the first bishop of Charleston, a diocese which in the 1820s and 1830s consisted of 11,000 Catholics in three states: Georgia and the Carolinas. England became an inveterate traveler, roaming on horseback from small town to small town in search of the few local Catholics, and frequently preaching to mostly Protestant audiences in courtrooms and churches. Although in general a liberal, he was a supporter of slavery, which the Roman Catholic Church did not officially condemn until the late nineteenth century. Most of the clergy in the antebellum South agreed with England, and northern Catholics—who associated Protestant abolitionists with nativism—were generally lukewarm on the issue. Here England writes several open letters to John Forsyth, the Secretary of State, disputing the Secretary's assertion that an 1839 encyclical of Pope Gregory XVI was abolitionist —in fact, England argues, it had condemned only the Atlantic trade in slaves, and not the "peculiar institution" itself. Using scriptural evidence and natural law (see No. 29), England demonstrates the orthodoxy of his position according to the theology of his day.

To the Honorable John Forsyth, Secretary of State, United States
Charleston, October 7, 1840

Sir: I proceed to give additional reasons to show that the letter of our holy father, Pope Gregory XVI, regarded only the "slave trade." . . . It is against

[the] desperate traffic, in which Portugal and Spain have had so enormous a share that the Pope's letter is directed, and not against domestic slavery, of the existence of which he is conscious, but respecting which he uses no action, and which rests upon a totally different basis as it is perfectly unconnected with cruelty such as is above described. . . .

Respecting domestic slavery, we distinguish it from the compulsory slavery of an invaded people in its several degrees. I shall touch upon the varieties separately. The first is "voluntary"; that which exists amongst us is not of that description, though I know very many instances where I have found it to be so; but I regard not the cases of individuals, I look to the class. In examining the lawfulness of voluntary slavery, we shall test a principle against which abolitionists contend. They assert, generally, that slavery is contrary to the natural law. The soundness of their position will be tried by inquiring into the lawfulness of holding in slavery a person, who has voluntarily sold himself. Our theological authors lay down a principle, that man in his natural state is master of his own liberty, and may dispose of it as he sees proper; as in the case of a Hebrew (*Exodus* 21:5) who preferred remaining with his wife and children as a slave, to going into that freedom to which he had a right; and in the case of the Hebrew (*Leviticus* 25:47) who, by reason of his poverty, would sell himself to a sojourner or to a stranger. Life and its preservation are more valuable than liberty, hence when Esther addresses Assuerus (*Esther* 8:4) she lays down the principle very plainly and naturally. "For we are sold, I and my people, to be destroyed and slain, and to perish. But if we had been sold for bondsmen and bondswomen, I had held my tongue."

The natural law then does not prohibit a man from bartering his liberty and his services to save his life, to provide for his sustenance, to secure other enjoyments which he prefers to that freedom, and to that right to his own labor, which he gives in exchange for life and protection. Nor does the natural law prohibit another man from procuring and bestowing upon him those advantages, in return for which he has agreed to bind himself to that other man's service, provided he takes no unjust advantage in the bargain. Thus a state of voluntary slavery is not prohibited by the law of nature; that is, a state in which one man has dominion over the labor and ingenuity of another to the end of his life, and consequently in which that labor and ingenuity are the property of him who has the dominion, and are justly applicable to the benefit of the master and not the slave. All our theologians have from the earliest epochs sustained, that though in a state of pure nature all men are equal, yet the natural law does not prohibit one man from having dominion over the useful action of another as his slave; provided this dominion be obtained by a just title. . . .

In one point of view, indeed, we may say that the natural law does not establish slavery, but it does not forbid it. . . . I know many slaves who would not accept their freedom; I know some who have refused it; and though our domestic slavery must upon the whole be regarded as involuntary, still the exceptions are not so few as are imagined by strangers.

It may be asked why anyone should prefer slavery to freedom. I know many instances where the advantages to the individual are very great; and so, sir, I am confident do you, yet I am not in love with the existence of slavery. I would never aid in establishing it where it did not exist.

The situation of a slave, under a humane master ensures to him food, raiment, and dwelling, together with a variety of little comforts; it relieves him of the apprehensions of neglect in sickness, from all solicitude for the support of his family, and in return, all that is required is fidelity and moderate labor. I do not deny that slavery has its evils, but the above are no despicable benefits. Hence I have known many freedmen who regretted their manumission.

In examining the case of the voluntary slave, sir, we have discovered some of the grounds upon which Catholic divines, however they may deprecate its existence, teach that slavery is perfectly compatible with the natural law, and that it has been introduced by the law of nations. . . .

Slavery, then, sir, is regarded by that church of which the Pope is the presiding officer, not to be incompatible with the natural law, to be the result of sin by divine dispensation, to have been established by human legislation, and when the dominion of the slave is justly acquired by the master to be lawful, not only in the sight of the human tribunal, but also in the eye of Heaven; but not so the "slave trade," or the reducing into slavery the African and Indian in the manner that Portugal and Spain sanctioned, which they continue in many instances still to perpetuate, and which the apostolic letters have justly censured as unlawful.

[Letter of October 13, 1840]

Job possessed slaves, and he treated them with kindness (31:16).

How came these patriarchs to have property in those slaves? Many of them were born in their houses, that is, of their servants, and this was acknowledged to be a good title, not only by the law of nations, but clearly, in the case before us, by the law of God. But how came their parents slaves? Perhaps originally they voluntarily became so. They might have been bought from others who acquired a just dominion, by that or by some other good title. . . .

Thus God himself recognized the validity of the title to a slave founded upon purchase as well as birth. . . .

Thus, sir, all the divines of the Roman Catholic Church acknowledge that they find the divine legislation for the Hebrew people, the recognition of slavery, and the enactment of provisions for its regulation.

It was not contrary to the law of nature, or else the God of nature could not have permitted its sanction in that code which he gave his chosen people. It was not incompatible with the practices of pure and undefiled religion—because it was, at least, permitted by him who is the great and sole object of the highest religious homage. It was, in many cases, rather a source of protection than of evil to its unfortunate subjects.

[Letter of October 21, 1840]

Sir: The divine sanction for the existence of slavery, and for the various titles by which property in slaves may be acquired, being shown, it would rest upon those who deny its religious legality today to prove distinctly that this sanction had been withdrawn. . . . I proceed to examine what the divine legislator of Christianity [Jesus Christ] has done upon this subject.

He made no special law, either to repeal or to modify the former and still subsisting right; but he enforced principles that, by their necessary operation and gradual influence, produced an extensive amelioration. . . . In the New Testament we find instances of pious and good men having slaves, and in no case do we find the Savior imputing it to them as a crime, or requiring their servants' emancipation. . . .

In many of his parables, the Savior describes the master and his servants in a variety of ways, without any condemnation or censure of slavery. . . .

After the promulgation of the Christian religion by the Apostles, the slave was not told by them he was in a state of unchristian durance. . . . Nor did the Apostles consider the Christian master obliged to liberate his Christian servants. St. Paul in his epistle to Philemon, acknowledges the right of the master to the services of his slave, for whom, however, he asks, as a special favor, pardon for having deserted his owner. . . .

To the Christian slave was exhibited the humiliation of the incarnate

God, the suffering of the unoffending victim, the invitation of this model of perfection to that meekness, that humility, that peaceful spirit, that charity and forgiveness of injuries which constitutes the glorious beatitudes. He was shown the advantage of suffering, the reward of patience, and the narrow long road along whose rugged ascents he was to bear the cross, walking in the footsteps of his Savior. . . .

Thus, sir, did the legislator of Christianity, whilst he admitted the legality of slavery, render the master merciful, and the slave faithful, obedient, and religious, looking for his freedom in that region, where alone true and lasting enjoyment can be found. . . .

36. Cardinal Gibbons Defends the Knights of Labor (1887)

The full force of the Industrial Revolution hit the United States and Europe in the nineteenth century. Enormous technological advances were made—but working conditions for laborers became worse and worse. In most U.S. cities Catholic immigrants made up the bulk of the cheap labor force; they thus formed a natural constituency for nascent labor unions, including the largest organization in the country, the Knights of Labor. In 1884 the Vatican condemned the Canadian Knights of Labor; the hierarchy feared that the Knights, as a "secret society" (secrecy being necessary due to the absence of legal protections for union members), might take priority over Catholics' obligation to their church. A few American bishops desired that Catholics should also be barred from the American Knights. This would either have destroyed the Knights, who counted a Catholic as their president, or—more likely—have severely damaged the ascendancy of the Catholic Church in America. (In Europe, where the hierarchy tended to side with the capitalist class, workers left the Church in droves.) Thus, in 1887, Cardinal Gibbons submitted this document—probably actually written by Bishop John Ireland —to Rome. It was a potentially risky move for Gibbons, but it paid off: the American Knights were not condemned, and the working class has remained as the backbone of the Church to this day.

Your Eminence:

In submitting to the Holy See the conclusions which after several months of attentive observation and reflection, seem to me to sum up the truth concerning the association of the Knights of Labor, I feel profoundly convinced of the vast importance of the consequences attaching to this question, which forms but a link in the great chain of the social problems of our day, and especially of our country.

In weighing this question I have been very careful to follow as my constant guide the spirit of the Encyclicals, in which our Holy Father, Leo XIII, has so admirably set forth the dangers of our time and their remedies, as well as the principles by which we are to recognize associations condemned by the Holy See. . . .

In the following considerations I wish to state in detail the reasons which determined the vote of the great majority of the committee—reasons whose truth and force seem to me all the more evident today; I shall try at the same time to do justice to the arguments advanced by the opposition.

1. In the first place, in the constitution, laws and official declarations of the Knights of Labor, there can clearly be found assertions and rules . . . which we would not approve; but we have not found in them those elements so clearly pointed out by the Holy See, which places them among condemned associations.

(a) In their form of initiation there is no oath.

(b) The obligation to secrecy by which they keep the knowledge of their business from strangers or enemies, in no wise prevents Catholics from manifesting everything to competent ecclesiastical authority, even outside of confession. This has been positively declared to us by their president [their chief officers—leur president].

(c) They make no promise of blind obedience. The object and laws of the association are distinctly declared, and the obligation of obedience does not go beyond these limits.

(d) They not only profess no hostility against religion or the Church, but their declarations are quite to the contrary. The Third Plenary Council commands that we should not condemn an association without giving a hearing to its officers or representatives: "auditis ducibus, corypheis vel sociis praecipuis." Now, their president in sending me a copy of their constitution, says that he is a Catholic from the bottom of his heart; that he practices his religion faithfully and receives the sacraments regularly; that he belongs to no Masonic or other society condemned by the Church; that he knows of nothing in the association of the Knights of Labor contrary to the laws of the Church; that, with filial submission he begs the Pastors of the Church to examine all the details of their organization [their constitution and laws—tous les details de leur organisation], and, if they find anything worthy of condemnation, they should indicate it, and he promises its correction. Assuredly one does not perceive in all this any hostility to the authority of the Church, but on the contrary a spirit in every way praiseworthy. . . .

2. That there exist among us, as in the other countries of the world, grave and threatening social evils, public injustices, which call for strong resistance and legal remedy, is a fact which no one dares to deny, and the truth of which has been already acknowledged by the Congress and the President of the United States. Without entering into the sad details of these wrongs,—which does not seem necessary here,—it may suffice to mention only that monopolies on the part of both individuals and of corporations, have already called forth not only the complaints of our working classes, but also the opposition of our public men and legislators; that the efforts of these monopolists, not always without success, to control legislation to their own profit, cause serious apprehension among the disinterested friends of liberty; that the heartless avarice which, through greed of gain, pitilessly grinds not only the men, but particularly the women and children in various employments, makes it clear to all who love humanity and justice that it is not only the right of the laboring classes to protect themselves, but the duty of the whole people to aid them in finding a remedy against the dangers with which both civilization and the social order are menaced by avarice, oppression and corruption.

It would be vain to deny either the existence of the evils, the right of legitimate resistance, or the necessity of a remedy. At most doubt might be raised about the legitimacy of the form of resistance and the remedy employed by the Knights of Labor. This then ought to be the next point of our examination.

3. It can hardly be doubted that for the attainment of any public end, association—the organization of all interested persons—is the most efficacious means, a means altogether natural and just. This is so evident, and besides so conformable to the genius of our country, of our essentially popular social conditions, that it is unnecessary to insist upon it. It is almost the only means to invite public attention, to give force to the most legitimate resistance, to add weight to the most just demands.

Now there already exists an organization which presents a thousand attractions and advantages, but which our Catholic workingmen, with filial obedience to the Holy See, refuse to join; this is the Masonic organization, which exists everywhere in our country, and which, as Mr. Powderly has expressly pointed out to us, unites employer and worker in a brotherhood very advantageous for the latter, but which numbers in its ranks hardly a single Catholic. Freely [nobly—de grand coeur] renouncing the advantages which the Church and their consciences forbid, workingmen form associations [join—se forment], having nothing in common with the deadly designs of the enemies of religion and seeking only mutual protection and help, and the legitimate assertion of their rights. But here they also find themselves threatened with condemnation, and so deprived of their only means of defense. Is it surprising that they should be astonished at this and that they ask *Why?*

4. Let us now consider the objections made against this sort of organization.

(a) It is objected that in these organizations Catholics are mixed with Protestants, to the peril of their faith. Naturally, yes, they are mixed with Protestants in the workers' associations, precisely as they are at their work; for in a mixed people like ours, the separation of religious in social affairs is not possible. But to suppose that the faith of our Catholics suffers thereby is not to know the Catholic workers of America who are not like the workingmen of so many European countries—misguided and perverted children, looking on their Mother the Church as a hostile stepmother—but they are intelligent, well-instructed and devoted children ready to give their blood, as they continually give their means (although small and hard-earned) for her support and protection.

(b) But it is said, could there not be substituted for such an organization confraternities which would unite the workingmen under the direction of the priests and the direct influence of religion? I answer frankly that I do not believe that either possible or necessary in our country. . . . We find that in our country the presence and explicit influence of the clergy would not be advisable where our citizens, without distinction of religious belief, come together in regard to their industrial interests alone. Without going so far, we have abundant means for making our working people faithful Catholics, and simple good sense advises us not to go to extremes.

(c) Again, it is objected that the liberty of such an organization exposes Catholics to the evil influences of the most dangerous associates, even of atheists, communists, and anarchists. That is true; but it is one of the trials of faith which our brave American Catholics are accustomed to meet almost daily, and which they know how to disregard with good sense and firmness. . . . In truth, the only grave danger would come from an alienation between the Church and her children, which nothing would more certainly occasion than imprudent condemnations.

(d) An especially weighty charge is drawn from the outbursts of violence, even to bloodshed, which have characterized several of the strikes inaugurated by labor organizations. Concerning this, three things are to be remarked: first, strikes are not an invention of the Knights of Labor, but a means almost everywhere and always resorted to by employees in our land and elsewhere to protest against what they consider unjust and to demand their rights; secondly in such a struggle of the poor and indignant multitudes against hard and obstinate monopoly, anger and violence [outbursts of anger—colere et le violence] are often as inevitable as they are regrettable; thirdly, the laws and chief authorities of the Knights of Labor, far from encouraging violence or the occasions of it, exercise a powerful influence to hinder it, and to keep strikes within the limits of good order and legitimate action. A careful examination of the acts of violence which have marked the struggle between capital and labor during the past year, leaves us convinced that it would be unjust to attribute them to the association of the Knights of Labor. . . .

The part of Christian prudence evidently is to try to hold the hearts of the multitude by the bonds of love, in order to control their actions by the principles of faith, justice and charity, to acknowledge frankly the truth and justice in their cause, in order to deter them from what would be false and criminal, and thus to turn into a legitimate, peaceable and beneficent contest what could easily become for the masses of our people a volcanic abyss, like that which society fears and the Church deplores in Europe.

Upon this point I insist strongly, because, from an intimate acquaintance with the social conditions of our country I am profoundly convinced that here we are touching upon a subject which not only concerns the rights of the working classes, who ought to be especially dear to the Church which our Divine Lord sent to evangelize the poor, but with which are bound up the fundamental interests of the Church and of human society for the future. This is a point which I desire, in a few additional words to develop more clearly.

5. Whoever meditates upon the ways in which divine Providence is guiding contemporary history cannot fail to remark how important is the part which the power of the people takes therein at present and must take

in the future. We behold, with profound sadness, the efforts of the prince of darkness to make this power dangerous to the social weal by withdrawing the masses of the people from the influence of religion, and impelling them towards the ruinous paths of license and anarchy. Until now our country presents a picture of altogether different [most consolingly different—tout different] character—that of a popular power regulated by love of good order, by respect for religion, by obedience to the authority of the laws, not a democracy of license and violence, but that true democracy which aims at the general prosperity through the means of sound principles and good social order.

In order to preserve so desirable a state of things it is absolutely necessary that religion should continue to hold the affections, and thus rule the conduct of the multitudes. . . . To lose influence over the people would be to lose the future altogether; and it is by the heart, far more than by the understanding, that we must hold and guide this immense power, so mighty either for good or for evil. Among all the glorious titles of the Church which her history has merited for her, there is not one which at present gives her so great influence as that of Friend of the People. Assuredly, in our democratic country, it is this title which wins for the Catholic Church not only the enthusiastic devotedness of the millions of her children, but also the respect and admiration of all our citizens, whatever be their religious belief. It is the power of precisely this title which renders persecution almost an impossibility, and which draws toward our holy Church the great heart of the American people.

And since it is acknowledged by all that the great questions of the future are not those of war, of commerce or finance, but the social questions, the questions which concern the improvement of the condition of the great masses of the people, and especially of the working people, it is evidently of supreme importance that the Church should always be found on the side of humanity, of justice toward the multitudes who compose the body of the human family. . . . Cardinal Manning very wisely wrote, "We must admit and accept calmly and with good will that industries and profits must be considered in second place; the moral state and domestic condition of the whole working population must be considered first. . . . The conditions of the lower classes as are found at present among our people, can not and must not continue. On such a basis no social edifice can stand." In our country, especially, this is the inevitable program of the future, and the position which the Church must hold toward the solution is sufficiently obvious. . . .

6. Now let us consider for a moment the consequences which would inevitably follow from a contrary course, from a lack of sympathy for the working class, from a suspicion of their aims, from a hasty condemnation of their methods.

(a) First, there is the evident danger of the Church's losing in popular estimation her right to be considered the friend of the people The logic of men's hearts goes swiftly to its conclusions, and this conclusion would be a pernicious one for the people and for the Church. To lose the heart of the people would be a misfortune from which the friendship of the few rich and powerful would be no compensation.

(b) There is a great danger of rendering hostile to the Church the political power of our country, which openly takes sides with the millions who are demanding justice and the improvement of their condition. The accusation of being, "un-American," that is to say, alien to our national spirit, is the most powerful weapon which the enemies of the Church know how to employ against her. It was this cry which aroused the Know-Nothing persecution thirty years ago, and the same would be quickly used again if the opportunity offered itself. . . . Now, to seek to crush by an ecclesiastical condemnation an organization which represents nearly 500,000 votes, and which has already so respectable and so universally recognized a place in the political arena, would to speak frankly, be considered by the American people as not less ridiculous as it is rash. To alienate from ourselves the friendship of the people would be to run great risk of losing the respect which the Church has won in the estimation of the American nation, and of destroying the state of peace and prosperity which form so admirable a contrast with her condition in some so-called Catholic countries. Already in these months past, a murmur of popular anger and of threats against the Church has made itself heard, and it is necessary that we should move with much precaution.

(c) A third danger, and the one which touches our hearts the most, is the risk of losing the love of the children of the Church, and of pushing them into an attitude of resistance against their Mother. The whole world presents no more beautiful spectacle than that of their filial devotion and obedience. But it is necessary to recognize that, in our age and in our country, obedience cannot be blind. We would greatly deceive ourselves if we expected it. Our Catholic working men sincerely believe that they are only seeking justice, and seeking it by legitimate means. A condemnation would be considered both false and unjust, and would not be accepted. We might indeed preach to them submission and confidence in the Church, but these good dispositions could hardly go so far. They love the Church, and they wish to save their souls, but they must also earn their living, and labor is now so organized that without belonging to the organization there is little chance to earn one's living.

Behold, then, the consequences to be feared. Thousands of the most devoted children of the Church would believe themselves repulsed by their Mother and would live without practicing their religion. The revenues of the Church, which with us come entirely from the free offerings of the people, would suffer immensely, and it would be the same with Peter's pence. The ranks of the secret societies would be filled with Catholics, who had been up to now faithful. The Holy See, which has constantly received from the Catholics of America proofs of almost unparalleled devotedness, would be considered not as a paternal authority, but as a harsh and unjust power. Here are assuredly effects, the occasion of which wisdom and prudence must avoid. . . .

Therefore, with complete confidence, I leave the case to the wisdom and prudence of your Eminence and the Holy See.

Rome, February 20, 1887.

J. Cardinal Gibbons,

Archbishop of Baltimore.

37. John A. Ryan and the Bishops' Program for Social Reconstruction (1919)

John A. Ryan (1869–1945) was among the best-known social reformers of his day. He had already written several books on economic justice when, at the end of World War I, he put together a plan of general social reform. Many of the proposals Ryan made—which, in addition to those presented here, included a permanent federal Labor Board, housing projects for the working classes, a general reduction of the cost of living through monopoly-busting and cooperative stores, vocational training, and an end to child labor— seemed radical at the time, although most have now been put into practice to a greater or lesser degree. Ryan was nevertheless able to persuade a number of American bishops to support his program, in part because the Vatican was perceived as having come out strongly in favor of the rights of labor with Pope Leo XIII's famous encyclical of 1891, Rerum Novarum, the first of the so-called social encyclicals, which Ryan quotes in the last paragraph.

A Practical and Moderate Program

No attempt will be made in these pages to formulate a comprehensive scheme of reconstruction. Such an undertaking would be a waste of time as regards immediate needs and purposes, for no important group or section of the American people is ready to consider a program of this magnitude. Attention will therefore be confined to those reforms that seem to be desirable and also obtainable within a reasonable time, and to a few general principles which should become a guide to more distant developments. A statement thus circumscribed will not merely present the objects that we wish to see attained, but will also serve as an imperative call to action. It will keep before our minds the necessity for translating our faith into works. In the statements of immediate proposals we shall start, wherever possible, from those governmental agencies and legislative measures which have been to some extent in operation during the war. These come before us with the prestige of experience and should therefore receive first consideration in any program that aims to be at once practical and persuasive. . . .

Women War Workers

One of the most important problems of readjustment is that created by the presence in industry of immense numbers of women who have taken the places of men during the war. Mere justice, to say nothing of chivalry, dictates that these women should not be compelled to suffer any greater loss or inconvenience than is absolutely necessary; for their services to the nation have been second only to the services of the men whose places they were called upon to fill. One general principle is clear; No female worker should remain in any occupation that is harmful to health or morals. Women should disappear as quickly as possible from such tasks as conducting and guarding street cars, cleaning locomotives, and a great number of other activities for which conditions of life and their physique render them unfit. Another general principle is that the proportion of women in industry ought to be kept within the smallest practical limits. If we have an efficient national employment service, if a goodly number of the returned soldiers and sailors are placed on the land, and if wages and the demand for goods are kept up to the level which is easily attainable, all female workers who are displaced from tasks that they have been performing only since the beginning of the war will be able to find suitable employments in other parts of the industrial field, or in those domestic occupations which sorely need their presence. Those women who are engaged at the same tasks as men should receive equal pay for equal amounts and qualities of work. . . .

Present Wage Rates Should Be Sustained

The general level of wages attained during the war should not be lowered. In a few industries, especially some directly and peculiarly connected with the carrying on of war, wages have reached a plane upon which they cannot possibly continue for this grade of occupations. But the number of workers in this situation is an extremely small proportion of the entire wage-earning population. The overwhelming majority should not be compelled or suffered to undergo any reduction in their rates of remuneration, for two reasons: First, because the average rate of pay has not increased faster than the cost of living; second, because a considerable majority of the wage-earners of the United States, both men and women, were not receiving living wages when prices began to rise in 1915. . . . Even if the great majority of workers were now in receipt of more than living wages, there are no good reasons why rates of pay should be lowered. After all, a living wage is not necessarily the full measure of justice. All the Catholic authorities on the subject explicitly declare that this is only the minimum of justice. In a country as rich as ours, there are very few cases in which it is possible to prove that the worker would be getting more than that to which he has a right if he were paid something in excess of this ethical minimum. Why then, should we assume that this is the normal share of almost the whole laboring population? Since our industrial resources and instrumentalities are sufficient to provide more than a living wage for a very large proportion of the workers, why should we acquiesce in a theory which denies them this measure of the comforts of life? Such a policy is not only of very questionable morality, but is unsound economically. The large demand for goods which is created and maintained by high rates of wages and high purchasing power by the masses is the surest guarantee of a continuous and general operation of industrial establishments. It is the most effective instrument of prosperity for labor and capital alike. The principal beneficiaries of a general reduction of wages would be the less efficient among the capitalists, and the more comfortable sections of the consumers. The wage-earners would lose more in remuneration than they would gain from whatever fall in prices occurred as a direct result of the fall in wages. On grounds both of justice and sound economics, we should give our hearty support to all legitimate efforts made by labor to resist general wage reductions. . . .

Social Insurance

Until this level of legal minimum wages is reached the worker stands in need of the device of insurance. The State should make comprehensive provision for insurance against illness, invalidity, unemployment, and old age. So far as possible the insurance fund should be raised by a levy on industry, as is now done in the case of accident compensation. The industry in which a man is employed should provide him with all that is necessary to meet all the needs of his entire life. Therefore, any contribution to the insurance fund from the general revenues of the State should be only slight and temporary. For the same reason no contribution should be exacted from any worker who is not getting a higher wage than is required to meet the present needs of himself and family. Those who are below that level can make such a contribution only at the expense of their present welfare. Finally, the administration of the insurance laws should be such as to interfere as little as possible with the individual freedom of the worker and his family. Any insurance scheme, or any administrative method, that tends to separate the workers into a distinct and dependent class, that offends against their domestic privacy and independence, or that threatens individual self-reliance and self-respect, should not be tolerated. The ideal to be kept in mind is a condition in which all the workers would themselves have the income and the responsibility of providing for all the needs and contingencies of life, both present and future. Hence all forms of State insurance should be regarded as merely a lesser evil, and should be so organized and administered as to hasten the coming of the normal condition.

The life insurance offered to soldiers and sailors during the war should be continued, so far as the enlisted men are concerned. It is very doubtful whether the time has yet arrived when public opinion would sanction the extension of general life insurance by the Government to all classes of the community.

The establishment and maintenance of municipal health inspection in all schools, public and private, is now pretty generally recognized as of great importance and benefit. Municipal clinics where the poorer classes could obtain the advantage of medical treatment by specialists at a reasonable cost would likewise seem to have become a necessity. A vast amount of unnecessary sickness and suffering exists among the poor and the lower middle classes because they cannot afford the advantages of any other treatment except that provided by the general practitioner. Every effort should be made to supply wage-earners and their families with specialized medical care through development of group medicine. Free medical care should be given only to those who cannot afford to pay.

Labor Participation in Industrial Management

The right of labor to organize and to deal with employers through representatives has been asserted above in connection with the discussion of the War Labor Board. It is to be hoped that this right will never again be called in question by any considerable number of employers. In addition to this, labor ought gradually to receive greater representation in what the English group of Quaker employers have called the "industrial" part of business management—"the control of processes and machinery; nature of product; engagement and dismissal of employees; hours of work, rates of pay, bonuses, etc.; welfare work; shop discipline; relations with trade unions." The establishment of shop committees, working wherever possible with the trade union, is the method suggested by this group of employers for giving the employees the proper share of industrial management. There can be no doubt that a frank adoption of these means and ends by employers would not only promote the welfare of the workers, but vastly improve the relations between them and their employers, and increase the efficiency and productiveness of each establishment. There is no need here to emphasize the importance of safety and sanitation in work places, as this is pretty generally recognized by legislation. What is required is an extension and strengthening of many of the existing statutes, and a better administration and enforcement of such laws everywhere. . . .

Ultimate and Fundamental Reforms

Despite the practical and immediate character of the present statement, we cannot entirely neglect the question of ultimate aims and a systematic program; for other groups are busy issuing such systematic pronouncements, and we all need something of the kind as a philosophical foundation and as a satisfaction to our natural desire for comprehensive statements.

It seems clear that the present industrial system is destined to last for a long time in its main outlines. That is to say, private ownership of capital is not likely to be supplanted by a collectivist organization of industry at a date sufficiently near to justify any present action based on the hypothesis of its arrival. This forecast we recognize as not only extremely probable, but as highly desirable; for, other objections apart, Socialism would mean bureaucracy, political tyranny, the helplessness of the individual as a factor in the ordering of his own life, and in general social inefficiency and decadence.

Main Defects of the Present System

Nevertheless, the present system stands in grievous need of considerable modifications and improvement. Its main defects are three:

Enormous inefficiency and waste in the production and distribution of commodities; insufficient incomes for the great majority of wage-earners, and unnecessarily large incomes for a small minority of privileged capitalists. Inefficiency in the production and distribution of goods would be in great measure abolished by the reforms that have been outlined in the foregoing pages. Production would be greatly increased by universal living wages, by adequate industrial education, and by harmonious relations between labor and capital (the basis of adequate participation by the former in all the industrial aspects of business management). The wastes of commodity distribution could be practically all eliminated by co-operative mercantile establishments, and co-operative selling and marketing associations.

Co-operation and Co-partnership

Nevertheless, the full possibilities of increased production will not be realized so long as the majority of the workers remain mere wage earners. The majority must somehow become owners, or at least in part, of the instruments of production. They can be enabled to reach this stage gradually through co-operative productive societies and co-partnership arrangements. In the former the workers own and manage the industries themselves; in the latter they own a substantial part of the corporate stock and exercise a reasonable share in the management. However slow the attainments of these ends, they will have to be reached before we can have a thoroughly efficient system of production, for an industrial and social order that will be secure from the danger of revolution. It is to be noted that this particular modification of the existing order, though far-reaching and involving to a great extent the abolition of the wage system, would not mean the abolition of private ownership. The instruments of production would still be owned by individuals, not by the State.

Increased Incomes for Labor

The second great evil, that of insufficient income for the majority can be removed only by providing the workers with more income. This means not only universal living wages, but the opportunity of obtaining something more than that amount for all who are willing to work hard and faithfully. All the other measures for labor betterment recommended in the preceding pages would likewise contribute directly or indirectly to a more just distribution of wealth in the interest of the laborer.

Abolition and Control of Monopolies

For the third evil mentioned above, excessive gains by a small minority of privileged capitalists, the main remedies are prevention of monopolistic control of commodities, adequate government regulation of such public service monopolies as will remain under private operation, and heavy taxation of incomes, excess profits and inheritances. The precise methods by which genuine competition may be restored and maintained among businesses that are naturally competitive, cannot be discussed here; but the principle is clear that human beings cannot be trusted with the immense opportunities for oppression and extortion that go with the possession of monopoly power. That the owners of public service monopolies should be restricted by law to a fair or average return on their actual investment, has long been a recognized principle of the courts, the legislatures, and public opinion. It is a principle which should be applied to competitive enterprises likewise, with the qualification that something more than the average rate of return should be allowed to men who exhibit exceptional efficiency. However, good public policy, as well as equity, demands that these exceptional business men share the fruits of their efficiency with the consumer in the form of lower prices. The man who utilizes his ability to produce cheaper than his competitors for the purpose of exacting from the public as high a price for his product as is necessary for the least efficient business man, is a menace rather than a benefit to industry and society.

Our immense war debt constitutes a particular reason why incomes and excess profits should continue to be heavily taxed. In this way two important ends will be attained: the poor will be relieved of injurious tax burdens, and the small class of specially privileged capitalists will be compelled to return a part of their unearned gains to society.

A New Spirit, a Vital Need

"Society," said Pope Leo XIII, "can be healed in no other way than by a return to Christian life and Christian Institutions." The truth of these words is more widely perceived to-day than when they were written, more than twenty-seven years ago. Changes in our economic and political systems will have only partial and feeble efficiency if they be not reinforced by the Christian view of work and wealth. Neither the moderate reforms advocated in this paper, nor any other program of betterment or reconstruction will prove reasonably effective without a reform in the spirit of both labor and capital. The laborer must come to realize that he owes his employer and society an honest day's work in return for a fair wage, and that conditions cannot be substantially improved until he roots out the desire to get a maximum of return for a minimum of service. The capitalist must likewise get a new viewpoint. He needs to learn the long-forgotten truth that wealth is stewardship, that profit-making is not the basic justification of business enterprise, and that there arc such things as fair profits, fair interest, and fair prices. Above and before all, he must cultivate and strengthen within his mind the truth which many of his class have begun to grasp for the first time during the present war; namely, that the laborer is a human being, not merely an instrument of production; and that the laborer's right to a decent livelihood is the first moral charge upon industry. The employer has a right to get a reasonable living out of his business, but he has no right to interest on his investment until his employees have obtained at least living wages. This is the human and Christian, in contrast to the purely commercial and pagan, ethics of industry.

38. Joseph Nevins, "Education to Catholic Marriage" (1928)

Manuals on how to hear confession had grown out of early Irish penitential books, which catalogued the possible sins of monks. They tended to develop in a legalistic, act-based direction: there were a certain number of sins one might commit, each with its own penalty, and it was a confessor's duty to determine what sins a penitent had committed and how many times he or she had committed them. Before the 1920s, however, few confessors would have dreamed of raising the obscene subject of sex, including birth control; they were often advised that to do so might give their penitents ideas and advice they otherwise would not have thought of! However, with the use of artificial birth control on the rise in the wake of action by progressive feminists such as Margaret Sanger, Catholic priests began to feel that it was their duty—however disagreeable—to interrogate their female penitents about their sexual habits, in order to point out the sins against the Catholic faith they might be committing.

The laity are of the mind that contraception is forbidden only by the law of the Church—that it is only man-made law. This notion is hard to change, and it constitutes a very considerable handicap. To counteract this, they must be given to understand that the teaching of the Church is infallible and not debatable; that we are not arguing with them, we are teaching them, and what we say and preach is to be accepted on faith, unequivocally. They must be informed or reminded that this is necessary matter for confession, and be given to understand that they are tampering with a sacred institution. Confessors, too, will realize that as ministers of the Sacrament they are bound to interrogate upon this point, for there is solid ground for suspicion that adults generally are at fault herein. Our task is really to inculcate anew the reverence and docility of a truly Catholic mind toward the teaching of the Church on Matrimony. . . .

As to the assertion one occasionally hears made, even by priests, that married people are not questioned as to the fulfillment of their family obligation, we prefer to say that it is unbelievable, and we trust, utterly as unwarranted as such a practice is, in itself, a clear and serious default of a confessor's duty.

The giving of absolution to penitents who confess to contraception is of course at the discretion of the confessor. . . . If absolution be given, it should be with clear statement to the penitent that it is of doubtful worth and that the penitent must assure himself or herself whether or not his dispositions positively permit it to have any value. This much at least is required of the confessor. Then there is the further question, Is it advisable or even right to give absolution at all, short of moral certitude that the purpose of amendment is what it should be? There is at times a compelling reason for not absolving, but for refusing. Other people are as guilty of the same sin or are tempted to it, and it is certain in most cases that they know what their neighbors are doing in the way of family limitation, and they see and know that such approach the holy tribunal and appear at the altar rail, and they are scandalized in the true sense of the word. They comment on all this, and fix their own consciences. . . .

Absolution should be refused to all who do not give moral assurance of their purpose of amendment. Many are in a false conscience about the whole business of married life and seem to regard as the one important thing that they rate as practical Catholics in the eyes of the community where they are well known. It is imperative on the grounds of the common good that they be brought to their senses religiously, that they be treated as *recidivi,* and that no ordinary evidence of right dispositions will warrant giving them even conditional absolution; and they should be given to understand that conditional absolution is of doubtful value and of itself does not justify their receiving Holy Communion. It is to the credit of the clergy that they are very loth to refuse absolution, but we have come to a pass where the considerations are not individual and personal, and we must not be thought to compromise Catholic moral doctrine.

39. DOROTHY DAY, "LOAVES AND FISHES" (1933)

When Dorothy Day wrote this essay for her newspaper, The Catholic Worker, *the paper—and the movement it had begun—was more than thirty years old. But here she recalls the heady year of 1932–33, when she met the itinerant Frenchman Peter Maurin and with him founded a movement that changed the lives of thousands of Catholics. By this time Day had already lived a full life: after a career as a reformist journalist, and after having had a child out of wedlock, she converted to Catholicism. In late 1932 her relationship had failed, she was back in Manhattan after several years in a cottage on remote Staten Island, and she was unsure of her next move; then Maurin appeared on her doorstep. For the rest of her life Day was the driving force behind the Catholic Worker, living a richly traditional spiritual life and remaining fiercely attached to her ideals of poverty and pacifism, while inspiring the volunteers who thronged the two Worker houses on the Lower East Side of Manhattan as they made enormous pots of soup and coffee—and got the paper out on time.*

Someone once said that it took me from December until May to bring out the paper. The truth is that I agreed at once. The delay was due chiefly to the fact that Peter, in his optimism about funds, was relying on a priest he knew who had a very plush rectory uptown on the West Side. His clerical friend would give us a mimeograph machine, paper, and space in the rectory basement. None of these were forthcoming—they had been only optimistic notions of Peter's.

But in the meantime Peter was educating me. I had a secular education, he said, and he would give me a Catholic outline of history. One way to study history was to read the lives of the saints down the centuries. Perhaps he chose this method because he had noticed my library, which contained a life of St. Teresa of Avila and her writings, especially about her spiritual foundations, and a life of St. Catherine of Siena. "Ah, there was a saint who had an influence on her times!" he exclaimed. Then he plunged into a discussion of St. Catherine's letters to the Popes and other public figures of the fourteenth century, in which she took them to task for their failings.

The date I had met Peter is clear in my mind because it was just after the feast of the Immaculate Conception, which is on December 8. I had visited the national shrine at Catholic University in Washington to pray for the hunger marchers. I felt keenly that God was more on the side of the hungry, the ragged, the unemployed, than on the side of the comfortable churchgoers, who gave so little heed to the misery of the needy and the groaning of the poor. I had prayed that some way should open up for me to do something, to line myself up on their side, to work for them, so that I would no longer feel I had been false to them in embracing my newfound faith.

The appearance of Peter Maurin, I felt with deep conviction, was the result of my prayers. Just as the good God had used the farmer Habakuk to bring the mess of food intended for the reapers to Daniel in the lions' den, so had He sent Peter Maurin to bring me the good intellectual food I needed to strengthen me to work for Him.

I learned shortly how he had happened to come to see me. He had heard of me on a visit to the *Commonweal,* our famous New York weekly edited by laymen. It had been started by Michael Williams, a veteran journalist, who had worked in San Francisco on the same paper with my father years before. Peter had also been told of my conversion by a red-headed Irish Communist with whom he struck up a conversation on a bench in Union Square. The Irishman told Peter that we both had similar ideas—namely, that the Catholic Church had a social teaching which could be applied to the problems of our day. So Peter had set out to find me.

Now he had someone to whom he could propound his program. He must have proposed it many times before, at Social Action conferences, in visits to public figures and chancery offices around the country. But he seemed to have got nowhere. It might have been his shabbiness, it might have been his thick accent, that prevented him from getting a hearing.

Perhaps it was because of my own radical background that Peter brought me a digest of the writings of Kropotkin one day, calling my attention especially to *Fields, Factories and Worshops* [*sic*]. He had gone over to the Rand School of Social Science for this, and carefully copied out the pertinent passages. He also liked *Mutual Aid* and *The Conquest of Bread.*

I was familiar with Kropotkin only through his *Memoirs of a Revolutionist,* which had originally run serially in the *Atlantic Monthly.* (Oh, far-off day of American freedom, when Karl Marx could write for the morning *Tribune* in New York, and Kropotkin could not only be published in the *Atlantic,* but be received as a guest in the homes of New England Unitarians, and in Jane Addams' Hull House in Chicago!)

Peter came day after day. He brought me books to read and the newest of his phased writings. There was to be no end to my learning.

One day I chanced upon Peter in his friend's uptown church. I had dropped in to say a few prayers. After some minutes I looked up. There was Peter, sitting in front of the Blessed Sacrament, evidently in deep meditation. He seemed totally unconscious of the presence of anyone else in the church. He sat there in silence. Every now and then he would nod his head, and gesticulate with his hand, as though he were making one of his points to the Presence before Whom he sat so quietly. I did not want to disturb him.

Also, in my subconscious, I was probably tired of his constant conversation. His line of thought, the books he had given me to read, were all new to me and all ponderous. There was so much theory. I had read about Kropotkin the man, his life and adventures. In a way they told me much. I was not sure I wanted to know more. Peter read Kropotkin's theoretical works. It was the idea, the abstract thought, that got him and that he hoped would get me. Sitting there thinking back over the past weeks, I had to face the fact that Peter was hard to listen to. I would tune in some concert, some symphony, and beg him to be still. Tessa (my brother John's wife) and I both loved music, but Peter seemed to have no ear for it. He would be obedient for a time. But soon he would look at my forbidding face, and, seeing no yielding there, he would go over to the gentler Tessa, pulling a chair close to hers and leaning almost on the arm, he would begin to talk. He was incorrigible. Yet we were growing to love him, to greet him warmly when he came, to press food on him, knowing that he ate only one meal a day.

His willingness to talk to any visitor who dropped in, however, was a boon to us; it released us for our various chores. I, for example, could run into the front room to my typewriter and get some work done. I recall one visitor in particular, who came quite often, a sculptor named Hugh ———, a tall man, heavy and quiet, with big brown eyes. He used to take out a flute and play while Peter talked to him.

"You are quite right, Peter," he would say every now and then, nodding absently. Then he would go right on piping his simple tunes. He startled us one day, when a woman friend of ours came to call, by remarking after she had left that she used to come to his studio and sit in the nude on the mantelpiece. We concluded that she must have resembled some model who had once posed for him.

Usually by ten or eleven we urged our visitors to go. We were at home with them and felt free to send them on their way. On mild nights, Hugh and Peter would go on to Union Square to sit on a park bench. There they would continue their conversation—if it could be called that—with Hugh playing his flute, and Peter, gesticulating, haranguing him with his discussion of history, his analysis of ideas, old and new, and, in doing so, perhaps rehearsing his lessons for me the next day.

Placidly, Tessa awaited her baby, and I went on with my free-lancing. In the evenings, my brother and I (John was working days now) would talk over plans for the paper with Peter, who knew nothing about journalism. He would supply the ideas, and we would get out the paper for the "man in the street."

My mind and heart were full of the part I had to play, self-centered creature that I was. I planned the makeup and the type, and what stories I would write to go with Peter's easy essays. I don't think we even consulted Peter as to whether he liked the title we had given to his writings in the paper, "Easy Essays." He was so happy over the coming incarnation of his ideas in print that he never expressed himself on the subject. But he well knew that, in spite of the title, his essays were anything but easy. Like those in the Gospel, his were hard sayings—hard to work out in everyday life.

Having become convinced of this after several weeks, I went, on the advice of Father Joseph McSorley, former provincial of the Paulist Society and my good spiritual adviser at the time, to the Paulist Press. For an edition of two thousand copies, I was told, the price would be fifty-seven dollars.

I decided to wait until I had the cash in hand before getting out the first issue. I didn't want to run up any debts. I did no installment buying, although I didn't mind being late with the rent or skimping on groceries to speed the accumulation of enough money to pay the first bill. Father McSorley helped a lot by finding work for me to do. Father Harold Purcell gave me ten dollars, and Sister Peter Claver brought me a dollar which someone had just given to her.

All that winter Peter had come back and forth from Mt. Tremper in upstate New York, but by April he was in town all the time. Our plans were shaping up. Yet Peter was plainly not too well pleased with the way the paper was going.

I had sent my copy to the printer—news accounts of the exploitation of Negroes in the South, and the plight of the sharecroppers; child labor in our own neighborhood; some recent evictions; a local strike over wages and hours; pleas for better home relief, and so on—and we were waiting for proofs.

When they came we cut them out and started making a dummy, pasting them up on the eight pages of a tabloid the size of the Nation, writing headlines, and experimenting with different kinds of type. Peter looked over what I had written as it came back from the printer. I could see that, far from being happy about it, he was becoming more and more disturbed. One day, while looking over some fresh proofs, he shook his head. His expression was one of great sadness. "It's everyone's paper," he said. I was pleased. I thought that was what we both wanted. "And everyone's paper is no one's paper," he added with a sigh.

He rose without another word and went out the door. Later we learned indirectly that he had gone back upstate. It was some time before we heard from him again.

We kept hoping that he would be on hand for that historic May Day in 1933 when we ventured out in Union Square to sell the first issue. He wasn't. A friendly priest sent three young men to accompany me. One of them was Joe Bennett, a tall, gangling blond boy from Denver, who was to work closely with us for some months. The day was bright and warm and beautiful. The square was packed with demonstrators and paraders, listening to speeches, carrying on disputes among themselves, or glancing through the great masses of literature being given out or sold, which so soon were litter on the ground. The two younger men, intimidated and discouraged by the slighting comments of the champions of labor and the left, soon fled. Religion in Union Square! It was preposterous! If we had been representing Jehovah's Witnesses, we might have had a friendlier reception. But people associated with the Roman Catholic Church! Joe Bennett and I stuck it out, reveling in the bright spring sunshine. We did not sell many papers, but we did enjoy the discussions into which we were drawn. One Irishman looked at the masthead and rebuked us for the line which read "a penny a copy." We were in the pay of the English, he said. Next month we changed it to "a cent a copy" just to placate the Irish.

We knew Peter would not have let this go without making a point. He would have said, "When an Irishman met an Irishman a thousand years ago, they started a monastery. Now, when an Irishman meets an Irishman, you know what they start." Then he would have gone on with a long discourse on Gaelic culture, on how it was the Irish who kept civilization alive through the Dark Ages, and on and on, until his adversary would have forgotten all about his heat over the penny.

Another protest came from a Negro, who pointed out that the two workers on our masthead, standing on either side of our title, the *Catholic Worker,* were both white men. One had a pick and the other had a shovel. "Why not have one white and the other colored?" he wanted to know.

We thought it was a good suggestion. Before our next issue came out we found an artist who made a new masthead for us, a white man and a colored man, each with his implements of toil, clasping hands, with the figure of Christ in the background, uniting them. Joe Bennett and I sat on park benches that first day, got our first touch of sunburn and gradually relaxed. In spite of our small sales and the uncertain prospects for the future, it was with a happy feeling of accomplishment that I returned to East Fifteenth Street that evening.

But I missed Peter Maurin. We had been so excited at the idea of launching a new paper, small though it was, and we had had so many details to attend to, that there was not much time to miss him before the paper came out. But now I did. His absence gave me an uneasy feeling, reminding me that our paper was not reflecting his thought, although it was he who had given us the idea.

Then, for a while, I was too busy again to think much about it. Copies had to be mailed out to editors of diocesan papers and to men and women prominent in the Catholic world. Mail began to come in praising our first effort. Some letters even contained donations to help us continue our work. I was lighthearted with success. We had started. . . .

More and more people began to come. Two constant visitors at the office of the *Catholic Worker* were a thin, shabby, and rather furtive-looking pair whom Peter had picked up in Union Square earlier in the spring before he went away. To him they represented "the worker." They would listen to him untiringly and without interrupting. They were the beginning of an audience, something to build on—not very promising, but something. After one of Peter's discussions in the square, they usually followed him to my place, where, if there was not a bit of change forthcoming, there was at least bread and sweet tea. Peter would say each time, "They have no place to sleep." He was sure that I would produce the dollar needed for two beds on the Bowery. But often there was no dollar, so they stayed for lunch instead.

All the while Peter was in the country I was visited regularly by the pair of them. They always announced themselves before I opened the door: "Dolan and Egan here again." It got so that my personal friends, knowing how exasperated I was becoming at having my time taken up, used to call out upon arriving, "Dolan and Egan here again."

Thus it was with repressed impatience that I heard one day a knock on the door of my apartment above the barbershop. I stood there, braced for the familiar greeting. When it did not come, I opened the door anyway— there stood Peter Maurin.

"Peter! Where have you been?" My relief was so great that my welcome was ardent. "Where were you on May Day? Thousands of people in Union Square and not a sign of Peter!"

"Everyone's paper is no one's paper," he repeated, shaking his head. Peter seemed rested and not so dusty as usual. His gray eyes told me that he was glad to be back. While I prepared coffee and soup and put out the bread, he went on and on, and I let him, content to wait until he was eating his soup to tell him all that had been happening. When his mouth was full he would listen.

I got no explanation from him as to why he had gone away. The closest he came to it was to say wryly, with a shrug, "Man proposes and woman disposes." But he looked at me and smiled and his eyes warmed. I could see that he was happy to be back and ready to get on with his mission. He was full of patience, ready to look at me now not as a Catherine of Siena, already enlightened by the Holy Spirit, but as an ex-Socialist, ex-I.W.W., ex-Communist, in whom he might find some concordance, some basis on which to build. But unions and strikes and the fight for better wages and hours would remain my immediate concern. As St. Augustine said, "The bottle will still smell of the liquor it once held." I continued on this track until Peter had enlightened my mind and enlarged my heart to see further, more in accord with the liberty of Christ, of which St. Paul was always speaking.

Peter . . . often spoke of what he called "a philosophy of work." "Work, not wages—work is not a commodity to be bought and sold" was one of his slogans. "Personal responsibility, not state responsibility" was another. "A personalist is a go-giver, not a go-getter," he used to say. "He tries to give what he has instead of trying to get what the other fellow has. He tries to be good by doing good to the other fellow. He has a social doctrine of the common good. He is alter-centered, not self-centered."

Much later, when I had a look at that first issue, I could see more clearly what bothered Peter. We had emphasized wages and hours while he was trying to talk about a philosophy of work. . . . It must have appeared to him that we were just urging the patching-up of the industrial system instead of trying to rebuild society itself with a philosophy so old it seemed like new. Even the name of the paper did not satisfy him. He would have preferred Catholic Radical, since he believed that radicals should, as their name implied, get at the roots of things. The second issue of the paper, the June-July number, showed that we had been talking things over. My editorial said:

Peter Maurin (whose name we misspelled in the last issue) has his program which is embodied in his contribution this month. Because his program is specific and definite, he thinks it is better to withdraw his name from the editorial board and continue his contact with the paper as a contributor.

Then came Peter's editorial:

As an editor, it will be assumed that I sponsor or advocate any reform suggested in the pages of the Catholic Worker. I would rather definitely sign my own work, letting it be understood what I stand for.

My program stands for three things: Round-table discussions is one and I hope to have the first one at the Manhattan Lyceum the last Sunday in June. We can have a hall holding 150 people for eight hours for ten dollars. I have paid a deposit of three. I have no more money now but I will beg the rest. I hope everyone will come to this meeting. I want Communists, radicals, priests, and laity. I want everyone to set forth his own views. I want clarification of thought.

The next step in the program is houses of hospitality. In the Middle Ages it was an obligation of the bishop to provide houses of hospitality or hospices for the wayfarer. They are especially necessary now and necessary to my program, as halfway houses. I am hoping that someone will donate a house rent-free for six months so that a start may be made. A priest will be at the head of it and men gathered from our roundtable discussions will be recruited to work in the houses cooperatively and eventually be sent out to farm colonies or agronomic universities. Which comes to the third step in my program. People will have to go back to the land. The machine has displaced labor. The cities are overcrowded. The land will have to take care of them.

My whole scheme is a Utopian, Christian communism. I am not afraid of the word communism. I am not saying that my program is for everyone. It is for those who choose to embrace it. I am not opposed to private property with responsibility. But those who own private property should never forget it is a trust.

This succinct listing of his aims was not even the lead editorial. Perhaps it sounded too utopian for my tastes; perhaps I was irked because women were left out in his description of a house of hospitality, where he spoke of a group of men living under a priest. . . .

There were other articles on more mundane matters. One stated that readers had contributed $156.50. That, with what money I got from free-lancing, would keep us going. There was also a report on distribution: papers were being mailed out all over the country in bundles of ten or twenty; Dolan and Eagan had been selling on the streets (they kept the money to pay for their "eats and tobacco"); and I too had embarked on the great adventure of going out to face up to "the man on the street."

So we continued through the summer. Since this was the depression and there were no jobs, almost immediately we found ourselves a group, a staff, which grew steadily in numbers. Joe Bennett, our first salesman, was still with us. Soon we were joined by Stanley Vishnewski, a seventeen-year-old Lithuanian boy from the Williamsburg section of Brooklyn who used to walk to New York over the bridge every day and then twenty-five blocks uptown to Fifteenth Street. He sold the paper, too, and ran errands and worked without wages despite the urging of his father, a tailor, that he ought to be looking for a job. (Stanley has remained with us ever since.) . . .

40. KATHARINE M. BYRNE, "HAPPY LITTLE WIVES AND MOTHERS" (1956)

In the postwar years Catholic families were part of the general movement from working class to middle class, from city to suburb; women who during the war years might have held office or factory jobs or even been in military service now married returning GIs and, in many cases, had large families. Catholic newspapers and magazines supported this development, featuring editorials and profiles that portrayed marriage, motherhood, and housekeeping as the path to virtue and sanctity for women. Katharine Byrne's ironic response to the exaltation of the home as the woman's sphere was ahead of its time: not until the 1960s would large numbers of women begin to reject the notion that the home was the only appropriate outlet for their talents and energies.

The happy little wife and mother is really busy these days, and she is making my life no easier. You cannot turn many pages of a Catholic magazine without running into the brave and cheerful story of her life. Her days are filled with worthy projects at home and abroad, and the modest recital of her successes ("Of course, I can't do very much as I have eight children under six years of age") must have some good purpose in mind. Perhaps she rushes into print as an encouragement to the spiritually-lagging or hollering-at-the-kids type of female. That a quite opposite effect may follow is certainly no fault of hers.

The Life Beautiful

Most of us females of a lower order have a hard enough time learning to live with the lady in the House Gracious ads. You know the one. She sits smiling on her sun-drenched patio reading House Gracious. In the out-of-doors recreation area, some distance removed, her two roguish children ("We will raise a family, a boy for you, a girl for me") are engaged in constructive and compatible play. Or she may be sitting at a desk in the meal-planning area of her kitchen, her gourmet cookbook at her fingertips, a pink telephone at her elbow. No child has ever hurled a bowl of Pablum at these walls, nor is this gleaming floor ever awash with spilled Wheaties.

Poor banished children of Eve, we look with longing at all the Things which seem to fill her life so nicely. Only after a spiritual struggle which may last for years do we learn to rise above this girl, and to reject her way of life as false, materialistic and secular. Besides, we tell ourselves, she couldn't be that happy. Maybe she has a mean mother-in-law.

But we are faced at times with a different and more difficult problem.

There is another Happy Little Wife and Mother who sits on no sun-drenched patio. She lives, usually, in a huge lovable wreck of a house, distracted by few modern conveniences. In some cases her numerous brood may be tucked in to a three-room apartment. No matter. Cheerful as a well-worn cliché, she makes out nobly. While you pale at the thought of 48 hours with a non-operating Bendix, she wouldn't mind beating the blue-jeans on rocks.

Her children are good. Her curly-headed two-year-old folds dimpled hands in prayer. Yours has just sunk savage teeth into the arm of her little brother, and followed up his screams with a soothing kiss. No such ambivalent behavior ruffles the spiritual calm of her household.

You may think you are doing a fair job in human relations, but your efforts never work out quite as beautifully as hers. If she is good to the little boy nobody in the neighborhood likes, he blossoms under her kindly ministrations, is diverted from his objectionable hobby (stealing small articles from the local dime store) and now writes her grateful letters from a monastery.

There was a little boy who hung around your swings and sandbox one summer. Nobody knew where he lived and the other children weren't very kind to him. When you brought out the milk and sandwiches for yard picnics, you used to bring some for him, too. You urged the children to share toys and popsicles with this outlander. One day when it was time to put the rolling stock away, you noticed that one fairly new 24-inch bike was missing. You never saw the little boy again either.

Nothing like this ever happens to the Happy Little Wife and Mother.

Hers is a simplicist's world of easy and invariable answers to life's questions, a kind of you-too-can-learn-to-play-the-Hawaiian-guitar or *Readers' Digest* world in which formulas are neat and all the experiments behave as they should.

And yet, you know that life cannot be so simple even for her. She probably leads the same soul-buffeted life that we do. She may be better at it, but she's human, and I wish she'd break down and admit it. It would be a real comfort to me to hear the H. L. W. and M. admit that once, after three bleak winter weeks of unalleviated pressures, she walked out on her whole family and took a bus ride to the end of the line, alone.

When I was a little girl we had a remarkable neighbor named Mrs. Mulholland. Because she was the oldest person in the community, her birthday was always the occasion for a newspaper interview. When she reached her 100th year the usual questions were asked. But Mrs. Mulholland, God love her, had none of the usual answers. Did she drink? Well, yes, a little. She had had her first cocktail at 95. Wasn't that a bit late in life to start drinking? "Well, no. Before that I just took a straight nip when I needed it." Wasn't it hard for her to raise all those children alone, since her husband had died when she was in her thirties? Well, no, not as hard as you might think. Her husband, though a good man, you understand, had never really been too much help to her. But she had had a bachelor brother, Joe, with a good civil service job with the city, and he had turned over his check for years. Dear Mrs. Mulholland, I salute your honest virtues.

The Human Touch

When a woman whose dieting efforts have largely failed reads a "You, too . . ." article by a lady who lost 50 pounds in 50 weeks, she is heartened by the author's rueful admission that once, in the midst of this rigorous regimen, she locked herself in the bathroom and devoured a pound of butter-creams.

In much the same way, perhaps, we would welcome from the Happy

Little Wife and Mother the admission that while the way of life which she chose, and the one which, with God's grace she is trying to live well, is the one she wants, it is nevertheless a somewhat monotonous life. And often very lonely.

And on occasion, as she kisses her immaculate, clean-shaven, whitecollared husband goodbye, and turns to face the montage of congealed eggyolks, unbraided braids, ankle-deep cereal and damp baby which constitute her first order of the day, might she not indulge even briefly, her Cool Sewer Complex? (This complex was inspired by Ed Young's famous cartoon depicting the fat and harassed wife who greets her Art Carney–type husband with the classic plaint, "Here I am, standing all day over this hot stove, while you're down in that cool sewer.") Or think, even fleetingly, "Lord, life was good in the dime store." Or the Acme Tool and Die Works. Or the dust and dimness of the Modern Language Library stacks.

While I am often plunged into sadness by a comparison of my own inadequacies with the lives led in print by all Happy Little Wives and Mothers, I would feel a real spiritual affinity for the woman who will give us groundlings a work-in-progress report of her efforts toward the Good Life, an account written not from the peak of Everest, but from halfway up, where the going is still rough and the backslides many.

41. JOHN F. KENNEDY, "ADDRESS TO SOUTHERN BAPTIST LEADERS" (1960)

In 1928 the Democrat Al Smith's bid to win the presidency had been ruined at least partly by the public perception that his Catholicism would require him to subordinate United States interests to those of the Pope. John F. Kennedy was beset by similar accusations in the 1960 campaign, particularly in the conservative Protestant strongholds of the rural South. Two months before the election, Kennedy addressed the issue head-on in a short, pointed, and utterly convincing speech to a group of ministers in Houston, Texas. He went on to defeat Richard Nixon in November.

I am grateful for your generous invitation to state my views.

While the so-called religious issue is necessarily and properly the chief topic here tonight, I want to emphasize from the outset that I believe that we have far more critical issues in the 1960 election. . . . They are not religious issues—for war and hunger and ignorance and despair know no religious barrier.

But because I am a Catholic and no Catholic has ever been elected President, the real issues in this campaign have been obscured—perhaps deliberately, in some quarters less responsible than this. So it is apparently necessary for me to state once again—not what kind of church I believe in, for that should be important only to me, but what kind of America I believe in.

I believe in an America where the separation of church and state is absolute—where no Catholic prelate would tell the President (should he be a Catholic) how to act and no Protestant minister would tell his parishioners for whom to vote—where no church or church school is granted any public funds or political preference—and where no man is denied public office merely because his religion differs from the President who might appoint him or the people who might elect him.

I believe in an America that is officially neither Catholic, Protestant nor Jewish—where no public official either requests or accepts instructions on public policy from the Pope, the National Council of Churches or any other ecclesiastical source—where no religious body seeks to impose its will directly or indirectly upon the general populace or the public acts of its officials—and where religious liberty is so indivisible that an act against one church is treated as an act against all. . . .

Finally, I believe in an America where religious intolerance will someday end—where all men and all churches are treated as equal—where every man has the same right to attend or not to attend the church of his choice—where there is no Catholic vote, no anti-Catholic vote, no bloc voting of any kind—and where Catholics, Protestants and Jews, both the lay and the pastoral level, will refrain from those attitudes of disdain and division which have so often marred their works in the past, and promote instead the American ideal of brotherhood.

That is the kind of America in which I believe. And it represents the kind of Presidency in which I believe—a great office that must be neither humbled by making it the instrument of any religious group, nor tarnished by arbitrarily withholding its occupancy from the members of any religious group. I believe in a President whose views on religion are his own private affair, neither imposed upon him by the nation or imposed by the nation upon him as a condition to holding that office. . . .

I want a chief executive whose public acts are responsible to all and obligated to none—who can attend any ceremony, service or dinner his office may appropriately require him to fulfill—and whose fulfillment of his Presidential office is not limited or conditioned by any religious oath, ritual or obligation.

This is the kind of America I believe in—and this is the kind of America I fought for in the South Pacific and the kind my brother died for in Europe. No one suggested then that we might have a "divided loyalty," that we did "not believe in liberty" or that we belonged to a disloyal group that threatened "the freedoms for which our forefathers died."

And in fact this is the kind of America for which our forefathers did die when they fled here to escape religious test oaths, that denied office to members of less favored churches, when they fought for the Constitution, the Bill of Rights, the Virginia Statute of Religious Freedom—and when they fought at the shrine I visited today—the Alamo. For side by side with Bowie and Crockett died Fuentes and McCafferty and Bailey and Bedillio and Carey—but no one knows whether they were Catholics or not. For there was no religious test there.

I ask you tonight to follow in that tradition, to judge me on the basis of fourteen years in the Congress—on my declared stands against an ambassador to the Vatican, against unconstitutional aid to parochial schools, and against any boycott of the public schools (which I attended myself)—and instead of doing this do not judge me on the basis of these pamphlets and publications we have all seen that carefully select quotations out of context from the statements of Catholic Church leaders, usually in other countries, frequently in other centuries, and rarely relevant to any situation here—and always omitting of course, that statement of the American bishops in 1948 which strongly endorsed church-state separation.

I do not consider these other quotations binding upon my public acts —why should you? But let me say, with respect to other countries, that I am wholly opposed to the state being used by any religious group, Catholic or Protestant, to compel, prohibit or prosecute the free exercise of any other religion. And that goes for any persecution at any time, by anyone, in any country. . . .

But let me stress again that these are my views—for, contrary to common newspaper usage, I am not the Catholic candidate for President [but the candidate] who happens also to be a Catholic. I do not speak for my church on public matters—and the church does not speak for me.

Whatever issue may come before me as President, if I should be elected —on birth control, divorce, censorship, gambling, or any other subject—I will make my decision in accordance with these views, in accordance with what my conscience tells me to be in the national interest, and without regard to outside religious pressure or dictate. And no power or threat of punishment could cause me to decide otherwise.

But if the time should ever come—and I do not concede any conflict to be remotely possible—when my office would require me to either violate my conscience, or violate the national interest, then I would resign the office, and I hope any other conscientious public servant would do likewise.

But I do not intend to apologize for these views to my critics of either Catholic or Protestant faith, nor do I intend to disavow either my views or my church in order to win this election. If I should lose on the real issues, I shall return to my seat in the Senate satisfied that I tried my best and was fairly judged. But if this election is decided on the basis that 40,000,000 Americans lost their chance of being President on the day they were baptized, then it is the whole nation that will be the loser in the eyes of Catholics and non-Catholics around the world, in the eyes of history, and in the eyes of our own people.

But if, on the other hand, I should win this election, I shall devote every effort of mind and spirit to fulfilling the oath of the Presidency—practically identical, I might add with the oath I have taken for fourteen years in the Congress. For, without reservation, I can, and I quote "solemnly swear that I will faithfully execute the office of President of the United States and will preserve, protect, and defend the Constitution so help me God."

42. "Dignity and the Priest" (1961)

The Civil Rights Movement of the 1950s and 1960s was, especially in its early years, an almost entirely Protestant affair. Although a few Southern bishops showed great courage during early struggles over school desegregation, and many large cities featured Catholic Interracial Councils or similar organizations, most white Catholics in both South and North were either anti-integration or profoundly ambivalent. Liberal priests and nuns, who made a point of attending demonstrations in religious attire and were frequently photographed in the front lines of marchers, were an especially sore point for the Catholics who argued, with Bishop Thomas Toolen of Montgomery, that northern priests should be "at home doing God's work" instead of getting involved in the politics of civil rights. This editorial from the Boston Pilot, *the oldest Catholic newspaper in the country, contests Toolen's interpretation of "God's work."*

Sometimes people wonder why it is that clergymen get involved in matters of social action like sit-ins and bus rides that defy segregation laws and customs. The pulpit is the place for the preacher, they argue; let some one else take action in the field. This is pretty old-fashioned thinking, but even when it was in style it was dead wrong.

Bishop Reed of Oklahoma City put it on the line last week in a sermon closing the National Catholic Conference on Interracial Justice. The Bishop spoke of a picture widely circulated some months ago showing a priest being forcibly ejected from a public restaurant by two police officers. It was in his See city and the priest was a member of the clergy of his diocese. "I was uneasy," the bishop said, "since it was not a very dignified sight, and I place considerable importance on personal dignity, above all, on priestly dignity." But the bishop was prompt in coming to the support of the ejected priest. "If a priest must occasionally suffer indignity to call reluctant public attention to the indignity of racial discrimination, then I feel the breach of decorum is justified."

This kind of commentary puts the race situation in its proper focus. Most of us dislike controversy; we dislike public protests; we don't want anything to happen that can provoke violence. As a result, we are slow to take our positions in troubled and volatile situations for fear we will suffer a loss of personal dignity. Basically, this is a good instinct and prudence favors it. But there are times when the values under assault are so precious, when the injustices are so unbearable, when the hope for redress is so distant, that we must take dramatic and bold action, EVEN AT THE EXPENSE OF OUR OWN EMBARRASSMENT AND LOSS OF DIGNITY.

It is because we believe in human dignity, because we acknowledge the spiritual nature of man, that we have to rise and protest the historic injustices that have plagued the Negro in America, even if we rise at the expense of our own sense of propriety and decorum. Americans should be proud of those clergymen who have stood shoulder to shoulder with the Negroes in their pacific protests against racial inequality. They stand again with the Lord at the well of Jacob and offer a cup to the woman of Samaria. Moreover, they give an example to the rest of us to be bold without being foolhardy, to be active without being imprudent, and to respect the law of God above the customs of men.

As Bishop Reed pointed out in his sermon, and in his own life, it is not easy for some Americans to see the race situation in clear, committed lines. "I was reared in a segregated society . . ." the bishop said and it has been difficult to set aside the ways so long taken for granted in favor of those based on an authentic interpretation of the Christian faith. When we say that justice will prevail in our country, we do not say that it will be accomplished easily; we have already enough evidence to understand this. But easily or not, justice will win in America and men of every race and color and background will be full citizens, politically, economically, and socially. If churchmen, high and low, assist in providing leadership, we will not have to wait very long.

43. Dr. John Rock, "The Pill" (1963)

John Rock (1890–1984) was a professor of obstetrics at Harvard Medical School, one of the inventors of both the birth control pill and in vitro fertilization, and a practicing Catholic. In numerous interviews on television and in the press, and in his widely read book The Time Has Come, *he advocated his thesis that "the pill" should be acceptable to the Catholic Church because (unlike spermicides, condoms, and sterilization) it did not block normal procreation nor damage any part of the body. Rather, it imitated the natural suppression of ovulation during pregnancy. Rock argued that this was akin to the "rhythm method," approved for Catholics since 1951.*

The steroid compounds are the first physiologic means of contraception; that is, they prevent reproduction by modifying the time sequences in the body's own functions, rather than by use of an extraneous device or by a wholly artificial chemical action. In the decade during which I have been associated with the development of these compounds, it has been my consistent feeling that, when properly used for conception control, they merely serve as adjuncts to nature, but the Catholic moralists who thus far expressed themselves on the subject certainly do not share my belief.

My reasoning is based, in part, on the fact that the rhythm method, which is sanctioned by the Church, depends precisely on the secretion of progesterone from the ovaries, which action these compounds merely duplicate. It is progesterone, in the healthy woman, that prevents ovulation and establishes the pre- and post-menstrual "safe period." The physiology underlying the spontaneous "safe period" is identical to that initiated by the steroid compounds and is equally harmless to the individual. Indeed, the use of the compounds for fertility control may be characterized as a "pill-established safe period" and would seem to carry the same moral implications.

It must be emphasized that the pills, when properly taken, are not at all likely to disturb menstruation, nor do they mutilate any organ of the body, nor damage any natural process. They merely offer to the human intellect the means to regulate ovulation harmlessly, means which heretofore have come only from the ovary and, during pregnancy, from the placenta. These organs supply progesterone at those times when nature seeks to protect a fertilized ovum, from jeopardy. Since the intellect is also part of a woman's natural being, surely it too is charged with the duty of protection against potential danger. The ovary and placenta respond automatically to remove the internal danger to mother and fetus which would stem from a second fertilized ovum. But only the intellect can perceive the external dangers to mother and children which would derive, at a particular time in a marriage, from an additional pregnancy. Indeed, the serious consideration of medical, eugenic, economic, and social indications for family limitation which Pius XII stipulated in his allocution to midwives can be undertaken only by the intellect. It is difficult not to believe that God gave man his intellect to safeguard him whenever his inner biology is inadequate. One might even tend to think it immoral for husband and wife, aware of the indications Pius XII listed, to reject their God-given intellect and trust only to the automatic action of female sex glands or to their ability to suppress the powerful love urge which their Creator fused with their sex instinct.

The Church has approved the use of the steroid compounds for therapeutic purposes. "Disorders of the endocrine system can result in miscarriage, menstrual irregularity and other difficulties," writes Thomas J. O'Donnell, S.J., university regent of the School of Medicine at Georgetown University. "There is no moral objection to the progestational compounds when they are used for the treatment and correction of such disorders, even though temporary sterility may result as a by-product of such treatment."

Moreover, John J. Lynch, S.J., considers as licit the use of the steroids for three or four months by women whose menstrual cycles have been "so irregular, and consequently so unpredictable, as to make the practice of rhythm unreliable as a means of avoiding a pregnancy." A majority of theologians, he writes, believe this procedure is permissible, on the assumption by the physicians who prescribe it that after the drug is withdrawn, "there will follow . . . a regular and predictable cycle of ovulation," thus making it possible to practice the rhythm method.

Apart from the use of the pills to establish menstrual cycles of uniform length with the intention of facilitating the use of the rhythm method, however, the moralists have not found sanction for the use of these compounds in fertility control. . . . With regard to the use of the pills, the position of Catholic moralists, as summed up by Father Gibbons, is that "such use of drugs or serums raises grave moral questions since it involves deliberate and direct suppression of normal reproductive function solely for contraceptive purposes. . . . This is temporary sterilization," which the Church condemns just as much as permanent sterilization.

Let us attempt to analyze this concept of "deliberate and direct suppression of normal reproductive function solely for contraceptive purposes." Consider the case of a husband and wife who want another baby but for valid reasons should not start the pregnancy at a particular time, and therefore employ the rhythm method in accordance with Church doctrine. Assume, for purposes of discussion, that without pregnancy or medication, the wife would enjoy regularity of menstruation at intervals of four weeks, and also experience the intercurrent ovulations which would establish this periodicity. Let us realize, too, that physiologically ovulation is but the release of an ovum, and that the ovum cannot exert its reproductive function unless it is fertilized. What is the effect of the rhythm method at this juncture? Would we say that the husband "sterilizes" his wife if, in accord with the calculation of the fertile period, he deprives this ovum of the function of growth by willfully omitting coital insemination? But is he not "deliberately and directly" suppressing normal reproductive function by doing so, since he precludes the possibility of fertilization indispensable for the ovum's functioning? Can the wife be said to undergo "temporary sterilization" through the same process?

Under these conditions, a fertilizable ovum is released but dies, its function unfulfilled. Now, if the wife uses medication to maintain her menstrual regularity, this treatment will, at the same time, prevent the destruction of an ovum during each cycle. The ova, instead of maturing to a condition where they must die if they are not fertilized, will rest in the ovary, to become available later when, on omission of medication, nature calls them forth. Completely without attention to moral implications, is it semantically correct to stigmatize this condition as "temporary sterilization" or should it rather be called conservation of reproductive function against the time when the couple can properly have more children? Is not the essence of sterilization elimination of future reproductive function; and, of administration of oral steroids, simply its deferment? Can the two processes meaningfully be considered identical? . . .

In ethics, one perhaps would make the distinction that after ovulation or during pregnancy the final purpose for the secretion of progesterone is not suppression of ovulatory function per se. No, the direct object in both such instances is a good one. In each, progesterone is supplied by the wife's organs in order to exclude another ovum, which, fertilized, would jeopardize the safety of one previously fertilized, by the dangerous competition for maternal nourishment which this follower might exercise.

Surely, when her tissues effect progesterone-induced security in this manner, it is excusable because in these circumstances the organs are merely fulfilling their natural protective functions. One wonders if this kind of protection could be equally excusable when directly occasioned towards the same good end by the natural protective functioning of her brain instead of her ovary. This would be the situation if, with her husband's approval, she wills through medication to influence her hormonal situation in the same manner and for the same essential purpose; that is, to prevent a competing pregnancy, so that, as responsible parents, she and her husband will be able to nourish, physically and mentally, the children they already have. Certainly, these are as deserving as are the potential fetus in a liberated ovum and the actual fetus in the uterus.

Meditation on the morality of the use of the steroids for family limitation brings out another point which may be even more fundamental. This is the question of intent, which is well presented in two citations. Father Gibbons puts it this way: "The Church's pressing concern in the matter of fertility regulation is that the ends of marriage, as traditionally defined, be not confused or distorted. She does not wish to see sexual expression regarded as an independent good unrelated to the procreation and rearing of offspring." John R. Connery, S.J., referring to mechanical contraceptives, writes: The church "condemns such devices because they interfere with the natural orientation of the marriage act—the very purpose intended by nature and the Creator. When the new steroids are used for contraceptive purposes, they are intended to produce the same interference as that achieved by the external devices."

These statements, like many others, condemn the use of the "pill" for implementing the subjective intent to avoid conception, that sex may be used, perhaps only for love. Does such an attitude easily conform with the Church's justification of the rhythm method? The Papal documents sanctioning rhythm refer explicitly to the licitness of satisfying (by coitus) the secondary ends of marriage—sexual harmony and the allaying of concupiscence—when procreation should be avoided for serious reasons; that is, when, properly, there should be the subjective intent to avoid conception. Is this not a regard for sexual expression as a completely independent good, totally apart from procreation? Father Connery later in his article calls for the discovery of "some simple and reliable method of detecting and predicting ovulation" to make rhythm more reliable, a project which is, theoretically, entirely possible. Is he not implying that when such means are found, their use will be intended to produce exactly "the same interference" as do the oral pills, separating sexual expression, as an independent good, from procreation?

I am persuaded that the Church has not concluded its examination of the morality of the progestational steroids when used for fertility control. . . .

44. KAY TOY FENNER, "AMERICAN CATHOLIC DATING GUIDELINES" (1963)

For Catholics as for other Americans, the 1950s and early 1960s were years when "morality" bore more than a passing resemblence to conventional middle-class behavior. Etiquette manuals such as this one covered a wide variety of topics, from how to entertain at a baptism or dress when receiving the eucharist ("Willfully to choose to wear sloppy or overly-informal clothing is always wrong; so is immodest dress of any nature") to the correct way to address clergymen. The most fruitful topic, however, was romance: dating and marriage guidelines occupied a full third of this 1963 manual.

For Boys

a) Call for a girl at her house. Ask her to meet you elsewhere only in special circumstances. If you live in one suburb and she in another, you might ask a girl with whom you have a theater date to meet you at a respectable place in town, to avoid being late for the performance. But you take her to her door when going home, regardless of how far it is. You may not ask a girl to meet you anywhere, even under these circumstances, unless you have previously called at her home, and met one of her parents. . . .

c) Do not use her car, even though she has one and you do not. To use hers makes you seem less the man and the escort—it puts you in a false position. . . .

d) Plan your dates in advance whenever possible—and plan to *do* something. It is more fun and less moral risk to go dancing, see a show, or play cards than it is to drive aimlessly about the countryside or lounge in a tavern. . . .

m) Always remember: an escort is, in one sense, a guardian. For the space of an evening, a girl's immortal soul is in your care. Cherish it!

For Girls

a) Never date a boy you do not know. You may be said to "know" a boy who is in your classes at school or lives neighbor to you, with whom you have a speaking acquaintance, even though no one has actually introduced you. You could safely date such a boy if he asks you. Otherwise, never date a boy who has not been introduced to you by someone who knows him and knows you. This is not merely a social rule. It is physically and morally dangerous to date a stranger, no matter how attractive he seems or how romantic the circumstances under which you first saw him. . . .

c) Going on a date with a boy puts you under no obligation to him. He has the power to choose whom he will ask for a date and to determine what the evening's entertainment will be. . . . When you accept, you are doing him a favor. His return for the money he expends on a date is the pleasure of your company for the evening—nothing more. Kisses are not doled out to "pay" for a pleasant evening; they are a proof of liking or affection. Any boy who thinks otherwise is a boor.

d) . . . Well-bred boys understand that a girl must have parental permission to go out with a "new" boy, or to some place where she has never gone before. It is proof that she is cherished and *looked after* by her family, and quickly puts the relationship on the right plane, as being something open and above-board. . . .

f) It is the girl who sets the "tone" for the relationship between herself and her escort. It is really true that people usually treat one as one expects to be treated. If a girl is friendly, amiable, and well-bred, she will be treated like the lady she is. If she is boisterous, overly-familiar and vulgar in speech, her escort will still treat her as she seems to expect to be treated. It is up to you.

Of course there are exceptions. Every girl will sometimes have the experience of finding herself on a first date with a boy who is simply not her sort. Disregarding all her signs of displeasure, he is familiar, crude, tells off-color stories. What to do? If possible: be sick, have a sudden headache, and insist on going home immediately. . . .

h) Help make dates successful. Try to enjoy—and show you enjoy the entertainment offered you, no matter how elaborate or simple. Don't constantly apologize if you are a poor swimmer or golfer—ask your partner for tips and admire his skill. Don't criticize food or service anyplace or infer that you are used to much finer places. Don't hang back or fail to take part in any games or amusements as best you can, unless they are improper. Don't monopolize the conversation. Draw your escort out if you can. Don't strive to appear sophisticated if you are not. Don't talk about imaginary trips and engagements. Don't tell a Manhattan man what a divine time you had at Holy Cross last winter! . . .

k) Avoid the appearance of being the aggressor in any dealings boys. The pursued always has the advantage over the pursuer. You ask a boy who has never taken you out to a party or dance—once he does not return the compliment, don't ask him again, no matter how much fun the first date was. . . .

m) Promise yourself that no boy will ever be injured by association with you. Never intentionally dress or behave so as to inflame his passions. Never permit intimacies such as to impose too great a strain on his self-control. The better you like a boy, the greater your responsibility in this matter.

45. Sister Jean Reidy, C.H.M., "Nuns in Ordinary Clothes" (1967)

The Vatican II "Decree on the Adaptation and Renewal of Religious Life" called on vowed male and female religious to re-examine their rules in a spirit of renewal, stripping away accreted practices that had grown obsolete or counterproductive in the present day. One paragraph that garnered particular attention read: The religious habit, an outward mark of consecration to God, should be simple and modest, poor and at the same becoming. In addition it must . . . be suited to the circumstances of time and place and to the needs of the ministry involved. The habits of both men and women religious which do not conform to these norms must be changed. *Accordingly, many orders of nuns in the United States, who had worn a highly distinctive dress and headpiece that usually left only the face showing and disguised the shape of both head and body, began a period of experimentation. Some orders discarded the habit altogether, simply wearing ordinary modest clothing; others moved to a modified "habit" of identical blouse and skirt, sometimes with a small veil. Here a sister assesses public reaction to her new clothing.*

[Comments]

A theologian-author, internationally known, exclaimed his approval saying, "You belong to the twenty-second century! Wonderful! Build buildings quickly because young women will storm your novitiate. I approve (a certain sister's) vow renewal when I see this."

A famous priest-writer wrote his decided approbation to our superior general. He pointed out that the contemporary clothing fulfilled the Council's religious habit requirement in the "Decree for Religious." He saw the habit change as a sign of deep renewal in the community.

An instructor from India praised me for "getting down from the pedestal." He compared our sisters to Gandhi who dressed like his beloved people.

Three seventh-grade girls, in the presence of their much admired, traditionally dressed sister teacher, said to me without prompting, "You seem more human in those clothes." "I think I would feel more at home with you."

Two Catholic teen-agers in public schools told me they had "hated" my other "outfit" and that they felt "a lot better" with me now. One fifteen-year-old now wants to correspond.

A young wife, acquainted with me before the habit change, said when she saw me, without warning, in ordinary clothes for the first time, "Why, you're a *person!*" Later she analyzed her emotional reaction this way: "You always knew who you were but you did not let us know. In a way you deceived us without realizing it. After all, we saw only your face and hands." She has since invited me to work with teen-agers at evening meetings in her home.

Several mothers with teen-age and smaller children have invited me to their homes and to discussion groups. Almost all approve the ordinary clothes. A few older women, and some not old, have disapproved. These usually disapprove of the liturgy changes. At the close of an evening discussion club session centering on a serious theology book, several women said that they had felt at home with me and that I had not, by a habit and its associations, dominated the scene. I am becoming friends with some of these women in a way unfeasible before—and with obvious mutual benefit.

One older woman, conversing with me at a conference, said, "Now you can reach the contemporary adult woman. You can tell us what we cannot tell you, and we can tell you what you cannot tell us."

University undergraduate and graduate students have given me almost unqualified approval. A few suggest more identification. All seem to like my silver, third-finger-left-hand ring which indicates that I am "not available." There is no doubt that we communicate better and more naturally. A symbol with, for some, bad associations has disappeared. Yet respect remains—not the Victorian lady type, but a new respect, more natural, personal, and adult.

Visiting professors from other universities have given me decided approbation. Among professors at my own university, some disapprove while others give high praise and add considered reasons. One said of the experimenters, "We can tell you are nuns by your behavior." Another said, "People say they know you are nuns by the way you talk and act."

Among priests, the great majority of whom approve, the following have given special commendation: several senior theologians, the director of an academic institute of international reputation, several seminary teachers of philosophy and theology, a vicar general, chancery officials, the national director of a famous apostolic association, the dean of a college theology department, and a college president. A few priests thought I should be more recognizable. Two disapproved of the entire idea. When I objected to one priest that the traditional habit makes people think of God, he answered,

"Sister, when people look at the habit they think of the habit."

[Sisters' Views]

Many sisters expressing disapproval have feared loss of respect, date problems, loss of vocation, trouble with hair, vanity, expense, unsightliness of figure, too much attention to dress. One said, "I know it's right to change, but I'm afraid."

Some sisters tell me that after seeing the contemporary clothes on a sister they have changed their minds and have become more open to the idea. Some have become strong advocates of the change.

One sister feared that the more natural and spontaneous communication I was receiving from lay people resulted from my placing myself "on their level." Several think I should wear a veil, but more say to me that I should not.

Most approving among the sisters are those women in their thirties and forties—yet there are some in every age group who feel that the traditional habit no longer expresses the kind of friendliness and mission religious sisters are called to. Some feel that the habit symbolizes an older culture pattern and that it hinders communication especially with lay adults.

One aging missionary sister-superior, stationed in a Southern ghetto, went out of her way at a conference to encourage me and to say how much help she thought contemporary dress would bring to her apostolate.

A concluding personal note: In ordinary clothes I feel more myself, more adult, more natural, less tense, more responsibly religious. I am very happy with the Christian communication to which a plain suit admits me. I did not dream that new presence through a rather easy switch in symbols could so unlock the beautiful and dedicated lives of other people. Clothes indeed are a language of interpersonal communication.

46. "Statement by Catholic Theologians" and "Dissent In and For the Church" (1968 & 1969)

The 1968 encyclical Humanae Vitae *disagreed with the arguments of John Rock (see No. 43) and Catholic couples like the Crowleys (see No. 24), condemning the pill along with all other artificial methods of birth control. Only abstinence during the woman's fertile periods (the "rhythm method") remained acceptable to the Church as a way of limiting family size. In mak-*

ing the final decision—which contradicted the opinion of sixty-five of the seventy-two members of the papal commission set up to study the issue— Pope Paul VI stated that he felt unable personally to overturn nearly two thousand years of Christian teaching that birth control was contrary to God's law. Global reaction to the encyclical was swift and, in many cases, extremely negative. Some bishops hinted or stated outright that Catholics should follow their own consciences on the birth control issue, and many theologians argued that the papal decision had been incorrect, including the eighty-seven American Catholic theologians who publicly released a statement of dissent two days after the encyclical appeared. Called to explain their actions to a board of inquiry at Catholic University (where many of them taught), the theologians mounted a defense of their public action; the second excerpt is from their book, primarily written by Charles E. Curran and Robert E. Hunt of CUA.

[Statement by Catholic Theologians]

1. As Roman Catholic theologians we respectfully acknowledge a distinct role of hierarchical magisterium (teaching authority) in the Church of Christ. At the same time, Christian tradition assigns theologians the special responsibility of evaluating and interpreting pronouncements of the magisterium in the light of the total theological data operative in each question or statement. We offer these initial comments on Pope Paul VI's Encyclical on the Regulation of Birth.

2. The Encyclical is not an infallible teaching. History shows that a number of statements of similar or even greater authoritative weight have subsequently been proved inadequate or even erroneous. Past authoritative statements on religious liberty, interest-taking, the right to silence, and the ends of marriage have all been corrected at a later date.

3. Many positive values concerning marriage are expressed in Paul VI's Encyclical. However, we take exception to the ecclesiology implied and the methodology used by Paul VI in the writing and promulgation of the document: they are incompatible with the Church's authentic self-awareness as expressed in and suggested by the acts of the Second Vatican Council itself. The Encyclical consistently assumes that the Church is identical with the hierarchical office. No real importance is afforded the witness of the life of the Church in its totality; the special witness of many Catholic couples is neglected; it fails to acknowledge the witness of the separated Christian churches and ecclesial communities; it is insensitive to the witness of

many men of good will; it pays insufficient attention to the ethical import of modern science.

4. Furthermore, the Encyclical betrays a narrow and positivistic notion of papal authority, as illustrated by the rejection of the majority view presented by the Commission established to consider the question, as well as by the rejection of the conclusion of a large part of the international Catholic theological community.

5. Likewise, we take exception to some of the specific ethical conclusions contained in the Encyclical. They are based on an inadequate concept of natural law: the multiple forms of natural law theory are ignored and the fact that competent philosophers come to different conclusions on this very question is disregarded. Even the minority report of the papal commission noted grave difficulty in attempting to present conclusive proof of the immorality of artificial contraception based on natural law.

6. Other defects include: overemphasis on the biological aspects of conjugal relations as ethically normative; undue stress on sexual acts and on the faculty of sex viewed in itself, apart from the person and the couple; a static worldview which downplays the historical and evolutionary character of humanity in its finite existence, as described in Vatican II's Pastoral Constitution on the Church in the Modern World; unfounded assumptions about "the evil consequences of methods of artificial birth control"; indifference to Vatican II's assertion that prolonged sexual abstinence may cause "faithfulness to be imperiled and its quality of fruitfulness to be ruined"; an almost total disregard for the dignity of millions of human beings brought into the world without the slightest possibility of being fed and educated decently.

7. In actual fact, the Encyclical demonstrates no development over the teaching of Pius XI's Casti Connubii whose conclusions have been called into question for grave and serious reasons. These reasons, given a muffled voice at Vatican II, have not been adequately handled by the mere repetition of past teaching.

8. It is common teaching in the Church that Catholics may dissent from authoritative, non-infallible teachings of the magisterium when sufficient reasons for so doing exist.

9. Therefore, as Roman Catholic theologians, conscious of our duty and our limitations, we conclude that spouses may responsibly decide according to their conscience that artificial contraception in some circumstances is permissible and indeed necessary to preserve and foster the values and sacredness of marriage.

10. It is our conviction also that true commitment to the mystery of Christ and the Church requires a candid statement of mind at this time by all Catholic theologians.

[Public Dissent In and For the Church]

. . . The fact that many of the manualists do not allow for public dissent cannot be taken, therefore, as an absolute norm always obliging in all conceivable circumstances. The controlling value in all cases appears to be the good of the Church. Service of the Church is the enduring value which pervaded the manualist tradition on this point, and should constitute the dominant concern of every approach to the contemporary question of public manifestation of dissent in the Church; dissent in the Church must always be dissent for the Church.

It is well to recall here also that the question of dissent in the manualist tradition is properly cast in the category of the interpretive function of the theologian. Theological dissent is itself a part of the theological tradition which must constantly be reinterpreted! . . .

[In addition to his or her obligation to the truth, to the hierarchy, to individuals touched by particular questions, to priests, to the university community, to the public, to non-Catholics in general, and so forth,] the theologian has an obligation to all men of good will. In Catholic theology itself a universalism, which was strong in the teachings and writings of Pope Pius XII, became even more explicit in the encyclicals of John XXIII, which were also addressed for the first time to "all men of good will." *Humanae Vitae* is likewise addressed by Paul VI to all men of good will. Thus all men of good will were also in need of the interpretation of the Encyclical. Likewise, Catholic theologians have the obligation to show the credibility of the Church to all mankind. This becomes more necessary in our own day when even some Catholics have attacked the credibility of the Church. This obligation to make the Church and the teachings of the Church more credible is the work of interpretation. However, dissent itself can also serve the credibility of the Church, especially among those who incorrectly understand the Church as an authoritarian institution denying true freedom and, in particular, freedom of discussion in theological matters. They frequently fail to realize that the Church has traditionally allowed for such freedom of discussion by theologians in areas of non-infallible teaching.

The responsible theologian must be cognizant of all these diverse obligations which are incumbent upon him. To neglect any of these responsibilities would be irresponsible. The manifold responsibilities of the theologian to truth, to the whole Church, to the bishops, to fellow theologians, to the individuals directly involved, to priests generally, to his academic community, to the communications media, to non-Catholics and to all men of good will provide the constant factors with respect to which the theologian must evaluate his declarations and actions. The interpretive possibility of public dissent must be weighed with respect to all the foregoing factors in the light of prudence. Thus, the existing norm of public dissent consists not in a simple, verbal formula in the former manualist style but rather in the prudent balancing of the accepted values represented by each of the foregoing constant constituencies of the theologian.

In the contemporary ecclesiological context, therefore, theologians are conscious of their co-responsibility for the entire Church and their many different relationships with the other people of God. Contemporary ecclesiology is conscious of the different roles and functions in the Church which work together to build up the whole body of Christ. The hierarchical office and function, though necessary for the Church and of great importance, is not the only functioning role in the Church.

In the contemporary understanding of the modern age of communications, theologians realize that there are abundant and effective means available for the communication of theological interpretations. On other questions the subject professors themselves have often been asked to appear on radio and television programs and to grant interviews to the press. Requests for such communication of theological interpretations have come from the University itself and from official agencies of the United States Catholic Conference under the auspices of the American bishops.

Ecclesiology and the modern communications media have made both theologians and the magisterium aware of the function of public opinion in the Church. Pope Pius XII asserted the role of public opinion in the Church, even though at times an earlier generation rejected such a notion. Theologians, taking their lead from Pius XII, have developed the notion and place of such public opinion in the Church. . . .

Thus the Roman Catholic theologian has a responsibility and an obligation to interpret the teachings of the Church even to the point of dissenting from "authoritative, noninfallible teachings of the magisterium when sufficient reasons for so doing exist." Such dissent must be expressed in a responsible manner, which for the Roman Catholic means a way in which the good of the Church is ultimately helped and not hindered.

Public Nature and Practical Urgency of the Issue

The fact that *Humanae Vitae* concerns a matter that is not speculative and not practically indifferent such as, for example, subsistent relations in the Trinity, or the quality of Adam's original justice, but rather a matter of immediate and urgent practical consequence for millions of persons, both Catholic and non-Catholic, placed the subject matter, of its very nature, into the forum of public concern. It thus involves the "right to know," and the correlative "duty to inform," pertaining to a category of persons coextensive with the audience of the mass communication media. The class of persons vitally interested in *Humanae Vitae* is so vast that the ordinary channel of communication with such persons would be the mass communications media. Perhaps in recognition of the urgency of this question, theological interpretations approving the Encyclical's ethical conclusion have been made public to and through the mass communications media, beginning with Professor Lambruschini's press conference on July 29.

The possibility of mistake in papal teaching on this urgent matter, however, raises the question, in turn, of whether theological interpretation critical of the Encyclical should be communicated to the same public by the same means. Catholics believe eventually that the truth or error of the papal teaching will emerge. The process of confirmation or of correction could take a critically long time, however, if the necessary dialogue is conducted in private. Although the Church might not suffer if the process of confirmation of *Humanae Vitae* were to be prolonged, it would be most difficult to maintain that values protected by private discussion outweigh the harm that could be done to the Church if the process of correction were unduly prolonged, especially in this issue of immediate, urgent and practical consequence for the daily lives of millions of persons. If there is a real possibility of error, furthermore, the Church has nothing to fear from public discussion! If the teaching is correct, Catholics believe that the Spirit will confirm their teaching. If the teaching is incorrect, it can best be corrected if the freedom to consider the matter further is enjoyed by hierarchical magisterium and theologians alike.

Since collaboration and communication is a necessary part of the theological endeavor, the exercise of such freedom can hardly remain "private." No theological journal is so abstruse and no language so arcane as to prevent immediate (not merely eventual) publication of critical theological views of the Encyclical by the modern press, which was even able to obtain the papal statement days ahead of the official release. It is not certain that one can even speak of "private" theological discussion on such critical issues. In fact, the mass media began disseminating information throughout the world concerning *Humanae Vitae* and its content on July 27, two days before its official release to the public press at the Vatican, from an official English translation. The news media were not hesitant to give their own untrained "interpretations" of the normative significance of the Encyclical for Roman Catholics. These facts at least make clear that theological discussion, in these days of the pervasive presence of the press, cannot be confined quietly to the "speculative" pages of scholarly journals. The communications enterprises of today subscribe to such journals, and when an issue for speculative inquiry has dynamic effect on the lives of millions, the mass journals will be quick to expose and analyze significant scholarly opinion. Theologians must recognize this possibility if they are to prevent the scandal which may result from a misinterpretation of their own or others' scholarly views by well-meaning but not necessarily well-trained media reporters. Any notion that scholarly theological opinion written in journals can generally be quietly confined to private distribution is today a myth. In the face of the reality of likely exposure of his scholarly views on topical issues, the theologian acts with prudence when he chooses to issue a candid statement of legitimate views on his own motion, lest his position be misconstrued by press interpretation.

Respect for Hierarchical Teaching Authority

Responsible theological interpretation is not disrespectful to the hierarchical teaching authority. Nor will the laity lose respect for the teaching authority of the Church if such "dissenting" interpretation becomes generally known, if the faithful have generally and accurately been taught the respective and mutual roles of teacher and believer in the Church, that generally all pronouncements on religious matters are not of equal authoritative weight and that the responses they owe differ accordingly. Danger of scandal and disrespect in the wake of public dissent would be considerably mitigated by accurate and adequate instruction on the nature and function of the papal teaching office. It was the strong recommendation of the Vatican Synod of Bishops in 1967 that "clearly and in ways adapted to the contemporary mentality" the faithful be taught their responsibilities before the magisterium. A clear and intelligent explanation of the various responses a Catholic owes to the various exercises of the Church's teaching office, including a discussion of the circumstances under which it is quite legitimate and even necessary for a Catholic to suspend his assent, is an exercise of theological responsibility recognizing an existing "need to know" in the Church.

Public Dissent as a Balance of Values

Development in the science of theology, the methodology practiced by contemporary theologians and the ecclesiological insights of Vatican II and postconciliar theology contribute to a full theological understanding of the "right of dissent" which was articulated to a limited context by the manualist authors. In the era of mass communications, in the context of a co-responsible Church and in respect of moral issues with immediate practical consequences for millions of persons, the propriety of publication of "dissenting" theological opinion cannot be judged by inference to a fixed general formula in the manualist style. That is not to say that one's right to publish dissent is as broad as his opinion requires. The interpretative task of the theologian requires him not only to eschew simplistic formulas but also to identify the factors that must be weighed and balanced to determine whether publication of dissent is proper in a particular case. Thus, the theologian exercises the right to dissent in the living context, taking into consideration the substance and impact of the views in question as a key factor, but not the only factor, determining the manner in which such dissent should be expressed. . . .

47. Phyllis Schlafly, "What's Wrong with 'Equal Rights' for Women?" (1972)

Phyllis Schlafly, the controversial founder of the Eagle Forum, became a household name in the United States during her ultimately successful crusade against the Equal Rights Amendment (ERA), which if added to the Constitution would have guaranteed strict equality between men and women. The ERA's proponents argued that it was necessary to overturn women's historic oppression in law and in the workplace, but Schlafly responded that, on the contrary, it would eviscerate traditional femininity by requiring women to fight on the front lines and take jobs instead of being able to stay home with their children. A devout Catholic, a trained lawyer, and an experienced campaigner, Schlafly almost single-handedly turned the tide against the ERA in state legislatures across the country by asking women who agreed with her to pressure their local representatives. Her partisans—many of them middle-aged suburban housewives who had never set foot in a political meeting before—became radicalized, and would go on to help sweep Ronald Reagan and the Republican Party into national office during the 1980s and 1990s.

Of all the classes of people who ever lived, the American woman is the most privileged. We have the most rights and rewards, and the fewest duties. Our unique status is the result of a fortunate combination of circumstances.

1. We have the immense good fortune to live in a civilization which respects the family as the basic unit of society. This respect is part and parcel of our laws and our customs. It is based on the fact of life—which no legislation or agitation can erase—that women have babies and men don't.

If you don't like this fundamental difference, you will have to take up your complaint with God because He created us this way. The fact that women, not men, have babies is not the fault of selfish and domineering men, or of the establishment, or of any clique of conspirators who want to oppress women. It's simply the way God made us.

Our Judeo-Christian civilization has developed the law and custom that, since women must bear the physical consequences of the sex act, men must be required to bear the other consequences and pay in other ways. These laws and customs decree that a man must carry his share by physical protection and financial support of his children and of the woman who bears his children, and also by a code of behavior which benefits and protects both the woman and the children.

The Greatest Achievement of Women's Rights

This is accomplished by the institution of the family. Our respect for the family as the basic unit of society, which is ingrained in the laws and customs of our Judeo-Christian civilization, is the greatest single achievement in the entire history of women's rights. It assures a woman the most precious and important right of all—the right to keep her own baby and to be supported and protected in the enjoyment of watching her baby grow and develop.

The institution of the family is advantageous for women for many reasons. . . . After all, what do we want out of life? To love and be loved? Mankind has not discovered a better nest for a lifetime of reciprocal love. A sense of achievement? A man may search 30 to 40 years for accomplishment in his profession. A woman can enjoy real achievement when she is young—by having a baby. She can have the satisfaction of doing a job well —and being recognized for it.

Do we want financial security? We are fortunate to have the great legacy of Moses, the Ten Commandments, especially this one: "Honor thy father and thy mother that thy days may be long upon the land." Children are a woman's best social security—her best guarantee of social benefits such as old age pension, unemployment compensation, workman's compensation, and sick leave. The family gives a woman the physical, financial and emotional security of the home—for all her life.

The Financial Benefits of Chivalry

2. The second reason why American women are a privileged group is that we are the beneficiaries of a tradition of special respect for women which dates from the Christian Age of Chivalry. The honor and respect paid to Mary the Mother of Christ, resulted in all women, in effect, being put on a pedestal.

This respect for women is not just the lip service that politicians pay to "God, Motherhood, and the Flag." It is not—as some youthful agitators seem to think—just a matter of opening doors for women, seeing that they are seated first, carrying their bundles, and helping them in and out of automobiles. Such good manners are merely the superficial evidences of a total attitude toward women which expresses itself in many more tangible ways, such as money.

Women's Libbers Do NOT Speak for Us

The "women's lib" movement is not an honest effort to secure better jobs for women who want or need to work outside the home. This is just the superficial sweet-talk to win broad support for a radical "movement." "Women's lib" is a total assault on the role of the American woman as wife and mother, and on the family as the basic unit of society.

Women's Libbers are trying to make wives and mothers unhappy with their career, make them feel that they are "second class citizens" and "abject slaves." Women's libbers are promoting free sex instead of the "slavery" of marriage. They are promoting "Federal" day care-centers for babies instead of homes. They are promoting abortions instead of families. . . .

And why should the men acquiesce in a system which gives preferential rights and lighter duties to women? In return, the men get the pearl of great price: a happy home, a faithful wife, and children they adore.

If the women's libbers want to reject marriage and motherhood, it's a free country and that is their choice. But let's not permit these women's libbers to get away with pretending to speak for the rest of us. Let's not permit this tiny minority to degrade the role that most women prefer. Let's not let these women's libbers deprive wives and mothers of the rights we now possess.

Tell your Senators NOW that you want them to vote no on the Equal Rights Amendment. Tell your television and radio stations that you want equal time to present the case for marriage and motherhood.

48. JOSEPH CARDINAL BERNARDIN, "A CONSISTENT ETHIC OF LIFE" (1983)

Cardinal Bernardin of Chicago (1928–1996) was the unofficial leader of the U.S. bishops for many years. His most important contribution to American Catholic thinking may have been his proposal, in a speech at Fordham University, of a "seamless ethic of life," which would combine opposition to abortion and nuclear war with social-justice-oriented domestic and foreign policy. The overriding principle in all cases would be respect for the inherent dignity and worth of each human life, regardless of age, nationality, or economic status. In the following excerpt from Bernardin's speech, he proposes that the U.S. Bishops' recent pastoral letter, "The Challenge of Peace" (see No. 25), should be seen as defending such an ethical stance.

. . . Today I will discuss the pastoral letter in terms of the relationship of our Catholic moral vision and American culture. Specifically, I wish to use the letter as a starting point for shaping a consistent ethic of life in our culture. In keeping with the spirit of a university, I have cast the lecture in the style of an inquiry, an examination of the need for a consistent ethic of life and a probing of the problems and possibilities which exist within the Church and the wider society for developing such an ethic.

I do not underestimate the intrinsic intellectual difficulties of this exercise nor the delicacy of the question—ecclesially, ecumenically and politically. But I believe the Catholic moral tradition has something valuable to say in the face of the multiple threats to the sacredness of life today, and I am convinced that the Church is in a position to make a significant defense of life in a comprehensive and consistent manner.

Such a defense of life will draw upon the Catholic moral position and the public place the Church presently holds in the American civil debate. The pastoral letter links the questions of abortion and nuclear war. The letter does not argue the case for linkage; that is one of my purposes today. It is important to note that the way these two issues are joined in the pastoral places the American bishops in a unique position in the public policy discourse of the nation. No other major institution presently holds these two positions in the way the Catholic bishops have joined them. This is both a responsibility and an opportunity. . . .

I. The Church in Public Debate: The Pastoral in Perspective

. . . Early in the letter the bishops say that they are writing in order to share the moral wisdom of the Catholic tradition with society. In stating this objective the American bishops were following the model of the Second Vatican Council which called dialogue with the world a sign of love for the world.

I believe the long-term ecclesiological significance of the pastoral rests with the lessons it offers about the Church's capacity to dialogue with the world in a way which helps to shape the public policy debate on key issues. During the drafting of the pastoral letter one commentator wrote in the editorial section of the *Washington Post*:

"The Catholic bishops . . . are forcing a public debate on perhaps the most perplexing nuclear question of them all, the morality of nuclear deterrence. . . . Their logic and passion have taken them to the very foundation of American security policy."

This commentary accurately captures the purpose of the pastoral letter.

The bishops intended to raise fundamental questions about the dynamic of the arms race and the direction of American nuclear strategy. We intended to criticize the rhetoric of the nuclear age and to expose the moral and political futility of a nuclear war. We wanted to provide a moral assessment of existing policy which would both set limits to political action and provide direction for a policy designed to lead us out of the dilemma of deterrence. . . .

II. A Consistent Ethic of Life: A Catholic Perspective

"The Challenge of Peace" provides a starting point for developing a consistent ethic of life but it does not provide a fully articulated framework. The central idea in the letter is the sacredness of human life and the responsibility we have, personally and socially, to protect and preserve the sanctity of life.

Precisely because life is sacred, the taking of even one human life is a momentous event. Indeed, the sense that every human life has transcendent value has led a whole stream of the Christian tradition to argue that life may never be taken. That position is held by an increasing number of Catholics and is reflected in the pastoral letter, but it has not been the dominant view in Catholic teaching and it is not the principal moral position found in the pastoral letter. What is found in the letter is the traditional Catholic teaching that there should always be a presumption against taking human life, but in a limited world marked by the effects of sin there are some narrowly defined exceptions where life can be taken. This is the moral logic which produced the "Just War" ethic in Catholic theology.

While this style of moral reasoning retains its validity as a method of resolving extreme cases of conflict when fundamental rights are at stake, there has been a perceptible shift of emphasis in the teaching and pastoral practice of the Church in the last 30 years. To summarize the shift succinctly, the presumption against taking human life has been strengthened and the exceptions made ever more restrictive. Two examples, one at the level of principle, the other at the level of pastoral practice, illustrate the shift.

First, in a path-breaking article in 1959 in *Theological Studies*, John Courtney Murray, S.J., demonstrated that Pope Pius XII had reduced the traditional threefold justification for going to war (defense, recovery of property and punishment) to the single reason of defending the innocent and protecting those values required for decent human existence. Second, in the case of capital punishment, there has been a shift at the level of pastoral practice. While not denying the classical position, found in the writing of Thomas Aquinas and other authors, that the state has the right to employ capital punishment, the action of Catholic bishops and Popes Paul VI and John Paul II has been directed against the exercise of that right by the state. The argument has been that more humane methods of defending the society exist and should be used. Such humanitarian concern lies behind the policy position of the National Conference of Catholic Bishops against capital punishment, the opposition expressed by individual bishops in their home states against reinstating the death penalty, and the extraordinary interventions of Pope John Paul II and the Florida bishops seeking to prevent the execution in Florida last week.

Rather than extend the specific analysis of this shift of emphasis at the levels of both principle and practice in Catholic thought, I wish to probe the rationale behind the shift and indicate what it teaches us about the need for a consistent ethic of life. Fundamental to the shift is a more acute perception of the multiple ways in which life is threatened today. Obviously questions like war, aggression and capital punishment have been with us for centuries and are not new to us. What is new is the context in which these ancient questions arise, and the way in which a new context shapes the content of our ethic of life. Let me comment on the relationship of the context of our culture and the content of our ethic in terms of: 1) the need for a consistent ethic of life; 2) the attitude necessary to sustain it; and 3) the principles needed to shape it.

The dominant cultural fact, present in both modern warfare and modern medicine, which induces a sharper awareness of the fragility of human life is our technology. To live as we do in an age of careening development of technology is to face a qualitatively new range of moral problems. War has been a perennial threat to human life, but today the threat is qualitatively different due to nuclear weapons. We now threaten life on a scale previously unimaginable. As the pastoral letter put it, the dangers of nuclear war teach us to read the Book of Genesis with new eyes. From the inception of life to its decline, a rapidly expanding technology opens new opportunities for care but also poses new potential to threaten the sanctity of life. . . . The essential question in the technological challenge is this: In an age when we can do almost anything, how do we decide what we ought to do? The even more demanding question is: In a time when we can do anything technologically, how do we decide morally what we never should do?

Asking these questions along the spectrum of life from womb to tomb creates the need for a consistent ethic of life. For the spectrum of life cuts across the issues of genetics, abortion, capital punishment, modern warfare and the care of the terminally ill. These are all distinct problems, enormously complicated, and deserving individual treatment. No single answer and no simple response will solve them. My purpose, however, is to highlight the way in which we face new technological challenges in each one of these areas; this combination of challenges is what cries out for a consistent ethic of life.

Such an ethic will have to be finely honed and carefully structured on the basis of values, principles, rules and applications to specific cases. It is not my task today, nor within my competence as a bishop, to spell out all the details of such an ethic. It is to that task that philosophers and poets, theologians and technicians, scientists and strategists, political leaders and plain citizens are called. I would, however, highlight a basic issue: the need for an attitude or atmosphere in society which is the pre-condition for sustaining a consistent ethic of life. The development of such an atmosphere has been the primary concern of the "Respect Life" program of the American bishops. We intend our opposition to abortion and our opposition to nuclear war to be seen as specific applications of this broader attitude. We have also opposed the death penalty because we do not think its use cultivates an attitude of respect for life in society. The purpose of proposing a consistent ethic of life is to argue that success on any one of the issues threatening life requires a concern for the broader attitude in society about respect for human life.

Attitude is the place to root an ethic of life, but ultimately ethics is about principles to guide the actions of individuals and institutions. It is therefore necessary to illustrate, at least by way of example, my proposition that an inner relationship does exist among several issues not only at the level of general attitude but at the more specific level of moral principles. Two examples will serve to indicate the point.

The first is contained in The Challenge of Peace in the connection drawn between Catholic teaching on war and Catholic teaching on abortion. Both, of course, must be seen in light of an attitude of respect for life. The more explicit connection is based on the principle which prohibits the directly intended taking of innocent human life. The principle is at the heart of Catholic teaching on abortion; it is because the fetus is judged to be both human and not an aggressor that Catholic teaching concludes that direct attack on fetal life is always wrong. This is also why we insist that legal protection be given to the unborn.

The same principle yields the most stringent, binding and radical conclusion of the pastoral letter: that directly intended attacks on civilian centers are always wrong. The bishops seek to highlight the power of this conclusion by specifying its implications in two ways: first, such attacks would be wrong even if our cities had been hit first; second, anyone asked to execute such attacks should refuse orders. These two extensions of the principle cut directly into the policy debate on nuclear strategy and the personal decisions of citizens. James Reston referred to them as "an astonishing challenge to the power of the state."

The use of this principle exemplifies the meaning of a consistent ethic of life. The principle which structures both cases, war and abortion, needs to be upheld in both places. It cannot be successfully sustained on one count and simultaneously eroded in a similar situation. When one carries this principle into the public debate today, however, one meets significant opposition from very different places on the political and ideological spectrum. Some see clearly the application of the principle to abortion but contend the bishops overstepped their bounds when they applied it to choices about national security. Others understand the power of the principle in the strategic debate, but find its application on abortion a violation of the realm of private choice. I contend the viability of the principle depends upon the consistency of its application.

The issue of consistency is tested in a different way when we examine the relationship between the "right to life" and "quality of life" issues. I must confess that I think the relationship of these categories is inadequately understood in the Catholic community itself. My point is that the Catholic position on abortion demands of us and of society that we seek to influence an heroic social ethic.

If one contends, as we do, that the right of every fetus to be born should be protected by civil law and supported by civil consensus, then our moral, political and economic responsibilities do not stop at the moment of birth. Those who defend the right to life of the weakest among us must be equally visible in support of the quality of life of the powerless among us: the old and the young, the hungry and the homeless, the undocumented immigrant and the unemployed worker. Such a quality of life posture translates into specific political and economic positions on tax policy, employment generation, welfare policy, nutrition and feeding programs, and health care. Consistency means we cannot have it both ways. We cannot urge a compassionate society and vigorous public policy to protect the rights of the unborn and then argue that compassion and significant public programs on behalf of the needy undermine the moral fiber of the society or are beyond the proper scope of governmental responsibility.

Right to life and quality of life complement each other in domestic social policy. They are also complementary in foreign policy. "The Challenge of Peace" joined the question of how we prevent nuclear war to the question of how we build peace in an interdependent world. Today those who are admirably concerned with reversing the nuclear arms race must also be those who stand for a positive U.S. policy of building the peace. It is this linkage which has led the U.S. bishops not only to oppose the drive of the nuclear arms race, but to stand against the dynamic of a Central American policy which relies predominantly on the threat and the use of force, which is increasingly distancing itself from a concern for human rights in El Salvador and which fails to grasp the opportunity of a diplomatic solution to the Central American conflict. . . .

III. Catholic Ethics and the American Ethos: The Challenge and the Opportunity

A consistent ethic of life must be held by a constituency to be effective. The building of such a constituency is precisely the task before the Church and the nation. There are two distinct challenges, but they are complementary.

We should begin with the honest recognition that the shaping of a consensus among Catholics on the spectrum of life issues is far from finished. We need the kind of dialogue on these issues which the pastoral letter generated on the nuclear question. We need the same searching intellectual exchange, the same degree of involvement of clergy, religious and laity, the same sustained attention in the Catholic press.

There is no better place to begin than by using the follow-through for the pastoral letter. Reversing the arms race, avoiding nuclear war and moving toward a world freed of the nuclear threat are profoundly "pro-life" issues. The Catholic Church is today seen as an institution and a community committed to these tasks. We should not lose this momentum; it provides a solid foundation to relate our concerns about war and peace to other "pro-life" questions. The agenda facing us involves our ideas and our institutions; it must be both educational and political; it requires attention to the way these several life issues are defined in the public debate and how they are decided in the policy process.

The shaping of a consensus in the Church must be joined to the larger task of sharing our vision with the wider society. Here two questions face us: the substance of our position and the style of our presence in the policy debate.

The substance of a Catholic position on a consistent ethic of life is rooted in a religious vision. But the citizenry of the United States is radically pluralistic in moral and religious conviction. So we face the challenge of stating our case, which is shaped in terms of our faith and our religious convictions, in non-religious terms which others of different faith convictions might find morally persuasive. Here again the war and peace debate should be a useful model. We have found support from individuals and groups who do not share our Catholic faith but who have found our moral analysis compelling.

In the public policy exchange, substance and style are closely related. The issues of war, abortion, and capital punishment are emotional and often divisive questions. As we seek to shape and share the vision of a consistent ethic of life, I suggest a style governed by the following rule: We should maintain and clearly articulate our religious convictions but also maintain our civil courtesy. We should be vigorous in stating a case and attentive in hearing another's case; we should test everyone's logic but not question his or her motives.

The proposal I have outlined today is a multi-dimensional challenge. It grows out of the experience I have had in the war and peace debate and the task I see ahead as Chairman of the Pro-Life Committee. But it also grows from a conviction that there is a new openness today in society to the role of moral argument and moral vision in our public affairs. I say this even though I find major aspects of our domestic and foreign policy in need of drastic change. Bringing about these changes is the challenge of a consistent ethic of life. The challenge is worth our energy, resources and commitment as a Church.

49. RICHARD JOHN NEUHAUS,
"THE CATHOLIC MOMENT" (1987)

When Richard Neuhaus wrote The Catholic Moment *he was still a Lutheran minister, but he already expressed a deep admiration for Pope John Paul II and then-Cardinal Joseph Ratzinger and soon thereafter became a Roman Catholic. Neuhaus argued that the correct stance of the Christian church is one of prophetic suspicion toward the world, and that despite the attempted hijacking of the church by liberal accommodationists after Vatican II, the Roman Catholic Church was still uniquely situated to play this role after the abdication of that responsibility by the mainline Protestant churches. Although most Catholic reviewers reacted ambivalently at best to this thesis, it became a widespread point of discussion among neoconservatives, including many of those who, with Neuhaus, founded the journal* First Things *in 1991.*

1. This Is the Catholic Moment

There are of course many moments in two millennia of Christian history and more than four centuries of Roman Catholicism as a church among the churches in the West. Each moment in time is equally close to God's purpose, and God's purpose equally close to each moment. But we are to read the signs of the times to discern the obligations, limits, and opportunities of our moment. This, I have argued, is the moment in which the Roman Catholic Church in the world can and should be the lead church in proclaiming and exemplifying the Gospel. This can and should also be the moment in which the Roman Catholic Church in the United States assumes its rightful role in the culture-forming task of constructing a religiously informed public philosophy for the American experiment in ordered liberty. The first obligation and opportunity is much the more important. Indeed the achievement of the second is entirely dependent upon giving careful priority to the first. The specifically Christian proposition, and the community of faith that it brings into being, must be held in relentless and dynamic tension with all other propositions, including the American proposition. Pope John Paul is this historical moment's most public witness to the truth that if this tension is relaxed, the Church has nothing distinctive or ultimately helpful to offer the world.

2. The Most Important Opening Effected by Vatican Council II Is the Opening to the Church

This opening to the Church is, above all, an opening to the Gospel by which the Church is created and sustained. This is the Gospel that forms and integrates what Joseph Cardinal Ratzinger calls "the structure of faith." In the Council's further development of the tradition, it is made much clearer than it was before that the Roman Catholic Church is vulnerable to the Gospel and to the entire community that is claimed by the Gospel. In subsequent official teaching the primacy of the Gospel is asserted with a force unprecedented in Roman Catholic history. In truth, the Reformation understanding of the Gospel as God's justifying grace centered in the scriptural kerygma of cross and resurrection is today more boldly proclaimed by Rome than by many of the churches that lay claim to the Reformation heritage.

3. The Catholic Moment Is to Alert the World to the True Nature of Its Crisis

The greatest threat to the world is not political or economic or military. The greatest problem in the Church is not institutional decline or disarray. The crisis of this time and every time is the crisis of unbelief. With a sense of urgency that the world, and much of the Church, find embarrassing, Rome persists in asking, "When the Son of Man comes, will he find faith on earth?" This Pope is exercised not about dissent but about apostasy. He is attempting to chart a Christian course that is not so much against modernity as it is beyond modernity. The only modernity to be discarded is the debased modernity of unbelief that results in a prideful and premature closure of the world against its promised destiny. This Pope is giving voice to the Christian correlate to the opening to the transcendent that in culture, philosophy, and science is the great intellectual and spiritual event of our time. The Christian correlate, of course, is Christ. In this respect, John Paul is far ahead of those Christians, including many Roman Catholics, who are only now learning to accommodate the faith to a debased modernity that history is fast leaving behind. It is said that John XXIII opened the windows of the Church to the modern world. John Paul has entered the modern world to help open the windows of the modern world to the worlds of which it is part.

4. Ecumenism, Inherent and Irreversible, Is Essential to the Realization of the Catholic Moment

The Roman Catholic decision to pursue the more visible unity of the Church is irreversible because it is based upon the understanding that Christian unity is inherent in being the Church. The only Christ and the only Gospel by which a community can be the Church is the Christ and Gospel of the entire Church. The only unity that is lasting and worth pursuing is a unity rooted in a shared confession of Christ and the Gospel. Theological integrity is therefore not an obstacle to unity but the servant of unity. Ecumenism is not so much a program with a timetable as a way of living together in the one Church. Unity is to be achieved not by ecclesiastical conquest but by reconciled diversity in obedience to the Gospel. The Roman Catholic Church has a singular ecumenical calling to take the lead in healing the breach between the churches of the East and those of the West. In the West, the foremost obligation and opportunity is the healing of the breach of the sixteenth century between Rome and the Reformation. In America and especially in the developing world, the forces of greatest Christian vitality are Roman Catholicism and evangelical Protestantism. In many parts of the world, notably in Latin America, these forces are at war with one another. Although the obstacles are daunting, the Catholic Moment requires that the ecumenical mandate of Vatican II be extended to evangelical and fundamentalist Protestantism. An ecumenical commitment indomitable and full-orbed is required if Christianity is believably to represent hope for the unity of humankind.

5. The Catholic Moment Requires a Renewed Demonstration of Unity in Diversity

Pluralism is not a fault. It is evidence of the incompleteness of the world and of the Church within the world. Pluralism in the Church should not be the result of dissent from the Gospel but of diverse forms of radical obedience to the Gospel. The Roman Catholic Church is by far the most diverse of churches. With its discrete orders of ministry, its monastic communities, its myriad works of mercy, its multifarious national and cultural traditions, its political and ideological inclusiveness, and even its different patterns of theological reflection, the Roman Catholic Church is the paradigmatic instance of the unity in diversity that other churches should emulate and to which the world aspires. John Paul now declares that unity in diversity is in jeopardy—not because a few dissent from juridical authority but because many have been led astray from the Gospel. He is engaged in a project of restoration that some view as a renewed oppression and others as an effort to restore coherence to a tradition shattered by the assaults of modernity. In Vatican II the Roman Catholic Church kept its long-delayed appointment with modernity. The future of Christianity in the world will be powerfully influenced by whether Catholicism emerges from this meeting with a unity that is not uniformity and a diversity that is not division.

6. The Catholic Moment Requires a Renewal of Theology in Service to the Community of Faith and Its Mission in the World

There are inevitable tensions between the magisterium, or official teaching authority, and the theological enterprise. The basic relationship between the two, however, is not one of tension but of mutual service under the Gospel. That at least is the argument of Joseph Cardinal Ratzinger. Theology is a continuing conversation in which the magisterium plays the essentially pastoral part of guiding but not controlling the discourse. This ecclesial understanding of the theological enterprise is radically at odds with patterns of academic theology that have emerged since Vatican II. Like liberal Protestant theology before it, Roman Catholic theology increasingly finds itself torn between two communities competing for loyalty: academe and the church. This competition engages a strong element of class conflict, for most theologians belong to what is accurately described as the new knowledge class whose interests are preeminently served by academe. Continuing disputes about intellectual freedom are typically not about intellectual freedom. They are disputes over which community and which tradition is given priority by the theologian. In a "postliberal" understanding of cultural-linguistic traditions, it is seen that academic freedom is also an imposed discipline, that putative universalisms are also particularistic, and that release from orthodoxies is yet another orthodoxy. The Catholic Moment depends in large part upon whether Roman Catholic theologians move toward a postliberal position of service to the Gospel and the community that bears the Gospel, or, as in most of Protestantism, become stalled in sterile contests between liberalism and traditionalism.

7. If the Catholic Moment Is Realized, It Will Enhance the Prospect for Freedom and Justice in the World

Among world figures today, John Paul is the foremost champion of freedom as the first component of justice. He proclaims the truth that "the free adherence of the person to God" is both the font and foundation, the source and safeguard, of all human rights. Without that transcendent referent, all talk about human rights is, as Bentham declared it to be, nonsense on stilts. Against the propensities of all states, and against the ideology of some states and movements, the Church must contend to secure social space for the personal and communal "aspiration to the infinite." In order to be more effective, however, Roman Catholic social teaching must more thoroughly integrate the moral and political wisdom of specific experiments in ordered freedom and justice. John Courtney Murray's long-neglected exploration into the meaning of the American proposition should be taken up again, and the Council's "Declaration on Religious Freedom" should be further elaborated to illumine the choices facing the modern world.

8. The Catholic Moment Challenges the Imperiousness of the Political

This thesis follows closely upon the last. The freedom of the person and of persons in community must be secured by right political order. Right political order requires setting sharp limitations upon the political, if political is understood as state power. A wide array of associations, including religion, are "public" institutions and essential to the vitality of the earthly polis. The Church makes its greatest public contribution when it is most true to its own nature and mission. In a democracy, the primary political contribution of church leadership is to "equip the saints" for the exercise of their ministry in the public arena. The Church itself is called to be a community of virtue and a zone of truth in a political world of viciousness and mendacity. A "partisan church" is an apostate church. The Church has a theology of politics, not a political theology. A theology of politics requires that pastoral leadership both affirm the political project while, at the same time, keeping all political proposals under moral judgment. The Church in all times and places has never done this very well. Religious leadership, including Roman Catholic leadership, in America today sometimes seems hardly to be trying. The results are that the Church is perceived as but one political actor among others, political discourse is inflamed rather than informed, and the integrity of both Church and political order are grievously violated.

9. The Catholic Moment Will Redirect the World's Passion for Liberation

With love for its proponents and even greater love for its victims, Christians must repudiate the proposal that politics is salvation and salvation is politics. With John Paul, and invoking Saint Paul, we must reject the now dominant forms of liberation theology as "another gospel." Contrary to certain ideologies, eternal destiny and temporal duty are not opposed to one another. It is empirically probable and logically persuasive that human development is best advanced by transcendent hope. It is historically undeniable that, where transcendent hope is denied, all development leads only to new forms of bondage. Because it is the only Gospel we have been given, and because it is the deepest truth about humanity, the Church must boldly proclaim our vocation to the radically "new politics" of the heavenly city. Short of the Kingdom Come, we are alien citizens. In contending against the idolatry of the political, the Roman Catholic Church is today contending on behalf of the Gospel and therefore on behalf of all Christians.

10. The Catholic Moment Is for the Duration

Even when, please God, all the churches are in full communion in the one Church Catholic, there will likely still be a Roman Catholic Church. By virtue of its size, tradition, structure, charisms, and energies, the Roman Catholic Church will have a singular part in shaping the world-historical future of Christianity. And if the Gospel is true, Christianity bears witness to the future of the world, who is Christ. Therefore the Catholic Moment is encompassed by an eschatological horizon. Before that final consummation the relationship between Church and world will always be problematic. The world is ever prone to premature closure, turning in upon itself and against its transcendent destiny. The Church is ever tempted to join the world in that fatal turning. This is the temptation represented by Dostoyevsky's Grand Inquisitor, and the Grand Inquisitor takes many forms—theological, philosophical, spiritual, political. The Grand Inquisitor would persuade the prodigal sons of earth that they can be at home in a world that is still far from the home of the waiting Father. Resisting that temptation, the Church must often appear to be against the world, but it will always be against the world for the world. The Church's view of reality is premised upon a promise and is therefore in tension with all views of reality premised upon the present alone. The Church too lives in the present, but it lives by a promise that is also the ultimate truth about the present. Thus the Church's relationship to the world is essentially paradoxical. It is a relationship of yes and no, now and not yet. The Church will endure until the End Time, but along the way it is ever being tested as to whether it has the courage to live in paradoxical fidelity. Nowhere is that testing so severe, nowhere is the outcome of that testing so ominous, as in the Roman Catholic Church. This Pope, we all have reason to believe and reason to hope, knows that the paradox cannot be resolved and must not be relaxed. It can only be superseded by the coming of the One who is both the consummation and companion of our common pilgrimage.

50. ANDREW SULLIVAN, "ALONE AGAIN, NATURALLY" (1994)

In the 1980s and 1990s, as the gay rights movement in the United States and Europe began to make major headway on both the legal and social fronts, gay and lesbian Catholics spoke out frequently about the Church's attitude toward both homosexual persons and homosexual acts, and about their desire to remain practicing Roman Catholics while simultaneously achieving personal sexual fulfillment. The American bishops have regarded this movement, overall, with suspicion; the gay and lesbian Catholic group Dignity USA has been banned from meeting on church property in most dioceses, and the bishops have strongly affirmed moral teachings against homosexual acts while continuing to maintain that they welcome celibate gay men and women within the Church.

Andrew Sullivan, the British-born conservative gay American Catholic commentator and former editor of The New Republic, *has written broadly on many issues affecting American life and politics. In his writings about his identity as a gay Catholic, however, the personal, the political, and the theo-*

logical are uniquely intertwined. This essay reacts to several Vatican docu-
ments of the 1970s and 1980s, including one written by then-Cardinal Joseph
Ratzinger (now Pope Benedict XVI), and wraps a theological argument into
a personal reflection on intimacy, sexuality, and faith.

I

I can remember the first time what, for the sake of argument, I will call my
sexuality came into conflict with what, for the sake of argument, I will call
my faith. It was time for Communion in my local parish church, Our Lady
and St. Peter's. . . . I must have been around 15 or so. . . . As I filed up to the
Communion rail to face mild-mannered Father Simmons for the ump-
teenth time, something else intervened. Please, I remember asking almost
offhandedly of God, after a quick recital of my other failings, help me with
that.

I didn't have a name for it, since it was, to all intents and purposes,
nameless. I don't think I'd ever heard it mentioned at home, except once
when my mother referred to someone who had behaved inappropriately
on my father's town rugby team. (He had been dealt with, she reported
darkly.) At high school, the subject was everywhere and nowhere: at the
root of countless jokes but never actualized as something that could affect anyone we knew. But this ubiquity and abstraction brought home
the most important point: uniquely among failings, homosexuality was so
abominable it could not even be mentioned. . . . Although my friends and
family never stinted in pointing out other faults on my part, this, I knew,
would never be confronted. So when it emerged as an irresistible fact of
my existence, and when it first seeped into my life of dutiful prayer and
worship, it could be referred to only in the inarticulate void of that Sunday
evening before Communion.

From the beginning, however—and this is something many outside the
Church can find hard to understand—my sexuality was part of my faith-
life, not a revolt against it. Looking back, I realize that that moment at the
Communion rail was the first time I had actually addressed the subject of
homosexuality explicitly in front of anyone; and I had brought it to God
in the moments before the most intimate act of sacramental Communion.
Because it was something I was deeply ashamed of, I felt obliged to confront it; but because it was also something inextricable—even then—from
the core of my existence, it felt natural to enlist God's help rather than his

judgment in grappling with it. There was, of course, considerable tension in this balance of alliance and rejection; but there was also something quite natural about it, an accurate reflection of anyone's compromised relationship with what he or she hazards to be the divine.

To the outsider, faith often seems a kind of cataclysmic intervention, a Damascene moment of revelation and transformation, and no doubt, for a graced few, this is indeed the experience. But this view of faith is often, it seems to me, a way to salve the unease of a faithless life by constructing the alternative as something so alien to actual experience that it is safely beyond reach. Faith for me has never been like that. The moments of genuine intervention and spiritual clarity have been minuscule in number and, when they have occurred, hard to discern and harder still to understand. In the midst of this uncertainty, the sacraments, especially that of Communion, have always been for me the only truly reliable elements of direction, concrete instantiations of another order. Which is why, perhaps, it was at Communion that the subject reared its confusing, shaming presence.

The two experiences came together in other ways, too. Like faith, one's sexuality is not simply a choice; it informs a whole way of being. But like faith, it involves choices—the choice to affirm or deny a central part of one's being, the choice to live a life that does not deny but confronts reality. It is, like faith, mysterious, emerging clearly one day, only to disappear the next, taking different forms—of passion, of lust, of intimacy, of fear. And like faith, it points toward something other and more powerful than the self. The physical communion with the other in sexual life hints at the same kind of transcendence as the physical Communion with the Other that lies at the heart of the sacramental Catholic vision.

So when I came to be asked, later in life, how I could be gay and Catholic, I could answer only that I simply was. What to others appeared a simple contradiction was, in reality, the existence of these two connected, yet sometimes parallel, experiences of the world. It was not that my sexuality was involuntary and my faith chosen and that therefore my sexuality posed a problem for my faith; nor was it that my faith was involuntary and my sexuality chosen so that my faith posed a problem for my sexuality. It was that both were chosen and unchosen continuously throughout my life, as parts of the same search for something larger. As I grew older, they became part of me, inseparable from my understanding of myself. My faith existed at the foundation of how I saw the world; my sexuality grew to be inseparable from how I felt the world.

I am aware that this formulation of the problem is theologically flawed.

Faith, after all, is not a sensibility; in the Catholic sense, it is a statement about reality that cannot be negated by experience. And there is little doubt about what the authority of the Church teaches about the sexual expression of a homosexual orientation. But this was not how the problem first presented itself. The immediate difficulty was not how to make what I did conform with what the Church taught me (until my early 20s, I did very little that could be deemed objectively sinful with regard to sex), but how to make who I was conform with what the Church taught me. This was a much more difficult proposition. It did not conform to a simple contradiction between self and God, as that afternoon in the Communion line attested. It entailed trying to understand how my adolescent crushes and passions, my longings for human contact, my stumbling attempts to relate love to life, could be so inimical to the Gospel of Christ and His Church, how they could be so unmentionable among people I loved and trusted.

So I resorted to what many young homosexuals and lesbians resort to. I found a way to expunge love from life, to construct a trajectory that could somehow explain this absence, and to hope that what seemed so natural and overwhelming could somehow be dealt with. . . . [This] sparked an intense religiosity that could provide me with the spiritual resources I needed to fortify my barren emotional life. So my sexuality and my faith entered into a dialectic: my faith propelled me away from my emotional and sexual longing, and the deprivation that this created required me to resort even more dogmatically to my faith. And as my faith had to find increasing power to restrain the hormonal and emotional turbulence of adolescence, it had to take on a caricatured shape, aloof and dogmatic, ritualistic and awesome. As time passed, a theological austerity became the essential complement to an emotional emptiness. And as the emptiness deepened, the austerity sharpened.

II

In a remarkable document titled "Declaration on Certain Questions Concerning Sexual Ethics," issued by the Vatican in 1975, the Sacred Congregation for the Doctrine of the Faith made the following statement regarding the vexed issue of homosexuality: "A distinction is drawn, and it seems with some reason, between homosexuals whose tendency comes from a false education, from a lack of normal sexual development, from habit, from bad example, or from other similar causes, and is transitory or at least not incurable; and homosexuals who are definitively such because of some kind of innate instinct or a pathological constitution judged to be incurable."

The Church was responding, it seems, to the growing sociological and psychological evidence that, for a small minority of people, homosexuality is unchosen and unalterable. In the context of a broad declaration on a whole range of sexual ethics, this statement was something of a minor digression (twice as much space was devoted to the "grave moral disorder" of masturbation); and it certainly didn't mean a liberalization of doctrine about the morality of homosexual acts, which were "intrinsically disordered and can in no case be approved of."

Still, the concession complicated things. Before 1975 the modern Church, when it didn't ignore the matter, had held a coherent view of the morality of homosexual acts. It maintained that homosexuals, as the modern world had come to define them, didn't really exist; rather, everyone was essentially a heterosexual and homosexual acts were acts chosen by heterosexuals, out of depravity, curiosity, impulse, predisposition or bad moral guidance. Such acts were an abuse of the essential heterosexual orientation of all humanity; they were condemned because they failed to link sexual activity with a binding commitment between a man and a woman in a marriage, a marriage that was permanently open to the possibility of begetting children. Homosexual sex was condemned in exactly the same way and for exactly the same reasons as premarital heterosexual sex, adultery or contracepted sex: it failed to provide the essential conjugal and procreative context for sexual relations.

The reasoning behind this argument rested on natural law. Natural law teaching, drawing on Aristotelian and Thomist tradition, argued that the sexual nature of man was naturally linked to both emotional fidelity and procreation so that, outside of this context, sex was essentially destructive of the potential for human flourishing. . . . But suddenly, a new twist had been made to this argument. There was, it seems, in nature, a group of people who were "definitively" predisposed to violation of this natural law; their condition was "innate" and "incurable." Insofar as it was innate—literally *innatus* or "inborn"—this condition was morally neutral, since anything involuntary could not be moral or immoral; it simply was. But always and everywhere, the activity to which this condition led was "intrinsically disordered and could in no case be approved of." In other words, something fundamentally in nature always and everywhere violated a vital part of the nature of human beings; something essentially blameless was always and everywhere blameworthy if acted upon.

The paradox of this doctrine was evident even within its first, brief articulation. Immediately before stating the intrinsic disorder of homosexuality, the text averred that in "the pastoral field, these homosexuals must certainly be treated with understanding and sustained in the hope of overcoming their personal difficulties. . . . Their culpability will be judged with prudence." This compassion for the peculiar plight of the homosexual was then elaborated: "This judgment of Scripture does not of course permit us to conclude that all those who suffer from this anomaly are personally responsible for it. . . ." Throughout, there are alternating moments of alarm and quiescence; tolerance and panic; categorical statement and prudential doubt.

It was therefore perhaps unsurprising that, within a decade, the Church felt it necessary to take up the matter again. The problem could have been resolved by a simple reversion to the old position, the position maintained by fundamentalist Protestant churches: that homosexuality was a hideous, yet curable, affliction of heterosexuals. But the Church doggedly refused to budge from its assertion of the natural occurrence of constitutive homosexuals—or from its compassion for and sensitivity to their plight. In Cardinal Joseph Ratzinger's 1986 letter, "On the Pastoral Care of Homosexual Persons," this theme is actually deepened, beginning with the title.

To non-Catholics, the use of the term "homosexual person" might seem a banality. But the term "person" constitutes in Catholic moral teaching a profound statement about the individual's humanity, dignity and worth; it invokes a whole range of rights and needs; it reflects the recognition by the Church that a homosexual person deserves exactly the same concern and compassion as a heterosexual person, having all the rights of a human being, and all the value, in the eyes of God. This idea was implicit in the 1975 declaration, but was never advocated. Then there it was, eleven years later, embedded in Ratzinger's very title. Throughout his text, homosexuality, far from being something unmentionable or disgusting, is discussed with candor and subtlety. It is worthy of close attention: "The phenomenon of homosexuality, complex as it is and with its many consequences for society and ecclesial life, is a proper focus for the Church's pastoral care. It thus requires of her ministers attentive study, active concern and honest, theologically well-balanced counsel." And here is Ratzinger on the moral dimensions of the unchosen nature of homosexuality: "The particular inclination of the homosexual person is not a sin." Moreover, homosexual persons, he asserts, are "often generous and giving of themselves." Then, in a stunning passage of concession, he marshals the Church's usual arguments in defense of human dignity in order to defend homosexual dignity:

> It is deplorable that homosexual persons have been and are the object of violent malice in speech or in action. Such treatment deserves condemnation from the Church's pastors wherever it occurs. It reveals a kind of disregard for others which endangers the most fundamental principles of a healthy society. The intrinsic dignity of each person must always be respected in word, in action and in law.

Elsewhere, Ratzinger refers to the homosexual's "God-given dignity and worth"; condemns the view that homosexuals are totally compulsive as a "demeaning assumption"; and argues that "the human person, made in the image and likeness of God, can hardly be adequately described by a reductionist reference to his or her sexual orientation."

Why are these statements stunning? Because they reveal how far the Church had, by the mid-1980s, absorbed the common sense of the earlier document's teaching on the involuntariness of homosexuality, and had had the courage to reach its logical conclusion. In Ratzinger's letter, the Church stood foursquare against bigotry, against demeaning homosexuals either by anti-gay slander or violence or by pro-gay attempts to reduce human beings to one aspect of their personhood. By denying that homosexual activity was totally compulsive, the Church could open the door to an entire world of moral discussion about ethical and unethical homosexual behavior, rather than simply dismissing it all as pathological. What in 1975 had been "a pathological constitution judged to be incurable" was, eleven years later, a " homosexual person," "made in the image and likeness of God."

But this defense of the homosexual person was only half the story. The other half was that, at the same time, the Church strengthened its condemnation of any and all homosexual activity. By 1986 the teachings condemning homosexual acts were far more categorical than they had been before. Ratzinger had guided the Church into two simultaneous and opposite directions: a deeper respect for homosexuals, and a sterner rejection of almost anything they might do.

At the beginning of the 1986 document, Ratzinger bravely confronted the central paradox: "In the discussion which followed the publication of the 1975 declaration . . . an overly benign interpretation was given to the homosexual condition itself, some going so far as to call it neutral or even good. Although the particular inclination of the homosexual person is not a sin, it is a more or less strong tendency ordered toward an intrinsic moral evil and thus the inclination itself must be seen as an objective disorder." Elsewhere, he reiterated the biblical and natural law arguments against homosexual relations. Avoiding the problematic nature of the Old Testament's disavowal of homosexual acts (since these are treated in the context of such "abominations" as eating pork and having intercourse during menstruation, which the Church today regards with equanimity), Ratzinger focused on St. Paul's admonitions against homosexuality: "Instead of the original harmony between Creator and creatures, the acute distortion of idolatry has led to all kinds of moral excess. Paul is at a loss to find a clearer example of this disharmony than homosexual relations." There was also the simple natural-law argument: "It is only in the marital relationship that the use of the sexual faculty can be morally good. A person engaging in homosexual behavior therefore acts immorally." The point about procreation was strengthened by an argument about the natural, "complementary union able to transmit life," which is heterosexual marriage. The fact that homosexual sex cannot be a part of this union means that it "thwarts the call to a life of that form of self- giving which the Gospel says is the essence of Christian living." Thus "homosexual activity" is inherently "self-indulgent." "Homosexual activity," Ratzinger's document claimed in a veiled and ugly reference to HIV, is a "form of life which constantly threatens to destroy" homosexual persons.

This is some armory of argument. The barrage of statements directed against "homosexual activity," which Ratzinger associates in this document exclusively with genital sex, is all the more remarkable because it occurs in a document that has otherwise gone further than might have been thought imaginable in accepting homosexuals into the heart of the Church and of humanity. Ratzinger's letter was asking us, it seems, to love the sinner more deeply than ever before, but to hate the sin even more passionately. This is a demand with which most Catholic homosexuals have at some time or other engaged in anguished combat.

III

It is also a demand that raises the central question of the two documents and, indeed, of any Catholic homosexual life: How intelligible is the

Church's theological and moral position on the blamelessness of homo-sexuality and the moral depravity of homosexual acts? This question is the one I wrestled with in my early 20s, as the increasing aridity of my emotional life began to conflict with the possibility of my living a moral life. The distinction made some kind of sense in theory; but in practice, the command to love oneself as a person of human dignity yet hate the core longings that could make one emotionally whole demanded a sense of detachment or a sense of cynicism that seemed inimical to the Christian life. To deny lust was one thing; to deny love was another. And to deny love in the context of Christian doctrine seemed particularly perverse. Which begged a prior question: Could the paradoxes of the Church's position reflect a deeper incoherence at their core?

One way of tackling the question is to look for useful analogies to the moral paradox of the homosexual. Greed, for example, might be said to be an innate characteristic of human beings, which, in practice, is always bad. But the analogy falls apart immediately. Greed is itself evil; it is prideful, a part of Original Sin. It is not, like homosexuality, a blameless natural condition that inevitably leads to what are understood as immoral acts. Moreover, there is no subgroup of innately greedy people, nor a majority of people in which greed never occurs. Nor are the greedy to be treated with respect. There is no paradox here, and no particular moral conundrum.

Aquinas suggests a way around this problem. He posits that some things that occur in nature may be in accordance with an individual's nature, but somehow against human nature in general: "for it sometimes happens that one of the principles which is natural to the species as a whole has broken down in one of its individual members; the result can be that something which runs counter to the nature of the species as a whole, happens to be in harmony with nature for a particular individual: as it becomes natural for a vessel of water which has been heated to give out heat." Forget, for a moment, the odd view that somehow it is more "natural" for a vessel to exist at one temperature than another. The fundamental point here is that there are natural urges in a particular person that may run counter to the nature of the species as a whole. The context of this argument is a discussion of pleasure: How is it, if we are to trust nature (as Aquinas and the Church say we must), that some natural pleasures in some people are still counter to human nature as a whole? Aquinas's only response is to call such events functions of sickness, what the modern Church calls "objective disorder." But here, too, the analogies he provides are revealing: they are bestiality and cannibalism. Aquinas understands each of these activities as an emanation of a predilection that seems to occur more naturally in some than in others. But this only reveals some of the special problems of lumping homosexuality in with other "disorders." Even Aquinas's modern disciples (and, as we've seen, the Church) concede that involuntary orientation to the same gender does not spring from the same impulses as cannibalism or bestiality. Or indeed that cannibalism is ever a "natural" pleasure in the first place, in the way that, for some bizarre reason, homosexuality is.

What, though, of Aquinas's better argument—that a predisposition to homosexual acts is a mental or physical illness that is itself morally neutral, but always predisposes people to inherently culpable acts? Here, again, it is hard to think of a precise analogy. . . .

This suggests another analogy: the sterile person. Here, too, the person is structurally barred by an innate or incurable condition from the full realization of procreative union with another person. One might expect that such people would be regarded in exactly the same light as homosexuals. They would be asked to commit themselves to a life of complete celibacy and to offer up their pain toward a realization of Christ's sufferings on the cross. But that, of course, is not the Church's position. Marriage is available to sterile couples or to those past child-bearing age; these couples are not prohibited from having sexual relations.

One is forced to ask: What rational distinction can be made, on the Church's own terms, between the position of sterile people and that of homosexual people with regard to sexual relations and sacred union? If there is nothing morally wrong, per se, with the homosexual condition or with homosexual love and self-giving, then homosexuals are indeed analogous to those who, by blameless fate, cannot reproduce. With the sterile couple, it could be argued, miracles might happen. But miracles, by definition, can happen to anyone. What the analogy to sterility suggests, of course, is that the injunction against homosexual union does not rest, at heart, on the arguments about openness to procreation, but on the Church's failure to fully absorb its own teachings about the dignity and worth of homosexual persons. It cannot yet see them as it sees sterile heterosexuals: people who, with respect to procreation, suffer from a clear, limiting condition, but who nevertheless have a potential for real emotional and spiritual self-realization, in the heart of the Church, through the transfiguring power of the matrimonial sacrament. It cannot yet see them as truly made in the image of God.

But this, maybe, is to be blind in the face of the obvious. Even with sterile people, there is a symbolism in the union of male and female that speaks to the core nature of sexual congress and its ideal instantiation. There is no such symbolism in the union of male with male or female with female. For some Catholics, this "symbology" goes so far as to bar even heterosexual intercourse from positions apart from the missionary—face to face, male to female, in a symbolic act of love devoid of all non-procreative temptation. For others, the symbology is simply about the notion of "complementarity," the way in which each sex is invited in the act of sexual congress—even when they are sterile—to perceive the mystery of the other; when the two sexes are the same, in contrast, the act becomes one of mere narcissism and self-indulgence, a higher form of masturbation. For others still, the symbolism is simply about Genesis, the story of Adam and Eve, and the essentially dual, male-female center of the natural world. Denying this is to offend the complementary dualism of the universe.

But all these arguments are arguments for the centrality of heterosexual sexual acts in nature, not their exclusiveness. It is surely possible to concur with these sentiments, even to laud their beauty and truth, while also conceding that it is nevertheless also true that nature seems to have provided a spontaneous and mysterious contrast that could conceivably be understood to complement—even dramatize—the central male-female order. In many species and almost all human cultures, there are some who seem to find their destiny in a similar but different sexual and emotional union. They do this not by subverting their own nature, or indeed human nature, but by fulfilling it in a way that doesn't deny heterosexual primacy, but rather honors it by its rare and distinct otherness. As albinos remind us of the brilliance of color; as redheads offer a startling contrast to the blandness of their peers; as genius teaches us, by contrast, the virtue of moderation; as the disabled person reveals to us in negative form the beauty of the fully functioning human body; so the homosexual person might be seen as a natural foil to the heterosexual norm, a variation that does not eclipse the theme, but resonates with it. Extinguishing—or prohibiting—homosexuality is, from this point of view, not a virtuous necessity, but the real crime against nature, a refusal to accept the pied beauty of God's creation, a denial of the way in which the other need not threaten, but may actually give depth and contrast to the self.

This is the alternative argument embedded in the Church's recent grappling with natural law, that is just as consonant with the spirit of natural law as the Church's current position. It is more consonant with what actually occurs in nature; seeks an end to every form of natural life; and upholds the dignity of each human person. It is so obvious an alternative to the Church's current stance that it is hard to imagine the forces of avoidance that have kept it so firmly at bay for so long.

IV

For many homosexual Catholics, life within the Church is a difficult endeavor. In my 20s, as I attempted to unite the possibilities of sexual longing and emotional commitment, I discovered what many heterosexuals and homosexuals had discovered before me: that it is a troubling and troublesome mission. There's a disingenuous tendency, when discussing both homosexual and heterosexual emotional life, to glamorize and idealize the entire venture. To posit the possibility of a loving union, after all, is not to guarantee its achievement. There is also a lamentable inclination to believe that all conflicts can finally be resolved; that the homosexual Catholic's struggle can be removed by a simple theological *coup de main*; that the conflict is somehow deeper than many other struggles in the Church —of women, say, or of the divorced. The truth is that pain, as Christ taught, is not a reason to question truth; it may indeed be a reason to embrace it.

But it must also be true that to dismiss the possibility of a loving union for homosexuals at all—to banish from the minds and hearts of countless gay men and women the idea that they, too, can find solace and love in one another—is to create the conditions for a human etiolation that no Christian community can contemplate without remorse. What finally convinced me of the wrongness of the Church's teachings was not that they were intellectually so confused, but that in the circumstances of my own life—and of the lives I discovered around me—they seemed so destructive of the possibilities of human love and self-realization. By crippling the potential for connection and growth, the Church's teachings created a dynamic that in practice led not to virtue but to pathology; by requiring the first lie in a human life, which would lead to an entire battery of others, they contorted human beings into caricatures of solitary eccentricity, frustrated bitterness, incapacitating anxiety—and helped perpetuate all the human wickedness and cruelty and insensitivity that such lives inevitably carry in their wake. These doctrines could not in practice do what they wanted to do: they could not both affirm human dignity and deny human love.

This truth is not an argument; it is merely an observation. But observations are at the heart not simply of the Church's traditional Thomist philosophy, but also of the phenomenological vision of the current pope. To observe these things, to affirm their truth, is not to oppose the Church, but to hope in it, to believe in it as a human institution that is yet the eternal vessel of God's love. It is to say that such lives as those of countless gay men and lesbians must ultimately affect the Church not because our lives are perfect, or without contradiction, or without sin, but because our lives are in some sense also the life of the Church.

I remember, in my own life, the sense of lung-filling exhilaration I felt as my sexuality began to be incorporated into my life, a sense that was not synonymous with recklessness or self-indulgence—although I was not immune from those things either—but a sense of being suffused at last with the possibility of being fully myself before those I loved and before God. I remember the hopefulness of parents regained and friendships restored in a life that, for all its vanities, was at least no longer premised on a lie covered over by a career. I remember the sense a few months ago in a pew in a cathedral, as I reiterated the same pre-Communion litany of prayers that I had spoken some twenty years earlier, that, for the first time, the love the Church had always taught that God held for me was tangible and redemptive. I had never felt it fully before; and, of course, like so many spiritual glimpses, I have rarely felt it since. But I do know that it was conditioned not on the possibility of purity, but on the possibility of honesty. That honesty is not something that can be bought or won in a moment. It is a process peculiarly prone to self-delusion and self-doubt. But it is one that, if it is to remain true to itself, the Church cannot resist forever.

FURTHER SUGGESTED READING

Patrick Allitt, *Catholic Intellectuals and Conservative Politics in America, 1950–1983* (Ithaca, N.Y.: Cornell University Press, 1993).

Steven M. Avella & Elizabeth McKeown, eds., *Public Voices: Catholics in the American Context* (Maryknoll, N.Y.: Orbis Books, 2001).

Jeffrey M. Burns, Ellen Skerrett, & Joseph White, eds., *Keeping Faith: European and Asian Catholic Immigrants* (Maryknoll, N.Y.: Orbis Books, 2001).

Cesar Chavez, *The Words of Cesar Chavez* (College Station: Texas A&M University Press, 2002).

Michael W. Cuneo, *The Smoke of Satan: Conservative and Traditionalist Dissent in Contemporary American Catholicism* (Oxford: Oxford University Press, 1997).

Charles Curran, *Dissent In and For the Church* (New York: Sheed & Ward, 1969).

Paula Kane, James Kenneally, & Karen Kennelly, eds., *Gender Identities in American Catholicism* (Maryknoll, N.Y.: Orbis Books, 2001).

Timothy Matovina & Gerald E. Poyo, eds., *¡Presente!: U.S. Latino Catholics from Colonial Origins to the Present* (Maryknoll, N.Y.: Orbis Books, 2001).

Leslie Tentler, *Catholics and Contraception* (Ithaca, N.Y.: Cornell University Press, 2004).

Mary Jo Weaver, ed., *What's Left? Liberal American Catholics* (Bloomington: Indiana University Press, 1999).

Mary Jo Weaver & R. Scott Appleby, eds., *Being Right: Conservative Catholics in America* (Bloomington: Indiana University Press, 1995).

Kenneth Zanca, ed., *American Catholics and Slavery, 1789–1866* (Lanham, Md.: University Press of America, 1994).

Part V

Worship & the Spiritual Life

American Catholics have always been known—and sometimes distrusted and despised—for the many forms their public piety has taken. Although private and home-based devotions have always been popular (No. 61), Catholic devotional life has indeed often had a group or public component. These group devotions have been seen as reinforcing the cohesiveness of ethnic neighborhoods (Nos. 55, 57, and 68).

This section seeks to balance institutional documents (instructions from the American hierarchy) with the raw materials for "history from below," focusing not on what Catholics were being told to do, or what their best theologians thought they should be doing, but on what they were actually thinking and doing in the areas of liturgy, devotional practice, and popular piety. These documents describe various aspects of lay piety: the experience of liturgy from a number of historical periods; popular lay practices; and "reports from the field" about devotional and liturgical change, as well as a sample of American mysticism as represented by Thomas Merton (No. 65). Particular focus is given to the turmoil surrounding the implementation of the Second Vatican Council's reforms in the United States; while some Catholics did prove uninterested in change (No. 64), many looked forward to a new day in the church (Nos. 63, 66, 67, and 69). Finally, a selection of photographs of American Catholics concentrates on the living of the spiritual life in the mid-twentieth century: at public worship, at private prayer, at home, and even at war (No. 62).

51. PREPARING FOR CONFESSION (1792)

The Pious Guide to Prayer and Devotion, *assembled by anonymous members of the English Catholic community in Maryland and published at Georgetown on the Potomac in 1792 (a component of the future Washington,*

D.C.), was the first and most popular of the early Catholic prayer-books in the United States. It was a complete guide to the standard forms of prayer and ritual for the laity, including sacraments as well as private devotions, and was so widely used that it went through nine gradually expanded editions in the nineteenth century. This excerpt is from the elaborate instructions on preparation for the sacrament of Penance, which included a number of prayers as well as a nine-page examination of conscience.

The sacrament of Penance, which the saints term "the second plank after shipwreck," is one of the greatest blessings we derive from the sufferings and death of Jesus Christ. But as its efficacy chiefly depends on the dispositions of those who approach the holy tribunal, of course preparation for confession becomes one of the most serious duties of a christian [*sic*]. That rigid justice, which so severely punished one mortal sin in the angels, and which rigorously inflicted on the eternal Son of God all the penalties due to man's offences, will not assuredly remit the real guilt of sin on those who only carelessly comply with the external form of confession, without taking the necessary pains to excite in their souls the dispositions which so holy an action requires. Those who are so happy as to have been early instructed in the method of preparing for confession, should be particularly grateful to God for so great a blessing, and endeavour, by exact compliance with all they know to be necessary, to draw from this Sacrament the graces which it infallibly bestows on those who receive it with due dispositions.

One of the best rules which can be followed with respect to confession, is to approach the sacred tribunal each time as if it were to be the last. What would be your disposition, if you were actually stretched on your death-bed, and about to prepare for a confession which you knew would be followed by that tremendous judgment that has caused the greatest saints to tremble? . . . Do now, what you would then do; for the confession you are about to make may be your last; and even though you should have many opportunities of recurring to the tribunal of penance, yet be convinced that at the hour of death there could not be a more serious subject of remorse, than multiplied, but careless confessions. On the other hand no tongue can describe the consolation and peace of those who have been wise enough to settle their accounts with God in time, and who did not put off to a season of sickness, anxiety, and mental as well as bodily weakness, the awful task of preparing for eternity. It is in your power now to ensure this happiness for yourself, by seriously attending to the five following requisites for a good confession:—1st, Serious examination of conscience.—2d, Sorrow for sin.—3d, A determined resolution never more to offend God, and to avoid the occasions of sin.—4th, A candid, humble confession to an approved priest.—5th, A sincere desire and intention to satisfy God's justice, and make reparation to your neighbour if injured by you in reputation or property. . . .

Beg God to make your sins known to you, and to give you a true sense of their malice. Prostrate yourself in spirit at the feet of your Redeemer, as Magadalen did, when she washed them with her tears; or transport yourself in idea to Mount Calvary, and there beneath his Cross, pour forth your prayers to him, resolved to acquit yourself of this confession, as if it were to be your last. . . .

Examine yourself carefully of the sins you have committed since your last confession, and also upon the faults you may have committed in making it, but do this without scrupulous anxiety. . . . It will be of great use in this examination to call to mind the different places you have been in; your occupations, and the persons you have conversed with, &c.

An Examination of Conscience

Sins Against God: In Matters of Faith: Have you been guilty of heresy, or disbelief of any article of faith, or of voluntary doubting any article of faith? Have you rashly exposed yourself to the danger of infidelity, by reading bad books, keeping wicked company, going into places of worship belonging to other communions during the time of their service, and joining with them in their worship? Have you by word, or deed denied your faith, or railed at or despised holy things? Have you been ignorant of the articles of your faith, and of the duties of your religion, or negligent in instructing, or procuring the necessary instructions for those under your care? Have you given credit to dreams, taken notice of omens, or made any other superstitious observations? Have you used charms or spells, or consulted fortune-tellers, or made use of any other superstitious practices, to find out things to come, recover things lost, &c., how often? and with what scandal, and ill example to others? . . .

Sins Against Our Neighbor. In Actions: Have you wronged, deceived, or circumvented your neighbor in buying or selling? Have you injured him by stealing, cheating, usury, extortion, or any unlawful contract? by passing false money, or using false weights or measures? Have you bought or received stolen goods? Have you contracted debts without design of paying them? You may also sin by wronging your creditors, or your own family, by prodigal expenses—by refusing to pay your just debts when able, or by culpable extravagance, rendering yourself unable to pay them. . . . In fine, by unjustly taking or keeping any thing of value belonging to another; in which case it is impossible to obtain forgiveness, without making restitution to the best of your power. . . .

Sins Against Ourselves: By Pride: Having too great esteem for ourselves, and haughtily despising others. Being too apt to speak of our own affairs, or in our own praise. Aspiring to honours and preferment through vanity. Affecting to be humble, or deceiving others by hypocrisy. Being influenced in what we do by human respects, for obtaining the applause and esteem of men. . . .

Resolution of Amendment. If your heart be really penetrated with the sentiments you have expressed in the foregoing act of contrition, it will not be necessary to suggest the obligation you are under of forming serious resolutions for the amendment of your life. This resolution of never sinning again, is so essential to contrition, that, without it, there can be no real sorrow. It is nevertheless a point on which many persons fail; the greater number contenting themselves with a sort of general intention of doing better in the future, an intention which costs nothing; which often is only in imagination; which, at best, is very weak and indeterminate. As this defect of a firm, decided purpose of amendment, and the want of foreseeing and resolving against habitual faults, is the great cause of so many fruitless confessions, you should be particularly careful in making your resolutions. . . .

52. "Sunday Morning Mass" (1868)

St. Stephen's Church on East 28th Street in Manhattan is a vast Romanesque edifice, designed by James Renwick (who also did St. Patrick's Cathedral and the Smithsonian's "castle" building on the National Mall) in 1850. In 1860 it had 24,000 parishioners (making it the largest parish in the country) and was pastored by the notorious liberal Edward McGlynn, whose battles with New York's archbishop ultimately resulted in his excommunication. This article, for the New England magazine the Atlantic Monthly *in 1868, captures both the distinctively American and perhaps more "progressive" aspects of parish life (such as the Sunday school), and the flavor of the ritualized Tridentine Latin Mass. With its smallest elements, such as the placement of chairs for the presider, specified by Rome, this Mass was both highly unifying in its reassuring sameness and, for the majority of the congregation that did not know Latin and in any case could not usually hear the presider, somewhat mysterious and even mystifying. Catholics dutifully and devotedly attended mass in droves—many attended every day—but often practiced private devotions such as the rosary for much of the brief service. Catholics' deep ambivalence about this style of liturgy would be exposed during the liturgical movement of the mid-twentieth century (see Nos. 59 & 63), but during the nineteenth century it was a vital tool for binding the immigrant community together.*

It was a very cold and brilliant morning, stars glittering, moon resplendent, pavement icy, roofs snowy, wind north-northwest, and, of course, cutting right into the faces of people bound up Third Avenue. . . . There was scarcely any one astir to keep an adventurer in countenance, and I began to think it was all a delusion about the six-o'clock mass. At ten minutes to six, when I stood in front of the spacious St. Stephen's Church in Twenty-Eighth Street, there seemed to be no one going in; and, the vestibule being unlighted, I was confirmed in the impression that the early mass did not take place on such cold mornings. To be quite sure of the fact, however, I did just go up the steps and push at the door. It yielded to pressure, and its opening disclosed a vast interior, dimly lighted at the altar end, where knelt or sat, scattered about one or two in a pew, about a hundred women and ten men, all well muffled up in hoods, shawls, and overcoats, and breathing visibly. There was just light enough to see the new blue ceiling and its silver stars; but the sexton was busy lighting the gas, and got on with his work about as fast as the church filled. . . . As six o'clock approached, female figures in increasing numbers crept silently in by several doors, all making the usual courtesy; and all kneeling as soon as they reached a pew. At last the lower part of the church was pretty well filled, and there were some people in the galleries; in all, about one thousand women and about one hundred men. Nearly all the women were servant-girls, and all of them were dressed properly and abundantly for such a morning. There was not a squalid or miserable looking person present. Most of the men appeared to be grooms or coachmen. . . . There were two or three men near me who might or might not have been ecclesiastics or theological students; upon the pale and luminous face of each was most legibly written, This man prays continually, and enjoys it.

There is a difference between Catholics and Protestants in this matter of praying. When a Protestant prays in public, he is apt to hide his face, and bend low in an awkward, uncomfortable attitude; and, when he would pray in private, he retires into some secret place, where, if any one should catch him at it, he would blush like a guilty thing. It is not so with our Roman Catholic brethren. They kneel, it is true, but the body above the knees is bolt upright, and the face is never hidden; and, as if this were not enough, they make certain movements of the hand which distinctly announce their purpose to every beholder. . . . Another thing strikes a Protestant spectator of Catholic worship, the whole congregation, without exception, observe the etiquette of the occasion. When kneeling is in order, all kneel; when it is the etiquette to stand, all stand; when the prayer book says bow, every head is low. . . . From the hour of baptism, every Catholic is a member of the church, and he is expected to behave as such. This is evidently one reason for that open, matter-of-course manner in which all the requirements of their religion are fulfilled. No one is ashamed of doing what is done by every one in the world whom he respects, and what he has himself been in the habit of doing from the time of his earliest recollection. . . .

On this cold morning the priest was not as punctual as the people. The congregation continued to increase till ten minutes past six; after which no sound was heard but the coughing of the chilled worshippers. It was not til seventeen minutes past six that the priest entered, accompanied by two slender, graceful boys, clad in long red robes, and walked to his place, and knelt before the altar. All present, except one poor heathen, in the middle aisle, shuffled to their knees with a pleasant noise, and remained kneeling for some time. The silence was complete, and I waited to hear it broken by the sound of the priest's voice. But not a sound came from his lips. He rose, he knelt, he ascended the steps of the altar, he came down again, he turned his back to the people, he turned his face to them, he changed from one side of the altar to the other, he made various gestures with his hands, but he uttered not an audible word. The two graceful lads in crimson garb moved about him, and performed the usual service, and the people sat, stood, knelt, bowed, and crossed themselves in accordance with the ritual. But still not a word was spoken. At the usual time the collection was taken, to which few gave more than a cent, but to which *every one* gave a cent. A little later, the priest uttered the only words audible during the whole service. Standing on the left side of the altar, he said, in an agreeable, educated voice: "The Society of the Holy Rosary will meet this afternoon after vespers. Prayers are requested for the repose of the souls of—"; then followed the names of three persons. The service was continued, and the silence was only broken again by the gong-like bell, which announced by a single stroke the most solemn acts of the mass, and which, toward the close of the service, summoned those to the altar who wished to commune. During the intense stillness which usually followed the sound of the bell, a low, eager whisper of prayer could occasionally be heard, and the whole assembly was lost in devotion. About twenty women and five men knelt round the altar to receive communion. Soon after this had been administered some of the women began to hurry away, as if fearing the family at home might be ready for breakfast before breakfast was ready for them. At ten minutes to seven the priest put on his black cap, and withdrew; and soon the congregation was in full retreat. But by this time another congregation was assembling for the seven-o'clock mass; the people were pouring in at every door, and hurrying along all the adjacent streets to the church. . . .

What an economy this is! The parish of St. Stephen's contains a Catholic population of twenty-five thousand, of whom twenty thousand, perhaps, are old enough and well enough to go to church. As the church will seat four thousand persons, all this multitude can hear mass every Sunday morning. . . . The church, too, in the intervals of service, and during the week, stands hospitably open, and is usually fulfilling in some way the end of its erection. . . . When [Catholics] have invested half a million in a building, they put that building to a use which justifies and returns the expenditure. Even their grand cathedrals are good investments; since, besides being always open, always in use, always cheering and comforting their people, they are splendid illustrations of their religion to every passer-by, to every reader of books, and to every collector of engravings. Such edifices as St. Peter's . . . do actually cheer and exalt the solitary priest toiling on the outskirts of civilization. Lonely as he is . . . he feels that he has a property in those grandeurs, and that an indissoluble tie connects him with the system which created them, and which will one day erect a gorgeous temple upon the site of the shanty in which now he celebrates the rites of his church in the presence of a few railroad workers.

While these successive multitudes have been gathering and dispersing something has been going on in the basement of St. Stephen's, a long, low room . . . fitted up for a children's chapel and Sunday-school room. . . . There is a particular reason why a Protestant should be pleased at a Catholic Sunday school. Imitation is the sincerest homage. The notion of the Sunday school is one of several which our Roman Catholic brethren have borrowed from us. This church, hoary and wrinkled with age, does not disdain to learn from the young and bustling churches to which it has given all they have. . . . Indeed, the energetic and truly catholic superintendent of St. Stephen's school, Mr. Thomas E. S. Dwyer, informed me, that, before beginning this school, he visited all the noted Sunday schools in New York, Protestant, Catholic, and Jewish, and endeavored to get from each whatever he found in it suitable to his purpose.

3. THE BALTIMORE CATECHISM (1885)

The Baltimore Catechism of 1885 may be the most famous document ever produced by the American Church. Until the late 1960s it was certainly the most widely read, and even today its famous opening lines are well-remembered by Catholics who were children prior to Vatican II. Mandated by the 3rd Council of Baltimore, the catechism quickly became standard in schools and sacramental preparation. A number of editions were prepared over the years, which served two purposes: to express the theology more accurately, and to make the catechism more appropriate for various age groups. (The expanded catechism for confirmation and post-confirmation students is considerably more complex than the text presented here, which was meant for young children preparing for first communion.)

Lesson First: On the End of Man

1. Q. Who made the world?
   A. God made the world.
2. Q. Who is God?
   A. God is the Creator of heaven and earth, and of all things.
3. Q. What is man?
   A. Man is a creature composed of body and soul, and made to the image and likeness of God.
6. Q. Why did God make you?
   A. God made me to know Him, to love Him, and to serve Him in this world, and to be happy with Him forever in the next.
9. Q. What must we do to save our souls?
   A. To save our souls, we must worship God by faith, hope, and charity; that is, we must believe in Him, hope in Him, and love Him with all our heart.

10. Q. How shall we know the things which we are to believe?
   A. We shall know the things which we are to believe from the Catholic Church, through which God speaks to us.
11. Q. Where shall we find the chief truths which the Church teaches?
   A. We shall find the chief truths which the Church teaches in the Apostles' Creed.
12. Q. Say the Apostles' Creed. . . .

Lesson Tenth: On the Church

114. Q. Which are the means instituted by our Lord to enable men at all times to share in the fruits of the Redemption?
   A. The means instituted by our Lord to enable men at all times to share in the fruits of His Redemption are the Church and the Sacraments.
115. Q. What is the Church?
   A. The Church is the congregation of all those who profess the faith of Christ, partake of the same Sacraments, and are governed by their lawful pastors under one visible Head.
116. Q. Who is the invisible Head of the Church?
   A. Jesus Christ is the invisible Head of the Church.
117. Q. Who is the visible Head of the Church?
   A. Our Holy Father the Pope, the Bishop of Rome, is the Vicar of Christ on earth, and the visible Head of the Church.
128. Q. Has the Church any marks by which it may be known?
   A. The Church has four marks by which it may be known: it is One; it is Holy; it is Catholic; it is Apostolic.
133. Q. In which Church are these marks found?
   A. These marks are found in the Holy Roman Catholic Church alone. . . .

54. James Cardinal Gibbons, "The Invocation of the Saints" (1892)

Cardinal Gibbons's book, Faith of Our Fathers, *published in 1892 and still in print, was intended as an explanation of the faith for Catholics; but it has often been noted that it is so carefully written as to contain hardly anything offensive to American Protestant sensibilities. As the Archbishop of Baltimore, Gibbons was the de facto head of the American Church from 1877 to his death in 1921. He was known as a moderate figure, neither a liberal "Americanist" bishop nor a Europeanized conservative, and his non-aggressive style paid off in the respect shown him by even skeptics like H. L. Mencken, though his attendant indecisiveness could also put him in the shadow of his more color- ful colleagues. This selection demonstrates his diplomatic style; he tackles one of the most distinctively Catholic practices, devotion to the saints, in a way designed both to reign in Catholic excesses and to present a convincing apolo- getic to curious outsiders.*

Christians of most denominations are accustomed to recite the following article contained in the Apostles' Creed: "I believe in the Communion of Saints." There are many, I fear, who have these words frequently on their lips, without an adequate knowledge of the precious meaning which they convey.

The true and obvious sense of the words quoted from the Creed is, that between the children of God, whether reigning in heaven or sojourning on earth, there exists an intercommunion, or spiritual communication by prayer; and, consequently, that our friends who have entered into their rest are mindful of us in their petitions to God.

In the exposition of her Creed the Catholic Church weighs her words in the scales of the sanctuary with as much precision as a banker weighs his gold. With regard to the invocation of Saints the Church simply declares that it is "useful and salutary" to ask their prayers. There are expressions addressed to the Saints in some popular books of devotion which, to criti- cal readers, may seem extravagant. But they are only the warm language of affection and poetry, to be regulated by our standard of faith; and notice that all the prayers of the Church end with the formula: "Through our Lord Jesus Christ," sufficiently indicating her belief that Christ is the Me- diator of salvation. A heart tenderly attached to the Saints will give vent to its feelings in the language of hyperbole, just as an enthusiastic lover will call his future bride his adorable queen, without any intention of worship- ping her as a goddess. This reflection should be borne in mind while read- ing such passages. . . .

We have, also, abundant testimony from Scripture to show that the Saints assist us by their prayers. Almighty God threatened the inhabitants of Sodom and Gomorrah with utter destruction on account of their crimes and abominations. Abraham interposes in their behalf and, in response to his prayer, God consents to spare those cities if only ten just men are found there. Here the avenging hand of God is suspended and the fire of His wrath withheld, through the efficacy of the prayers of a single man. . . .

Nay, is it not a common practice among ourselves, and even among our dissenting brethren, to ask the prayers of one another? When a father is about to leave his house on a long journey the instinct of piety prompts him to say to his wife and children: "Remember me in your prayers."

Now I ask you, if our friends, though sinners, can aid us by their prayers, why cannot our friends, the saints of God, be able to assist us also? If Abraham and Moses and Job exercised so much influence with the Almighty while they lived in the flesh, is their power with God diminished now that they reign with Him in heaven? . . .

But you will ask, are the saints in heaven so interested in our welfare as to be mindful of us in their prayers? Or, are they so much absorbed in the contemplation of God, and in the enjoyment of celestial bliss, as to be altogether regardless of their friends on earth? Far from us the suspicion that the saints reigning with God ever forget us. In heaven, charity is triumphant. And how can the saints have love, and yet be unmindful of their brethren on earth? If they have one desire greater than another, it is to see us one day wearing the crowns that await us in haven. If they were capable of experiencing sorrow, their grief would spring from the consideration that we do not always walk in their footsteps here, so as to make sure of our election to eternal glory hereafter. . . .

To ask the prayers of our brethren in heaven is not only conformable to Holy Scriptures, but is prompted by the instincts of our nature. The Catholic doctrine of the Communion of Saints robs death of its terrors, while the Reformers of the sixteenth century, in denying the Communion of Saints, not only inflicted a deadly wound on the Creed, but also severed the tenderest chords of the human heart. They broke asunder the holy ties that unite earth with heaven—the soul in the flesh with the soul released from the flesh. If my brother leaves me to cross the seas I believe that he continues to pray for me. And when he crosses the narrow sea of death and lands on the shores of eternity, why should he not pray for me still? What does death destroy? The body. The soul still lives and moves and has its being. It thinks and wills and remembers and loves. The dross of sin and selfishness and hatred are burned by the salutary fires of contrition, and nothing remains but the pure gold of charity

O far be from us the dreary thought that death cuts off our friends entirely from us! Far be from us the heartless creed which declares a perpetual divorce between us and the just in heaven! Do not imagine when you lose a father or mother, a tender sister or brother, who die in the peace of Christ, that they are forgetful of you. The love they bore you on earth is purified and intensified in heaven. Or if your innocent child, regenerated in the waters of baptism, is snatched from you by death, be assured that, though separated from you in body, that child is with you in spirit and is repaying you a thousand-fold for the natural life it received from you. Be convinced that the golden link of prayer binds you to that angelic infant, and that it is continually offering its fervent petitions at the throne of God for you, that you may both be reunited in heaven. But I hear men cry out with Pharisaical assurance, "You dishonor God, sir, in praying to the saints. You make void the mediatorship of Jesus Christ. You put the creature above the Creator." How utterly groundless is this objection! We do not dishonor God in praying to the saints. We should, indeed, dishonor Him if we consulted the saints independently of God. But such is not our practice. The Catholic Church teaches, on the contrary, that God alone is the Giver of all good gifts; that He is the Source of all blessings, the Fountain of all goodness. She teaches that whatever happiness or glory or influence the saints possess, all comes from God. As the moon borrows her light from the sun, so do the blessed borrow their light from Jesus, "the Sun of Justice," the one Mediator (of redemption) of God and men. Hence, when we address the saints, we beg them to pray for us through the merits of Jesus Christ, while we ask Jesus to help us through His own merits.

But what is the use of praying to the saints, since God can hear us? If it is vain and useless to pray to the saints because God can hear us, then Jacob was wrong in praying to the angel; the friends of Job were wrong in asking him to pray for them, though God commanded them to invoke Job's intercession; the Jews exiled in Babylon were wrong in asking their brethren in Jerusalem to pray for them; St. Paul was wrong in beseeching his friends to pray for him; then we are all wrong in praying for each other. You deem it useful and pious to ask your pastor to pray for you. Is it not, at least, equally useful for me to invoke the prayers of St. Paul, since I am convinced that he can hear me?

God forbid that our supplications to our Father in heaven should diminish in proportion as our prayers to the Saints increase; for, after all, we must remember that, while the Church declares it necessary for salvation to pray to God, she merely asserts that it is "good and useful to invoke the saints." To ask the prayers of the saints, far from being useless, is most profitable. By invoking their intercession, instead of one we have many praying for us. To our own tepid petitions we unite the fervent supplications of the blessed and "the Lord will hear the prayers of the just." To the petitions of us, poor pilgrims in this vale of tears, are united those of the citizens of heaven. We ask them to pray to their God and to our God, to their Father and to our Father, that we may one day share their delights in that blessed country in company with our common Redeemer, Jesus Christ, with whom to live is to reign.

55. The Sodality of the Blessed Virgin Mary (1897)

The word "sodality" is from a Latin root meaning "fellowship." In the Catholic Church, sodalities are associations of laymen and women for devotional and charitable purposes. Sodalities served a number of purposes in the close-knit ethnic neighborhoods of the major American cities prior to 1960: members inspired each other to greater personal devotion and prayed with and for each other, but also usually shared some kind of social work, such as aid to the sick, elderly, or indigent of their communities. The Sodality of the Blessed Virgin Mary, founded in Rome in 1563, was a major fixture on this scene; the Catholic Encyclopedia of 1912 described it as being uniquely capable, through the practices described in its manual, of making its members "not only loyal Catholics but also true lay apostles for the salvation and blessing of all around them."

II. Object of the Sodality

The chief aim of the Sodality is to foster in the hearts of the members a more than ordinary devotion to our Blessed Lady, in order that, helped by her special protection, they may lead a pure Christian life and prepare themselves to die a happy death. . . .

III. Practices of the Sodality

On a day and at an hour appointed the members hold their regular meetings. The usual practice of the Sodality, at its regular meetings, is to recite the Office of the Blessed Virgin, or the Little Office of the Immaculate Conception, if this is more convenient. In case of necessity, other prayers, hymns, and devotions may be substituted.

The Director, or some one appointed by him, should always give an instruction at these meetings on some topic connected with our Lady. . . . A vast amount of instruction can be conveyed in a year when the work is not allowed to become desultory. . . . In the true spirit of the Sodality, the members should frequently receive Holy Communion—if possible, all together—especially on feasts of the Blessed Virgin: they should practice the devotion of the Six Sundays of St. Aloysius, and it is advisable that they devote some days every year to the spiritual exercises of a Retreat.

The good works recommended are not obligatory, but all or any of them may be done with great profit:

Every day, to begin the day by some special prayers to their heavenly Patroness. In the *Prima Primeria* three *Hail Marys* are customary, morning and night. To be present, if possible, at the holy Sacrifice of the Mass. To give some time to pious meditation or to spiritual reading. To recite, at least in part, the Rosary or the Office of the Blessed Virgin. To make an examination of conscience before going to rest.

Once a month, at the very least, to receive the sacraments of Penance and the Holy Eucharist.

Once or twice a year, to make a general confession; that is, a review since the last one made.

At the death of a member of the Sodality, to accompany the body to the grave and fervently commend the soul to God.

At all times, to be earnest in furthering the interests of the Church and of religion; to strive, by example as well as by words, to lead back to the way of salvation those who have strayed from the faith or from the practice of virtue; to promote works of mercy, especially towards members of the Sodality in time of sickness; to aim not only at acquiring ordinary Christian virtue, but at excelling in piety, purity, humility, modesty, diligence and fidelity in the duties of one's state of life. . . .

In the history of the Sodality we find that its members have been the apostles of all good works, especially among men and boys. They should promote such undertakings, for example, as the Apostleship of Prayer, the Communion of Reparation, the Adoration of the Blessed Sacrament, the recitation of the Rosary, and the attendance at Retreats and Missions, such Catholic works as the Propagation of the Faith, the Holy Childhood, Catholic circulating libraries. . . . The socialistic tendencies of our age must be counteracted, or at least directed to seek the welfare, instead of the ruin, of human society. The Sodality, uniting men as it does, to influence one another for good, and that under the patronage of our Blessed Mother, is a most effectual means of doing this.

IV. Benefits of the Society

"We may apply to the Sodality," wrote Father Stephen Binet, S.J., "what St. Bernard said of the religious life. In it:

1. "Men lead a purer life.
2. "They fall into sin less often.
3. "If they do fall, the fall is less serious.
4. "They rise again more easily.
5. "They walk more cautiously.
6. "They enjoy more tranquil rest.
7. "Their souls are more abundantly watered with the dews of grace and the favors of heaven.
8. "They make satisfaction to God, and avoid purgatory more easily.
9. "They die with more confidence and resignation.
10. "They are more gloriously crowned in heaven.

"This," he says, "is the decalogue of our Lady's Sodality; these are the ten great privileges she grants to all those who practice faithfully what they promise when they are enrolled in the Sodality."

56. "Litany for the Conversion of America" (1908)

Missions, similar to Protestant revivals, were an important part of Catholic life in Europe beginning in the Counter-Reformation. Since the United States was technically a mission territory for the Catholic Church until 1908, the conversion of unchurched Catholics, Protestants, and non-Christians ranked high on the list of priorities. Isaac Hecker's Paulists, among the earliest religious orders to be founded in the United States, were dedicated to mission work, and their fervor was stoked by high-profile conversions such as that of

Hecker himself and of his contemporary, Orestes Brownson. Through their organization, the Catholic Missionary Union, the Paulists ran the Apostolic Mission House in Washington, D.C., where beginning in 1904 priests were trained in mission techniques and then sent to apostolates in many American dioceses. In its first decade its graduates, supported not by local bishops but by the Missionary Union, gave almost 2,500 missions to both Catholics and Protestants, and claimed as many as 25,000 converts a year. This litany was prayed at the AMH every day, and reached a wider audience when the Divine Word Fathers published it in 1914.

Lord, have mercy on us.
Christ, have mercy on us.
Lord, have mercy on us.
Christ, hear us.
Christ, graciously hear us.
God the Father, Creator of the world, have mercy on America.
God the Son, Redeemer of mankind, have mercy, etc.
God the Holy Ghost, perfector of the elect,
Holy Trinity, One God,
Holy Mary, conceived without sin, Pray for America.
Holy Angels, guardians of the souls of this people,
St. Michael, Prince of the church,
St. Gabriel, glorious messenger of Our Saviour's Incarnation,
St. Raphael, faithful guide of those who have lost their way,
St. John the Baptist, precursor of the Messiah and great example of
     penance,
St. Peter, prince of the Apostles and supreme pastor of Christ's
     sheep,
St. Paul, doctor of the Gentiles,
St. Augustine of Canterbury, apostle of the English,
St. Patrick, apostle of the Irish,
St. Boniface, apostle of the Germans,
St. Anscar, apostle of the Scandinavians,
SS. Cyril and Methodius, apostles of the Slavonians,
St. Francis Xavier, apostle of the Indies and the Far East,
St. Peter Claver, apostle of the Negroes,
All ye holy apostles of the nations.
St. Francis de Sales, patron of convert-makers,
St. Rose of Lima, first flower of American sanctity,

St. Turibius, glorious shepherd of the souls of the people,

St. Francis Solano, great apostle of the Western races,

All ye holy missionaries to the American people,

Be merciful, Spare us, O Lord.

Be merciful, Graciously hear us, O Lord.

From the consequences of our sins, O Lord, deliver America.

From the spirit of pride and apostasy, O Lord, etc.

From the spirit of hypocrisy, worldliness, and sacrilege,

From presumption and self-conceit,

From schism, heresy, and all blindness of heart,

From gluttony, drunkenness, and all uncleanness,

By Thy compassion on the multitude,

We sinners, We beseech Thee, hear us.

That it may please Thee to hasten the conversion of our country, and unite it to the ancient faith and communion of Thy Church, We beseech, etc.

That it may please Thee particularly to convert our relations, friends, and benefactors,

That it may please Thee to strengthen timid souls to be faithful to conscience,

That it may please Thee to give them grace boldly to take the step that leads from darkness to light,

That it may please Thee to inspire many apostolic vocations,

That it may please Thee to give all Thy priests a special grace for making converts,

That it may please Thee to fill Thy people with an ardent zeal for gaining souls,

That it may please Thee to inspire us all with zeal for the apostolate of prayer,

That it may please Thee to preserve the Catholics of this land from all sin of scandal,

That it may please Thee to convert the American people,

Son of God, Good Shepherd of souls,

Lamb of God, Who takst away the sins of the world, Spare us, O Lord.

Lamb of God, Who takst away the sins of the world, Graciously hear us, O Lord.

Lamb of God, Who takst away the sins of the world, Have mercy on us, O Lord.

Christ, hear us. Christ, graciously hear us. . . .

Look down, O Lord, with an eye of compassion on all those souls who, under the name of Christians, are yet far astray from Thy unity and truth, and wander in the paths of error and schism. Oh, bring the American people back to Thee and to Thy Church, we humbly beseech Thee. Dispel their darkness by Thy heavenly light. Remove their prejudices by the brightness of Thy convincing truth. Take away from them the spirit of obstinacy and pride and give them a meek and docile heart. Inspire them with a strong desire to find out Thy truth, and a strong grace to embrace it in spite of the opposition of the world, the flesh and the devil. We humbly pray Thee to raise up for them Catholic friends, whose burning zeal shall instruct them, and whose holy lives shall edify them, that all may be converted to Thy true faith, O Lord, who livest and reignest, world without end. Amen.

57. "The Passion Play of the West" (1910)

The Catholic Church in the United States has traditionally been a church of immigrants, with English, French, and Spanish colonists followed by Irish, German, Italian, Slavic, Hispanic, and Southeast Asian waves. Each group has brought its own devotional practices from home, retaining a strong cultural-religious identity even as it assimilated into "American" culture, and even as the various traditions cross-fertilized within the church. Although today we are familiar with the elaborate passion plays staged during Holy Week by Latino Catholics in the Southwest, these dramas have a long history in the American Church. Deriving ultimately from medieval liturgical dramas, they became especially popular in Germany; a German Catholic Franciscan imported the tradition, including a living crucifixion, to San Francisco several years after the 1906 earthquake that almost destroyed the city.

The co-ordination between pictorial religion and the masses is so well established that it would be mere futility to deny that the average man is more largely influenced by what he sees than by what he hears. . . . This faculty of visual remembrance is most apparent in the emotional and therefore plastic mind; and as an evidence of its use in the uplifting of mankind may be instanced the recent production of that mighty and majestic drama, the Passion Play, enacted at the San Francisco Coliseum, consuming four nights in its recital, and witnessed by audiences which filled the vast structure to its doors.

On the largest stage ever built west of Chicago, erected in the fashion of a central stage and two smaller flanking ones—a device adapted from the German dramas and used in the famous play at Oberammergau—the twenty-one acts of the Franciscan drama were presented. Twenty-five thousand dollars is the estimated cost of this stupendous production, to perfect which one hundred characters took part, three hundred supernumeraries aided, and a chorus of two hundred voices, led by an orchestra of forty pieces, furnished the musical setting. A net of finest piano wire was stretched from side to side of the great building, to further the acoustic properties, and scenery and costumes of historical accuracy filled in the impressive picture of Jerusalem at night, the wonderfully beautiful opening scene of the play. . . .

The first act of the play proper pictures the entrance of Christ into Jerusalem, with King Solomon also entering on the left, the city in its entirety being shown on the right.

The return of the prodigal son and the dining hall of Simon form the main features of the second act. . . . The impressive scene of the last supper and the sacrifice of Melchisedec mark the fourth act, and in the fifth, Judas sells the Saviour for thirty pieces of silver, while on the flanking stage the boy Joseph is being sold into captivity by his brothers. . . .

Ending this stupendous and wonderful presentation of the solemn scenes and incidents of Holy Week come the pictures of the crucifixion, the lonely burial, the triumphant resurrection and the sublime ascension. This magnificent and dramatic culmination, presenting the Saviour of mankind in all the agony of His tremendous sacrifice on the cross, made such an impression on the vast audience, breathless in their realization of its overwhelming import, that one great sigh arose from the thousands assembled, as if from a single throat. The most sublime sight of the ages—He Who died to save a world—was before their eyes, and, beyond that sigh of horror, the immense auditorium was silent as the rock-hewn tomb.

A great and tragic darkness overspreads the stage. An earthquake rends the ground. Deep and solemn peals of thunder weight the quivering air. The mob flees terror-stricken. The Saviour groans aloud. Death strikes the pierced body. Over the stricken face a luminous light softly glows. The light surrounds Mary Magdalen embracing the foot of the cross. A centurion, grim and harsh, thrusts a naked spear into the yet bleeding side. Joseph of Arimathea comes forward and asks the body of the persecutors. This granted, he bears the Christ tenderly away.

The Passion Play of the West is the production of Father Josaphat

Kraus, of the Franciscan Order. The drama, as originally planned, was to have been a totally different affair from what it came to be at the end. Father Kraus . . . wanted to reach the hearts of men, and he conceived the idea of presenting this sublime spectacle, rightly judging that the best way of influencing mankind was by the appeal through the emotions. It was to have been produced in the parish hall, and probably not more than a score of persons outside the congregation of the church would have known anything about it. But from a small beginning sprang one of the mightiest and most powerful stage presentations San Francisco has ever seen; a presentation that drew thousands night after night at a time when the gayest and merriest fete the city has witnessed was nightly going on, to sit awestricken and reverent, beholding the presentation of the story that has run through nineteen centuries and whose power never fails. Night after night men gathered before that great and often-darkened stage; night after night tears coursed silently down rough and gentle faces; night after night groans and choking sobs were heard on all sides of the crowded house; night after night men wrung each other's hands without a word of speech and went their way feeling in dumb fashion the uplifting power of Father Kraus' drama, and night after night the mighty truths there presented found an echo in many a heart to remain forever. . . . The musical setting for this masterpiece of Father Kraus was arranged by Father Peter Huesges, who made careful and appropriate selections from the compositions of Palestrina, Rossini, Handel, Gounod and Mendelssohn, and blended these into a score of remarkable unity and fitness. Some few of Father Huesges' own compositions of a fine and high order were interwoven into the themes chosen, and the least that can be said in praise of the musical factor is that it harmonized perfectly with the meaning and solemnity of the biblical incidents, enhancing and supporting them in a devotional and wholly satisfying manner. . . .

58. "Youth and Catholic Leadership" (1936)

In 1927 Pius XI defined Catholic Action as "the participation of the laity in the apostolate of the hierarchy." It is an umbrella term covering a number of organized lay apostolates which sought to exert a Catholic influence on society at large during the pre- and post-war periods. In the United States this general movement had the support of the National Catholic Welfare Council, the episcopal organization that preceded the United States Conference of Catholic Bishops. The laity were encouraged to develop a spiritual foundation and to express their piety through working to transform the world they lived in. Faith, Catholic Action leaders insisted, was not just for Sundays and private devotions; it ought to influence life in the secular world as well, not just for men and women, but (as this article describes) also for young people.

The Catholic Church today, probably as never before in her history, needs ... the growth of leaders into leadership all through their life in all parts of America's life and of the life of Catholics. It is crucial for Church and Country.

What was it that put the palsy on so many fine young Catholic men and women—born leaders—who a generation ago started out hopefully and bravely? ... Too many have slumped into mediocrity. Too many never grew. Too many have gone wrong. The reason seems to be (and the lesson is before us now to read) that while emphasis has been put, it has not been emphasis enough to put in a time like ours, upon an age-old truth of our Faith and of human nature. *Our Faith is to guide all our life and all our actions.* It is not narrow. It embraces all the actual things and all the possibilities in our nature, in our thoughts and deeds and in our surroundings. If it does not so live in persons' lives, then their lives become deformed and stunted and decay.

For leadership, here, embraces every phase of life. It means leadership in one's own work, whatever it is, to organize it and make it serve all the others who join in doing it and all who use the commodities or the services which it provides. Pius XI draws an analogy between an economic order, that would thus serve the common good, and the Mystical Body, itself. He enjoins us to create that order. We have been told over and over again that as Catholics we are thus obligated. But some way it has not penetrated enough of us. ... Many Catholics in all positions see only at intervals, or rarely, or not at all, that their work in all its conditions is subject to a law of God which they must try to live up to.

We glory in the ancient guilds and in the economic morality that they enforced. For our own time many in every occupation, and in every class within every occupation, seem content with paganism or at best are hazily restive. They should be leaders. They have, or have had, ability. They have, or have had, courage. They have still the Faith to guide them and strengthen them. They turn their backs or look somewhere else. And the world goes drunkenly on. ...

Our Catholic Responsibility

The development of talents is a responsibility and a duty. There is the duty of the individuals who possess the talents—and all of us possess them. There is the duty of parents, of the whole group, the whole body of Catholics, to help the individuals in their development. The burying of talents for the talents to rot and the stunting of talents for them to grow crooked and all awry is an offense against God and man. The human beings who possess the talents themselves become all twisted and eventually rot; and God is not glorified and man does not show the glory of God.

Leadership of youth by youth is one phase to be considered under the heading "Youth and Leadership." There is also that same leadership—these same persons—growing older and developing to meet the issues and the events as these change and as the methods change with the years. Youth is a time of idealism. Even youth's sins are a perverted search for the good, the true thing, and the beautiful. In helping the young to the opportunities to create the good, the true, and the beautiful and to lead and to share in leadership in so doing, the range of interests of the youth is found to be far wider than is usually suspected. The range of interests and activities becomes larger as children pass their 'teens and enter their twenties.

They are to take their part, and a growing part as their lives unfold, in creating a Catholic civilization; in restoring all things in Christ; in measuring their lives, opportunities, and environment by the standards of Christ and His Church; in working directly, for the salvation of their own souls and those of others; in working indirectly, to the same end and for the glory of God through fashioning a social and governmental order and a whole culture in accord with God's laws and the Christian spirit. They should become habitual to this when young, so that when young they will do their smaller work well and when older do their larger work better.

The home has its place in the development of this type of leadership. The school has its place. Mass and the sacraments and the liturgical round of the Church's year have their great place. But more and more in our day the necessity is being seen, again, of the place of the lay organization,— young people's organizations and organizations of adults.

"Youth and leadership" has a special meaning in relation to the lay organization. For the lay organization in Catholic Action, at work with and under the Hierarchy, gives youth the widest range of opportunities for leadership and joint action. The activities of the newer youth organizations that are now rapidly being formed are going far beyond the traditional emphasis upon recreation (although that rightly continues) and the traditional activity of the sodalities. Older organizations are modifying their programs. The trend is toward recognizing that the young are to take their part now, and to grow through sharing now, in the whole work of restoring all things in Christ . . . the chief aim is for the youth organizations to act in the consciousness that the Faith embraces all life.

Their formation of a right leadership will depend upon their honesty and thoroughness in facing American life in the spirit of true Catholics. There is no disguising the difficulty of this. And in attaining results, the home, the school and the teaching, guiding and sacramental power of the Church will be used to the utmost.

59. WILLIAM LEONARD, S.J., ON THE *MISSA RECITATA* IN WARTIME (1943–45)

During World War II, hundreds of Catholic priests became chaplains in the U.S. Armed Forces. Leonard, a Jesuit who served in the South Pacific, found that the young men under his care tended to compartmentalize their lives into "religious" and "secular" parts. Feeling that part of the problem might be the traditional style of the Latin Mass (see No. 52), Leonard began experimenting with the "Missa recitata," the dialogue mass, which gained great popularity in liturgical reform circles prior to Vatican II.

. . . The Army offered me an excellent proving-ground for some of my theories. One night after chow, I gathered some twenty of my best-disposed men.

"You've been listening patiently while I've been explaining the Mass," I said, "and I'm grateful. But now it's time to do something. If we Christians are a corporate unit, we ought to pray together, and our best prayer is the Mass. So from now on we're going to recite the Mass together. I asked you to come here tonight so that we could rehearse it a little. . . . OK?"

There was much nodding of heads.

"Good," I went on. "Let's try it. I'll begin the prayers at the foot of the altar, and you make the responses. Page 5 in your Stedman missals. Ready? *Introibo ad altare Dei . . .*"

There was a silence, and I looked around questioningly.

"What's the matter?"

"You mean in *Latin*, Father?"

"Sure," I said easily. "If those little altar boys at home can do it you should be able to. No problem, really."

Well, they tried. They stumbled and fell, repeatedly, over *laetificat* and *confitebor* and *vivificabis*, but they went gamely on, and I told myself that all they needed was practice. The odd part of it was that not one of them asked the perfectly obvious question, "What's the point of this? Why recite words when you don't know what they mean? Can you pray when you don't understand what you're saying?" It was just as well that they didn't ask because I couldn't have answered them—then.

The dialogue Mass never really caught on in New Guinea, in spite of my encouragement and the good will of my congregation. At the time I don't think I ever grasped how utterly unintelligible it was to the men. I had begun studying Latin in 1921, twenty-three years before . . . I loved it. I think I even believed that there were things you could express in Latin which English could not express. But by the time we reached Manila my disillusionment was complete, and I instituted a dialogue Mass in which the congregation responded in English. . . .

I remember a lieutenant-colonel who came up after Mass one Sunday to introduce himself. He was a convert, he told me, and wanted to say how much he had liked the sermon.

"Well, thanks," I said. "How do you like the dialogue Mass?"

"Oh, gosh, Father," he answered. "I was hoping you wouldn't ask me that."

"OK," I said. "Try not to make up your mind about it yet. Just keep doing it for a while."

Three months later he came up again to say good-bye. He had been ordered home.

"And by the way, Father, I've changed my mind completely about the dialogue Mass. I just hope my pastor back home in California will start it."

. . . More and more, the question of language in the liturgy bothered me. Every time I offered Mass I was conscious of how the *plebs sancta* was excluded. Once, after another priest had celebrated while I led the dialogue, I asked him to slow down during the Offertory and Canon; I myself could not keep pace with him. He was a devoted priest, but had no awareness whatever of the people's share. . . . I was learning day by day how irrelevant the liturgy was considered, even by professional liturgists, to the practice of virtue, to the apostolate, to the social mission of the Church, to the attainment of Christian holiness in oneself and others. After the War I encountered the same attitude among priests of outstanding intelligence and zeal. . . .

60. U.S. CATHOLIC BISHOPS, "REGULATIONS ON FAST AND ABSTINENCE" (1951)

On a day of fasting, Roman Catholics eat one full meal (which may include meat) and two very small, meatless meals, usually in the morning and evening. On a day of abstinence, they refrain from all meat. These two ascetic practices have traditionally been required of the faithful on specific days; prior to Vatican II these were relatively numerous, and American Catholics were well known for eating fish rather than meat on Fridays. Fasting and abstinence regulations are promulgated by the bishops (American Catholics now have only two mandatory days of fasting, Ash Wednesday and Good Friday, while Lenten Fridays are days of abstinence). In 1951, the U.S. Catholic bishops issued a guide for fasting and abstinence that, while conforming to canon law of the time, also represents a more personal approach to the matter: instead of precisely specifying the quantities of food per person, Catholics are to adjust their diets according to their needs, provided they stay within the guidelines for fasting and abstinence.

To foster the spirit of penance and of reparation for sin, to encourage self-denial and mortification, and to guide her children in the footsteps of Our Divine Savior, Holy Mother Church imposes by law the observance of fast and abstinence.

In accordance with the provisions of Canon Law, as modified through the use of special faculties granted by the Holy See, we herewith publish the following regulations:

On Abstinence:

Everyone over 7 years of age is bound to observe the law of abstinence.

Complete abstinence is to be observed on Fridays, Ash Wednesday, the Vigils of the Assumption and Christmas, and on Holy Saturday morning. On days of complete abstinence meat and soup or gravy made from meat may not be used at all.

Partial abstinence is to be observed on Ember Wednesdays and Saturdays and on the Vigils of Pentecost and All Saints. On days of partial abstinence meat and soup or gravy made from meat may be taken only *once* a day at the principal meal.

On Fast:

Everyone over 21 and under 59 years of age is also bound to observe the law of fast.

The days of fast are the weekdays of Lent, Ember Days, the Vigils of Pentecost, the Assumption, All Saints, and Christmas.

On days of fast only one full meal is allowed. Two other meatless meals, sufficient to maintain strength, may be taken according to each one's needs; but together they should not equal another full meal.

Meat may be taken at the principal meal on a day of fast except on Fridays, Ash Wednesday and the Vigils of the Assumption and Christmas.

Eating between meals is not permitted; but liquids, including milk and fruit juice, are allowed.

When health or ability to work would be seriously affected, the law does not oblige. In doubt concerning fast or abstinence, a parish priest or confessor should be consulted.

We earnestly exhort the faithful during the periods of fast and abstinence to attend daily Mass; to receive Holy Communion often; to take part more frequently in exercises of piety; to give generously to works of religion and charity; to perform acts of kindness towards the sick, the aged, and the poor; to practice voluntary self-denial especially regarding alcoholic drink and worldly amusements; and to pray more fervently, particularly for the intentions of the Holy Father.

61. PATRICK PEYTON & THE FAMILY ROSARY CRUSADE (1951)

Patrick Peyton (1909–1992) was born in Ireland, and as a teenager emigrated to the United States, where he was ordained in 1941. Devoted to the Blessed Virgin, he immediately began a ministry of preaching and prayer that made use of radio and television (along with old-fashioned local missions) to promote family prayer, especially of the Rosary. He famously—and frequently —proclaimed that "the family that prays together, stays together." His Family Rosary Crusade became a vast international organization that distributed free rosaries and instructional booklets to millions, while soliciting their pledges to pray the rosary daily with their families. In these two excerpts from his 1951 book The Ear of God, *Fr. Peyton first gives a few instructions on the nature of the rosary, and then describes a local "field crusade."*

[The Rosary]

The Rosary is far more indeed than a multiplication of Hail Marys, Our Fathers, and the variable prayers that we add to it. It has an essence of its own, and therefore a power of its own. To this power, it is true, is added the power of the prayers it contains. But the power of the Rosary cannot be calculated by arithmetic. The only measure of its power that we have is the history of marvels it has wrought. And although many popes besides Pius IX have recommended the Rosary to us in the strongest terms, its power is attested by an authority far greater even than theirs; for we say the Rosary on the advice of Mary herself.

Why it is so powerful we can only guess. . . .

The Rosary proper twines, in a garland, the two greatest prayers—the Our Father, the perfect prayer given to us by Jesus, and the lovely and mystic Hail Mary; yet the Rosary surpasses both these prayers together. It includes them and adds an original contribution from each sayer, an expression of each sayer's very nature, belief, and devotion. It is meditative prayer joined to vocal prayer, its soul an empathic participation in the greatest events in religion. Then what a wonderful device it is. It is more than prayer in the usual sense of the word: it is a kind of adventure in which we offer up a spiritual experience. When you look at the rosary in your hand, how simple it appears, that little string of beads, yet how far that short chain reaches, what a cosmos it encircles, how closely it binds us to God and to Mary: the single richest treasure in the Vatican—there, in your hand. . . .

No one must fall into the error of supposing that there is anything mystical about the number of prayers in the Rosary, nor about their numerical arrangement, nor about the mere beads. With all the mysticism inherent in the Rosary as a prayer, and in the prayers that are parts of it, the beads evolved from nothing else but devotion and convenience. . . .

It is a sublime spiritual experience for anyone. It is a school of religion which grades from kindergarten to heaven. This is why it is a perfect prayer for a family group. And it is a prayer for all states of the soul. It has the bells of Christmas in it, the solemn tolling of Good Friday, the rising sun of Easter. It has contrition, comfort, hope, and promise. From beginning to end it is all God's love and Mary's. And the richest single treasure in the Vatican can be had for nothing in any home.

[The Organization of the Family Rosary Crusade]

A field crusade of the Family Rosary, as the blueprint has been extended and refined since the crusade in London [Ontario], covers a period of nine weeks—four of preparation and five of active crusade. Not to tire the reader with the intricacies of its draftsmanship, this is but a broad outline of the plan:

A central office staffed partially with Family Rosary personnel and partially with help obtained locally is established in the area where the drive is to be held. The ordinary of each diocese appoints one or more priests to work full time with the crusade directors. Priests and laymen also are appointed as diocesan leaders, associate chairmen, and committee chairmen. Every pastor takes a census of his flock, including those who may have strayed. Then he appoints laymen as parish leaders, and these men are organized in divisions and teams consisting of one man for each five families in the parish. A crusade newspaper, *The Time,* is published for each week of the active crusade. Pastors preach the Family Rosary at every Mass each Sunday. In addition, special devotions such as Family Rosary triduums and novena services are arranged in all churches. Luncheons, dinners, and public rallies are held. Schools and hospitals are organized. And, meanwhile, every medium of publicity is employed—radio, diocesan and secular press, billboards, signs on streetcars and busses, car stickers, letter seals, even advertising in motion-picture theaters. The campaign is aimed at all levels, and the object is to make the crusade inescapable, so that even if a man does not read about it in his newspaper, hear about it over his radio or in his church, or see it advertised on the street, yet he will discover the Family Rosary in his morning mail or find his child entered in a Family Rosary essay contest in school. And during the final week canvassers go two by two from door to door with the Family Rosary pledge (not binding under pain of sin) :

I solemnly pledge the daily Family Rosary that our heavenly mother, Mary, may guard and protect my home.

So widespread is the love of Mary that nearly all doors are opened at once. Indeed, in every parish where crusades have so far been held, non-

Catholics also have asked to join in the pledge, particularly in cases of mixed marriage. In one parish alone, thirty-one non-Catholics pledged the daily Family Rosary. And out of the few cases where Catholics have rejected the pledge, there have come some touching stories of submission. There was, for example, the fallen-away Catholic, a salesman, who refused to sign. A week later he went down to the parish rectory and told the pastor: "Give me that pledge; I haven't been able to live with myself." And after he had signed: "Now I want to go to Confession." For although the canvassers go two by two, One unseen goes with them, and although the salesman had turned the two away, the Third had stayed behind and brought the lost sheep home. . . . As this is written, four and a half million pledges of the daily Family Rosary have been obtained.

62. American Catholics from World War II to the 1970s: Photographs from the Collections of the Library of Congress

An African-American Catholic parish on the South Side of Chicago, March 1942. Photographer: Jack Delano. Source: Library of Congress.

Top: The procession of the Blessed Sacrament at High Mass on Easter in a Polish Catholic church in Buffalo, New York, April 1943. Photographer: Marjory Collins. Source: Library of Congress.

Bottom: Mass on Memorial Day in the Lithuanian Cemetery of Pittsburgh, Pennsylvania, June 1943. Photographer: Marjory Collins. Source: Library of Congress.

Top: Chaplain Lawrence Calkins gives communion to two Detroit brothers during the invasion of Iwo Jima, February–March, 1945. The two (a marine and a navy ensign) had not met since the first months of the war. Source: U.S. Marine Corps.

Bottom: Cardinal Spellman says Mass at the Polo Grounds during a Family Rosary Crusade rally, 1952. Photographer: Associated Press. Source: Library of Congress, *New York World-Telegram* and the *Sun* Newspaper Photograph Collection.

The Knights of Columbus march in the Saint Patrick's Day Parade, Detroit, carrying sights with Irish family names. Ethnic pride has marked American Catholicism throughout its history—as, for example, with national parishes, March 1967. Photographer: Associated Press. Source: Library of Congress, *New York World-Telegram* and the *Sun* Newspaper Photograph Collection.

OPPOSITE PAGE:

Top: Nuns clamming on Long Island, 6 September 1957. Photographer: Toni Frissell. Source: Library of Congress.

Middle and bottom: Carl J. Breitfeller, chaplain of prisons in the Washington, D.C., area, saying Mass at the chapel of Christ the Prisoner at Lorton Prison, Virginia, 7 August 1964. Photographer: Douglas R. Gilbert. Source: Douglas R. Gilbert, photographer, *Look* Magazine Collection, Library of Congress, Prints and Photographs Division.

63. "How the 'People of God' Want to Worship" (1964)

As a part of the general reform movement before, during, and after Vatican II, the Christian Family Movement played a significant role in understanding the desires of the American Catholic laity through extensive surveys of its members. The question of the liturgical use of the vernacular had been discussed for decades (see No. 59 and 62), along with other potential changes. The largely middle-class young couples who formed the backbone of the CFM met regularly in their homes to discuss faith, practice, and the social issues of the day. This unusually active and well-informed group of Catholics contributed enthusiastically to a survey on liturgical reform in 1964; many of their desires would be met in the next few years.

"The liturgy must arouse in our people a real and intimate involvement in the life of the Church. The lay person must encounter Christ in the Liturgy so that he can become like Christ." This is a quote from one of the 58 reports that form the basis of this article—suggestions for liturgical reform by CFM members across the continent.

Background

Meeting 12 of the 1963–64 Inquiry Program proposed a parish study night on the Reform of the Liturgy. Having come to appreciate the value of worship as an aid to living a personal apostolic life, CFM members were asked to turn their attention to the form of worship as they had known it. In doing so they were to follow the lead of Vatican II where determined efforts to revitalize the Liturgy had recently been distilled into the now famous Constitution on the Sacred Liturgy.

This close look at the existing forms of worship was to seek to answer the same questions that confronted the bishops at the Council. . . . Each parish group was requested to list, in order of importance, those changes in the Liturgy that they would like to see introduced. . . .

Looking back now, a few months later, one can see how closely CFM was attuned to events taking place at the Council. . . . Bits of information were available through the ordinary news channels, of course, but full knowledge of the Constitution's contents was not widespread. Thus, it was a source of satisfaction to clergy and laity alike to see how many changes suggested in these reports—from a good cross section of U.S. and Canadian Catholics—have been fully anticipated by the Constitution. The Holy Spirit is indeed operating on all levels of today's Church.

Fifty-eight reports were received from parishes as widely separated as Sacramento, Calif., Providence, R.I., Ontario, Canada, and Miami, Fla. More than 2000 persons took part in the survey. The following are the changes in the Liturgy which these laymen feel would be most beneficial.

More Vernacular

Ninety per cent considered use of the vernacular the most important step towards more meaningful participation in the Liturgy. Overriding themes seemed to be:

"We want to worship in a language we can understand."

"We can repeat Latin, but cannot think in Latin."

"It is difficult to explain the use of Latin to Protestants, because we do not understand it either."

Some advanced that the Mass, Sacraments, and sacramentals (blessings) be conducted entirely in the vernacular. Others desired partial retention of the Latin. Holy week and funerals were singled out as services that would especially profit from a greater use of the vernacular.

Face the People

Highly favored was Mass facing the people, the use of a lector and commentator, a homily on the Mass, and more singing, particularly of hymns. If these suggestions were to be spiritually fruitful, it was noted time and again, the celebrant would have to make adjustments in his accustomed tone and his pace in reciting the prayers.

Make It Simple

The trend of the reports was definitely towards simplicity, avoiding duplications in the recital of Mass prayers by priest and by people. Requests for fixed dates for movable feasts, for a standardized missal, and for elimination of pulpit announcements, reflected the same yearning for the simple and uncluttered.

Some mentioned fewer statues and better taste in religious art. In addition it was suggested that less feasts of saints and more ferial days would serve the liturgical year more fruitfully.

64. Father Gommar De Pauw, J.C.D., "The Catholic Traditionalist Manifesto" (1964)

Not every American Catholic was thrilled with the liturgical changes that followed the Second Vatican Council. While the vast majority eventually reconciled themselves to the new style of communal worship, a small percentage continued to hold that the traditional Latin Tridentine mass (see No. 52) was the only valid manner of celebrating the Eucharist. Some members of this diverse group were so convinced of the new mass's illicitness that they eventually found themselves in schism with the Church, forming breakaway groups such as the Society of St. Pius X. Fr. Gommar De Pauw (1918–2005), a Belgian-born priest from Baltimore, founded the Catholic Traditionalist Movement in New York in 1964, shortly after releasing this manifesto.

Whereas the recently promulgated Constitution on the Church clearly states that "public opinion" has a vital role to play within the Catholic Church; Whereas the Catholic laity, according to this Ecumenical Council document, "should openly reveal . . . their needs and desires with that freedom and confidence which is fitting for children of God and brothers in Christ . . .";

Whereas the same Council document teaches that the Catholic laity "are permitted and sometimes even obliged to express their opinion on those things which concern the good of the Church . . .";

Whereas it cannot be denied that the new liturgical reforms and especially the changes in the Mass were introduced without the average Catholic man and woman being consulted;

Whereas these liturgical changes were not called for by "public opinion," but were rather subtly extorted from our Bishops by a small but well organized minority of self-appointed so-called liturgical experts, isolated in their ivory towers;

Whereas the greater number of the Catholic laity gratefully recognize true spiritual advantages in the partial use of English in the celebration of the Mass and the administration of certain sacraments, but at the same time wish to preserve some Latin in the Liturgy as an external sign of our unity with fellow Catholics all over the world;

Whereas the ever increasing use of the Latin-English missal by the laity and the inspiring success of the Latin Dialogue Mass in many parishes has shown how easily our Catholic people, if intelligently urged by their priests to do so, cope with the Latin;

Whereas the "active participation" in the Mass, introduced since November 1964, did not meet with the enthusiastic approval which certain press releases wishfully described, but instead generated sentiments ranging from passive resignation to outright resentment;

Whereas the principal fruit of the progressivistic agitation in the Liturgy and elsewhere in the Church has been the steadily increasing polarization of the radical minority and the traditionalist majority among God's people whose Christ-intended visible unity is thus becoming less and less apparent;

Whereas the liturgical progressivism is increasingly and alarmingly appearing to many as only the first phase of a broader scheme intent to "protestantize" the entire Catholic Church;

We, loyal and loving sons and daughters of our Holy Mother the Catholic Church, believing to represent the sentiments of the majority of American Catholics, urge all Catholic men and women who share the views expressed in this manifesto, to join us in forwarding to our beloved spiritual leaders, the Catholic Bishops of the United States, the divinely appointed guardians of our Catholic Faith, the following suggestions which we respectfully submit for their urgent consideration:

1. That, calling a halt to any further progress of vernacularism, English as now used in read Masses be allowed to continue while at the same time keeping our sung Masses entirely in Latin; that Latin be made a mandatory subject in all Catholic High Schools and continue to be recognized as the liturgical and theological language of the Latin rite Church and the supranational sign of unity among Catholics of various nations and cultures.

2. That in the seminaries where our future priests are being trained Latin regain the place of honor assigned to it by all the Popes of modern times, and that especially the open defiance of Pope John XXIII's apostolic constitution "Veterum Sapientia," now prevailing in many American seminaries, be immediately replaced with sensibly adapted but still obedient compliance.

3. That the permissive nature of the Liturgy Constitution of Vatican II be safeguarded on local levels so as to eliminate any form of regimented compulsion from innovations which this Constitution never made mandatory but simply permitted as "privileges," and that, consequently, priests and people be allowed to pursue the defense and promotion of the use of the traditional liturgical language and customs with the same freedom given to the proponents of vernacularism.

4. That the centuries-sanctioned liturgical Latin form of the Mass not be banned, but, if not given full priority, at least be allowed to co-exist with the new vernacular forms, so that priests and people be given full option and adequate opportunity to celebrate and assist at Mass in the traditional Latin form on Sundays as well as weekdays.

5. That the new methods of group participation at Mass not be made mandatory at all public Masses, but that individuals be allowed, to participate silently if they so desire, with such silent participation being recognized as equally fruitful and as praiseworthy as any form of group participation.

6. That in the new methods of community participation and especially in the field of sacred music and of architecture our Catholic heritage be preserved, and that strict control be exercised to eliminate and to prevent any features which are not conducive to preserve our Catholic identity, especially those practices or hymns marked by non-Catholic overtones or themes savoring of religious indifferentism or egalitarianism.

7. That the character of the Mass as the supreme act of worship to the most holy Trinity and the renewal of Christ's sacrifice on Calvary through the sacerdotal mediation of His ordained priests be duly emphasized, and that special caution be exercised to prevent the secondary social aspects of the Mass from being affected by the error of homocentricity or an exaggerated concept of the so-called lay-priesthood.

8. That the real presence of Christ in our tabernacles continue to be hailed as our greatest and uniquely Catholic possession; that reverences to the Blessed Sacrament, such as genuflections, will remain mandatory; that the custom of kneeling for the reception of Holy Communion will continue to be upheld; that the theologically less expressive communion formula "The Body of Christ" be replaced with "The living Christ"; that especially for sanitary reasons, Communion under both species not be introduced; and that our traditionally reverent customs in the handling of the altarbreads, destined for consecration, be preserved.

9. That our eminently Catholic devotion to the Blessed Virgin Mary,

mother of our divine Savior and mother of His Church, be continued and encouraged along lines derived from our traditional and theologically sound axiom "Through Mary to Jesus."

10. That respectfully mature loyalty and filial obedience to the Supreme Roman Pontiff as Christ's Vicar on earth and the visible Head of His Church continue to be preached and practiced by all Catholics, and that all open or veiled efforts to impede the practical acceptance of the Holy Father's supreme primacy over shepherds and faithful alike, will be effectively unmasked and vigorously met.

11. That our priests continue to live in celibacy and to wear their distinctive black street clothing with Roman collar, while our Sisters introduce only those dress changes that will still allow their uniform to remain indicative of their special dedicated position among God's people.

12. That, while truly respecting all non-Catholics who follow their conscience into what in candid honesty we must continue to call objective errors or partial truths, our bishops, priests, religious and laity alike renew their truly ecumenical efforts to proclaim the full unadulterated doctrine of Christ's Catholic Church in a world that desperately needs it.

65. Thomas Merton, "Fourth and Walnut Vision" (1966)

Thomas Merton (1915–1968) was one of the most important figures in postwar American Catholic spirituality. After a conventionally dissolute college career in England and at Columbia University, Merton—who had been studying medieval thought for some time and feeling an interior restlessness—converted to Catholicism and, several years later, became a monk at the Trappist Abbey of Gethsemeni in Kentucky. His first autobiography, The Seven Storey Mountain, *was published early in his monastic career and became an enormous bestseller; it portrays the young Merton as having finally found peace in the strict silence of the abbey. But Merton's intellectual restlessness led him, especially during the late 1950s and early 1960s, to question many of his earlier convictions. Although he remained a monk to the end of his life (he was accidentally killed while on a visit to Asia), he studied Buddhist as well as Christian mysticism, spoke out against racism, war, and social injustice, and corresponded widely with artists, intellectuals, and leftist Catholics. This excerpt from a 1966 book describes a vision he had on a rare trip out of the abbey, which was a part of his general growth into a more generous under-standing of what it meant to be holy, and what it meant to be human.*

In Louisville, at the corner of Fourth and Walnut, in the center of the shopping district, I was suddenly overwhelmed with the realization that I loved all those people, that they were mine and I theirs, that we could not be alien to one another even though we were total strangers. It was like waking from a dream of separateness, of spurious self-isolation in a special world, the world of renunciation and supposed holiness. The whole illusion of a separate holy existence is a dream. Not that I question the reality of my vocation, or of my monastic life: but the conception of "separation from the world" that we have in the monastery too easily presents itself as a complete illusion: the illusion that by making vows we become a different species of being, pseudo-angels, "spiritual men," men of interior life, what have you.

Certainly these traditional values are very real, but their reality is not of an order outside everyday existence in a contingent world, nor does it entitle one to despise the secular: though "out of the world" we are in the same world as everybody else, the world of the bomb, the world of race hatred, the world of technology, the world of mass media, big business, revolution, and all the rest. We take a different attitude to all these things, for we belong to God. Yet so does everybody else belong to God. We just happen to be conscious of it, and to make a profession out of this consciousness. But does that entitle us to consider ourselves different, or even *better,* than others? The whole idea is preposterous.

This sense of liberation from an illusory difference was such a relief and such a joy to me that I almost laughed out loud. And I suppose my happiness could have taken form in the words: "Thank God, thank God that I *am* like other men, that I am only a man among others." To think that for sixteen or seventeen years I have been taking seriously this pure illusion that is implicit in so much of our monastic thinking.

It is a glorious destiny to be a member of the human race, though it is a race dedicated to many absurdities and one which makes many terrible mistakes: yet, with all that, God Himself gloried in becoming a member of the human race. A member of the human race! To think that such a commonplace realization should suddenly seem like news that one holds the winning ticket in a cosmic sweepstake.

I have the immense joy of being *man,* a member of a race in which God Himself became incarnate. As if the sorrows and stupidities of the human condition could overwhelm me, now I realize what we all are. And if only everybody could realize this! But it cannot be explained. There is no way of telling people that they are all walking around shining like the sun.

This changes nothing in the sense and value of my solitude, for it is in fact the function of solitude to make one realize such things with a clarity that would be impossible to anyone completely immersed in the other cares, the other illusions, and all the automatisms of a tightly collective existence. My solitude, however, is not my own, for I see now how much it belongs to them—and that I have a responsibility for it in their regard, not just in my own. It is because I am one with them that I owe it to them to be alone, and when I am alone they are not "they" but my own self. There are no strangers!

Then it was as if I suddenly saw the secret beauty of their hearts, the depths of their hearts where neither sin nor desire nor self-knowledge can reach, the core of their reality, the person that each one is in God's eyes. If only they could all see themselves as they really are. If only we could see each other that way all the time. There would be no more war, no more hatred, no more cruelty, no more greed. . . . I suppose the big problem would be that we would fall down and worship each other. But this cannot be seen, only believed and "understood" by a peculiar gift.

66. Daniel Lowery, CSSR, "A 'Piety Void?'" (1966)

In 1965 the commentator Dan Herr published an article commenting on a number of currents in American church life in the wake of the first major successes of the liturgical reform movement as well as Vatican II. Among other things, Herr suggested that there was now a "piety void" in the lives of ordinary Catholics, who were ceasing to perform traditional devotions such as "visits to the Blessed Sacrament, devotional confession, novenas, missions, even retreats," although the new liturgy did not adequately fill their spiritual needs. Several months later, the Redemptorist Daniel Lowery responded to this charge of Herr's in the American Ecclesiastical Review.

Mr. Herr's statement twice refers to "many Catholics": "a 'piety void' in the lives of many Catholics" and "many Catholics feel a loss in their lives." He cites no empirical evidence, and I certainly can't cite any, but I have the impression that he is right in his estimate. My experience, and the experience of a number of priest friends, would prompt me to agree that "many Catholics" are involved.

It is noteworthy that the Catholics Mr. Herr refers to are not simply the "anti-liturgy" people. One would expect a "piety void" in the lives of those who are traumatized by the vernacular, fearful of the Pope's orthodoxy, and convinced that any change at all is the work of Satan. Apparently, though, a number of quite balanced people—people who like the new liturgy, conscientiously participate in it and even try to grasp more and more of the serious theology behind it—are also experiencing the "piety void."

In what is perhaps an understatement, Mr. Herr says that the Catholics who are aware of the void "are not happy about it." It seems to me that some of them are suffering deeply and others are quite confused. Some of the rigid traditionalists are certainly experiencing great anguish and even, in some cases, crises of faith. It is easy enough to laugh at such people; or to pity them. Either way, to confront them as individuals is to realize that they are suffering. Even the more balanced and progressive, though by no means as deeply disturbed as the traditionalists, are sometimes quite uneasy and perplexed. The current of this problem, it seems to me, runs deeper than some observers are willing to admit.

Schools of Thought

. . . The first school embraces those priests who would analyze the problem along these lines: "Yes, there is a 'piety void.' And I couldn't care less. In fact, it is a good thing. It is a sign of maturity among Catholics. It indicates that Catholics who have been brought up in an individualistic, formalistic, 'Jesus and I,' meritpiling Catholicism are finally growing up. There will be growing pains, of course, but these will pass. As the strong food of Vatican II gradually nourishes these people, they will have no difficulty at all with a 'piety void.'"

The second school includes those who might express themselves in this way: "Yes, there is a 'piety void.' And it's a shame. The people are confused, staggering, on the ropes. And all for no reason. Though the basic liturgical renewal is good and helpful, many other changes and opinions are the work of crackpots. Our job as priests is to place even stronger emphasis on the beautiful devotions and practices that have come down to us from our forefathers. If they were good enough for the saints, they ought to be good enough for us."

Expressing the divergent opinions in this unnuanced way may seem to make a caricature of them. Such is not my intention. Allowing for shades of opinion of both sides, I feel that these generalizations are fairly representative of the feelings of many priests.

I would like to submit that there is another approach, more balanced and realistic than any of the above. But before outlining it, I want to make some brief observations on the above opinions.

The first school (and apparently Mr. Herr would agree) contends that once the liturgy becomes completely renewed and once the people are really in tune with it, there will be no "piety void." The liturgy, in and of itself, will satisfy the people. I doubt this. I do not think that even an updated and flourishing liturgy will completely remove the "piety void" from the hearts of many Catholics. It seems to me that the history of religion testifies to the opposite. There is an observable tendency for people to come up with popular devotions and practices, even when the official worship is flourishing.

To take one example: The liturgy was flourishing in the early days of the Church. There was a rich Christian liturgy surrounding the burial of the dead. Yet many popular, quite non-liturgical devotions and practices grew up around Christian burial. These developments did not indicate that the people were ignorant of or opposed to the liturgy. They indicated, it seems to me, the very natural and normal tendency of worshipping man to intertwine the excellent and the ordinary, the official and the popular, the dogmatic and the sentimental. I do not think we have seen the ends of this tendency by any means.

The second school of thought makes the mistake of trying to "freeze" popular devotions and practices. It seems to forget that people, after all, instigate and develop popular devotions. But people are subject to their times, undergo many subtle psychological and sociological changes. What was a popular devotion for their forefathers, therefore, might not be a popular devotion for them. Or, what is more accurate, the basic devotion or practice might remain the same, but the approach to it may be quite different. Modern Catholics have a different approach from their ancestors.

To get back to my tertium quid proposal about the "piety void," I think there should be a renewal of popular devotions along with the liturgical renewal. There is no good reason why zealous priests cannot work towards a liturgical and non-liturgical updating at the same time. My proposal would emphasize the following points:

First of all, it is the responsibility of every priest to endorse the new liturgy intelligently and wholeheartedly. . . . Obviously included in the priest's responsibility is the obligation to instruct the people, in season and out of season, on the nature and importance of the liturgy. . . .

But secondly . . . there is no need to downgrade popular devotions. There is need, rather, to upgrade them: to make them harmonize with the liturgical seasons and accord as much as possible with the sacred liturgy, so that they are in some fashion derived from it and lead the people to it; to make them more flexible and more relevant to the people of our times, more in line with their aspirations and approaches.

I see no contradiction at all between these two emphases. I think that suffering, bewildered, confused Catholics would deeply appreciate this approach on the part of at least some priests.

To make my proposal more concrete, I will comment on the "popular, so-called pious devotions" listed by Mr. Herr.

1. Devotional Confession. Accurately speaking, the worthy reception of the sacrament of penance is not a popular devotion at all, but a liturgical celebration. Though I do not know why Mr. Herr included devotional confession in his list, I presume it has something to do with the fact that some priests have been discouraging the practice of frequent confession. The aim of these priests, as I understand it, is to offset a routine and mechanical approach to this sacrament.

The aim is certainly praiseworthy. But it seems to me that we have the opportunity today to take a more positive and dynamic approach to the problem. The Council has promised that "the rite and formulas for the sacrament of penance are to be revised so that they more clearly express both the nature and effect of the sacrament." While this revision is going on, there is much the individual priest can do to bring out the positive significance of this sacrament: an encounter with the merciful Christ and an entering into the death and resurrection of the Savior.

Surely, the people would appreciate a pastoral updating in the practice of giving penances. There are countless devout Catholics who long for a more imaginative and meaningful approach to sacramental penances. They are devoutly hoping that confessors will soon get over the "three Hail Marys" syndrome. Suiting the penance to the sin and to the real life of the penitent would do much to offset the problem of routine and formalism.

There is, in addition, the vast field of spiritual direction. Because of the shortage of priests and the heavy demands on their time, many Catholics hesitate even to ask a question of the confessor. Though one could argue that confession and spiritual direction are separate entities and should not be mixed, one could also suggest (and with solid historical backing) that much sound spiritual direction can be accomplished on the occasion of a confession of devotion. . . .

2. Visits to the Blessed Sacrament. One might argue that if there is a "piety void" here, the individual Catholic can blame no one but himself. After all, Christ is present in our Churches and the Churches are open. The Catholic who does not stop for a visit cannot blame a priest.

Or can he? Some of the sermonizing in this area has been less than dogmatically accurate, as Pope Paul's encyclical pointed out. And aside from the dogmatic aspects, there has been the insinuation that people who quietly visit the Blessed Sacrament are somehow being too individualistic in their piety and engaging in "comfortable" Catholicism. The assumption seems to be that those Catholics who make a habit of visiting the Church are the very ones who hide from the world, indulge in racial bigotry, hate Protestants, engage in shady business deals, etc.

The assumption is gratuitous. In my years as a priest, and long before, I have known many outstandingly apostolic and committed Catholics who made frequent visits to the Blessed Sacrament. These people were not "ghetto" Catholics. They were on fire with love for Christ and their fellowmen. But they savored those moments of silence in which they could rededicate themselves to Christ and remind themselves of Christ's undying love for all of us.

It is indeed a shame when mature and committed Catholics are made to feel, as even some priests and religious have been made to feel, that they are somehow un-liturgical, unprogressive and non-relevant because of their moments of prayer before the living Christ. . . .

4. Novenas. It seems commonly accepted that there have been some abuses in the matter of novenas: that some people have exaggerated the "numbers game," that others have developed an attitude perilously close to superstition. To the extent that this is true, it seems far more enlightened to correct the abuses than to "forbid" the people to attend novenas. One does not fill a void, even a "piety void," by forbidding things.

Some priests seem not to realize that many novena preachers have updated their approach to novenas and that several of the more popular "perpetual" or weekly novena devotions have been radically changed. The Perpetual Help devotion, with which I am most familiar, has been revised completely. With the assistance of Biblical and liturgical experts, the Redemptorist Fathers have drawn up a service that is more Biblical, more dialogal [*sic*] and more positive.

Such a service, designed to lead the people to the liturgy, is usually followed by benediction (part of liturgical worship) and provides an opportunity for confession. It can only be of spiritual profit to those who wish to attend. . . .

5. Missions and Retreats. . . . The modern "piety void" here is due mainly to two factors. One factor is that missions and retreats have too often been geared in the wrong direction, failing to meet the actual spiritual needs of modern people and failing to speak to them in a language they understand and appreciate. The second factor is that modern Americans, Catholics as well as others, easily become overly attached to diversions and recreations, such as bowling, pro football, golf, mystery stories, and TV. Nothing, but nothing, is allowed to interfere with their chosen pastimes.

Happily, many missionaries and retreat masters are now updating their material and their style. The chances are good that these spiritual exercises will have an enormous impact on modern Catholics, just as missions and retreats of former times had enormous impact on the Catholics of those days. Happily, too, more and more people, as they become more apostolic and more engaged in the problems of others, are finding a need for spiritual refreshment and reflection. . . .

The "piety void" in this area is, in my opinion, about ready to fill up. I think that the coming years will show a great upsurge in missions and retreats. As the missions and retreats become more relevant and understandable, the people will be more eager than ever to come.

To conclude: I agree with Mr. Herr that there is a "piety void." I think many Catholics, and not just the super pious, are experiencing it. I see no intrinsic reason why there should be a "piety void." I have offered a few suggestions as to what can be done about it.

67. MARY PAPA, "PEOPLE HAVING A GOOD TIME PRAYING" (1969)

The Catholic Pentecostal movement—also known as charismatic renewal—was one of a number of experimental prayer-and-worship practices that sprang up in the period following Vatican II. Intrigued by Protestant Pente-

costal claims to have received the "gifts of the Holy Spirit," two professors at Duquesne University prayed together for months and then, at a retreat in 1966, had a pentecostal experience. The movement spread rapidly first at universities, then among the general population, with 30,000 Catholics attending a conference at Notre Dame in 1973, and finally internationally. Despite some initial skepticism, Rome recognized the movement's essential validity and gave it an episcopal advisor of its own, Joseph Cardinal Suenens. One of the first sympathetic articles about the movement was written by Mary Papa of the National Catholic Reporter, *who interviewed movement leaders Kevin and Dorothy Ranaghan, attended several meetings of the group at Notre Dame, and came away a reluctant admirer.*

NOTRE DAME, Ind.—Friday nights being what they are on this all-male campus, many of the students who wandered into the prayer meeting were just sight-seeing. They had read that some of their classmates and professors were doing strange things such as "speaking in tongues" and driving out devils.

You could tell the sightseers. They wore "show-me" smirks.

As knowledge of the pentecostal prayer meetings at Notre Dame spread, so did misunderstanding.

To many it seemed incongruous that a movement previously associated with lower class Protestantism and fundamentalism should take root in a Catholic university ablaze with the progressive light of the Vatican Council.

In this context, the bizarre elements of the pentecostal meetings became the focus of both curiosity and downright concern.

I went to my first meeting, I think, hoping to be the first reporter in history to estimate the wingspan of the Holy Spirit. It didn't happen that way, though.

Things got off the ground with an invocation of the Holy Spirit, an invitation for him to come into our midst. After that, a hymn with guitar accompaniment. And then a long period of silence or silent prayer. I waited for something to happen. Finally, a student, who was smiling all over the place, spoke up; he thanked God and wanted to share with everyone the fact that God had helped him love a stranger in a way he never thought possible before now.

Some random scripture readings followed. These consisted of the reader opening his Bible, reading a passage aloud, then telling the group his particular insight into that passage.

The crowd by this time had swelled to about 80 persons. . . . We met in a classroom almost directly beneath the Notre Dame golden dome that to many symbolizes various forms of orthodoxy. It was a stormy night and the long periods of silence were shattered by umbrellas clattering to the floor.

As the storm progressed, the scene grew more appropriate for the strange happenings I had expected to see. But the prayers continued through a medium of cheerful conversation. A young couple held hands. A girl sipped Coke. A man offered a cigarette. And then they started singing ". . . they'll know we are Christians by our love . . ." I felt myself being taken in.

Five hours passed and I still had heard no one speaking in tongues. The sightseer types had left earlier, disappointed and still smirking.

These open prayer meetings are still held each Friday night, but any elements that might become spectacle are now being reserved for private gatherings. . . . A growing number of Catholics have been experiencing the same "Baptism in the Spirit" that Protestant pentecostals experience. Through the use of a symbolic gesture known as the "laying on of hands," they pray for the gifts of the Holy Spirit described in St. Paul.

These gifts include charity, wisdom, faith, prophecy, healing, discernment of spirits, speaking in tongues and interpretation of tongues. But, it is tongues—considered to be the least of the Holy Spirit's gifts—that has received the most attention.

When a person speaks in tongues his speech is said to be triggered into praising God in a foreign language unknown to the speaker or in a flow of indiscernible syllables. At Notre Dame, I was told, one occurrence of tongues was recognized as Japanese. A translation revealed that indeed it was a prayer. And the speaker disclaimed knowledge of Japanese.

While tongues is said to be a common occurrence in the pentecostal community at Notre Dame, it is considered only as an aid to the fruits of the Holy Spirit. These are catalogued as love, joy, peace, patience, kindness, and generosity. And, in all fairness, it must be said that these virtues are more pronounced in the pentecostal community than is the ability to speak in tongues.

They were particularly evident at the second meeting I attended. This time we met in a cheerful family room at the home of a Notre Dame physics professor and his wife. Though we were strangers, we were welcomed like old friends. Except for the fact that no one was drinking, it seemed like a cocktail party.

Among the 35 people there were four priests and two nuns. One of the priests was Father Jerome Wilson, Notre Dame's vice president for business affairs. Another was a visiting Trappist monk, white robe and all. There were a few undergraduates, but mostly the others were graduate students, professors and wives and a few businessmen.

What was to be another five-hour meeting got underway with a couple standard prayers and hymns. Then followed the scripture reading and individuals witnessing to the inspiration of the Spirit in their lives. They told how they had overcome this problem or that animosity, how they had suddenly experienced what it really means to love God.

There seemed to be no barriers, no inhibitions. No grim Sunday faces isolating their glances by staring into black-bound prayer books. They sat cross-legged on the floor. Ladies in slacks. White-robed monk. Cigarette smokers. Coffee drinkers. Praying in free-form, singing loudly to drown out a baby crying at the other end of the house. It occurred to me that these people were having a good time praying! Is this what they meant by the Holy Spirit dwelling amongst them?

When they began to prepare in earnest for the laying-on of hands, Father Edward O'Connor of the Notre Dame theology department pointed out that no one should feel pressured into participating in the laying on of hands.

A young man then talked of the need to rid oneself of the devil before one can receive the spirit. The negative aspect of the devil does not seem to be an overriding concern in this group, but it is one aspect that cannot be denied. And the laying on of hands seems to commonly begin with words like "In the name of Jesus of Nazareth, I command all unclean spirits to depart. . . ."

The laying on of hands began. The three men who had been chosen to pray over the candidates went together to each candidate and laid hands on his head. They commanded evil spirits to leave him that he might receive the Spirit. After a few minutes, their prayers sounded garbled. One of them seemed to be singing a sort of orientalized Gregorian chant. They were praying and singing in tongues.

When they finished praying over each candidate, other members of the group went together to pray with the one who had just received the laying on of hands. . . . The people upon whom hands were laid prayed quietly, none of them obviously spoke in tongues.

When the ceremony ended, anything else would have been anticlimactic. Besides that, it was long after midnight, so people began to leave. The host laughingly stopped the last group departing to tell them they couldn't leave until they had prayed over the host and hostess. They did, and the meeting ended with warm invitations to "please come back again."

There have been attempts to explain the Pentecostal movement at Notre Dame as a return to the devotional aspects of the Church. Some say the movement attracts people with emotional problems. Still others say it creates a false community that needs constant reinforcement. And of course, there are those who explain the whole phenomenon in terms such as "fanatic," "cracked," "off the deep end," or "nuts."

But the situation is not that simple.

It would be so convenient to say that these Catholic pentecostals were underfed, high-strung, groping intellectual misfits in a wholesome atmosphere of all-American footballhood. It would be convenient, but it would also be quite untrue. There seems to be no one level of conformity in this group except a common experience. . . . The pentecostal movement at Notre Dame now numbers about 100 persons.

They now meet somewhat regularly three times a week. Protestant pentecostal ministers have attended some of these meetings and the Catholics have prayed with the pentecostal group known as the Full Gospel Businessmen Fellowship International chapter in South Bend.

"There is an ecumenical element here," says Kevin. "Though there are still areas of strong theological disagreement, we can admit them and still pray together."

"We are not pentecostals," Dorothy says. "We are Catholics who have had a pentecostal experience . . . a deepened experience of the Holy Spirit."

Both defend the emotional aspect of the pentecostal movement. At Notre Dame no one worries about the emotion displayed in the football stadium, so what's wrong with a little emotion in religion? asks Kevin.

Among the misunderstandings circulating about Notre Dame's pentecostal movement was that its members were "fundamentalists and traditionalists." This particularly amuses the Ranaghans, who like to think of themselves as theological and social liberals. The misunderstanding, however, is perhaps a natural one, since Protestant pentecostals sprang from fundamentalist-type backgrounds.

"[Protestant pentecostals] have no sacramental system to fall back on," says Kevin. "But we come from a different tradition. The whole center of our life is the Eucharist. If this pentecostal experience doesn't lead to a fuller life in the Church, then it is worthless."

Dorothy explains that while the baptism in the Spirit cannot be considered a sacrament, she views it as a sort of adult reaffirmation of Baptism and Confirmation. "It's sort of the difference between what should happen in Confirmation and what does happen."

She views her ability to speak in tongues as a "quasi-tangible experience of loving God. This isn't something that has just come out of me. This is a gift God has given me."

But the Ranaghans feel that in order to be apostolic Christians, they are not to preach tongues, but preach Christ. "This isn't a movement. This is not a club. This is just a sharing of a Christian experience that should be a beginning rather than an end in itself," Dorothy said. "We do not know if it is significant for the Church, but it is significant for us."

68. GARRY WILLS, "MEMORIES OF A CATHOLIC BOYHOOD" (1972)

Garry Wills's text, written several years after the close of Vatican II and in the midst of the most sweeping period of experimentation in modern church history, looks back to his boyhood in the American Church of the 1940s. His ambivalence about that world—which the Council and the general cultural zeitgeist of the 1960s utterly destroyed—is founded on the ignorance and stasis he remembers along with the sometimes mystical joys it offered him (Wills studied in the seminary in his youth.) Wills's critique of preconciliar Catholicism is typical of liberal Catholics of his day—but his nostalgic memories were and are shared by many older Catholics, who are often deeply troubled by the direction the Church has taken. This text captures some of the conflicted attitude prevalent in the American Church of the early 1970s.

We grew up different. There were some places we went, and others did not —into the confessional box, for instance. There were also places we never went, though others could—we were told, from youth, to stay out of non-Catholic churches. Attendance there would be sinful, a way of countenancing error. It was forbidden territory—though tasted by some because prohibition gave tang to the experience: we were assisting at evil rites. We "born Catholics," even when we leave or lose our own church, rarely feel at home in any other. The habits of childhood are tenacious, and Catholicism was first experienced by us as a vast set of intermeshed childhood habits —prayers offered, heads ducked in unison, crossings, chants, christenings, grace at meals; beads, altar, incense, candles; nuns in the classroom alternately too sweet and too severe, priests garbed black on the street and brilliant at the altar; churches lit and darkened, clothed and stripped, to the rhythm of liturgical recurrences; the crib in winter, purple Februaries, and lilies in the spring; confession as intimidation and comfort (comfort, if nothing else, that the intimidation was survived), communion as reverie and discomfort; faith as a creed, and the creed as catechism, Latin responses, salvation by rote, all things going to a rhythm, memorized, old things always returning, eternal in that sense, no matter how transitory.

Such rites have great authority; they hypnotize. . . .

We spoke a different language from the rest of men—not only the actual Latin memorized when we learned to "serve Mass" as altar boys. We also had odd bits of Latinized English that were not part of other six-year-olds' vocabulary—words like "contrition" or "transubstantiation". . . .

The church judged things not out of a deeper antiquity, but from outside time altogether. That was borne in on us by an unanchored, anachronistic style (or mix of styles) in all things the church did. . . . Here one century, there another, and all jumbled together. Here the soutane, there the crozier. In the drone of Latin, sudden gabbles of Greek. Ancient titles (Pontifex Maximus) and an ancient familiarity of address (Paul our Pope, and Laurence our Bishop). The humble pilgrim hat for cardinals, proud mitre for bishops, triple tiara for a Pope, and absurd biretta for priests (made absurder, with purple poofs, for monsignors—yes, monsignori, for the patina of Italy was on all this merchandise, like the fuzzy encrustations on a shipwrecked cargo).

It all spoke to us of the alien. The church was stranded in America, out of place. And not only out of place here. It belonged to no age or clime, but was above them all; it had a "special dispensation" from history. History was a thing it did not have to undergo. Thus the church could pick and choose from any period, odd bits of all the ages clinging to her as she swept along, but none of them catching her, holding her back; she moved free of them all. . . .

We have yet to learn all the good wrought by "Vatican Two," and all the damage. But the main point about the Council can be put quite simply: it let out the dirty little secret. It forced upon Catholics, in the most startling symbolic way, the fact that the church changes. No more endless roll of saecula saeculorum. No more neat ahistorical belief that what one did on Sunday morning looked (with minor adjustments) like what the church had always done, from the time of the catacombs. All that lying eternity and arranged air of timelessness (as in Mae West's vestmented and massive pose) was shattered. . . .

But however bracing this experience of change has been to some, to the mass of Catholics it came as a shock, engendering disillusion. It threatened psychic ruin to them personally, as well as institutional jeopardy for the church. Not only had such people conceived of their church as timeless; they tried to approximate that state themselves. The readjustment all men undergo when there is growth was, for them, reorientation back to one immutable thing.

Catholics inhibited change, so far as they were able, in themselves and in their world. Perfect faith and trust would quiet the soul in a peaceful attitude of rest. After all, if one possesses the Truth already, any change is liable to be a departure from that truth, diminution of one's treasure. "Mysteries" remained, but were well posted—things one does not solve (or even, therefore, think much about). It would be the sin of presumption to ask for understanding of them. In heaven it would all be clear. Man's poor mind cannot grasp the high and deep things. A peasant's or old woman's faith was the ideal for which one should strive. There is an element of truth in this "wise peasant" school of thought; but that element is exaggerated and perverted by non-peasants striving back toward intellectual rusticity. Jacques Maritain calling himself "the peasant of the Garonne" is a bit like Marie Antoinette playing shepherdess to imbibe arcadian virtue. . . .

Burdened with the accounts of a large parish complex, then (if he succeeded) with all the schools in a diocese, the priest had little time for theology, or for study of any sort. He adopted the businessman's "no-nonsense" ways and practicality. He praised Simple Faith; he delivered a standard five-minute "ferverino" after the standard ten minutes of announcements and financial reporting on Sunday morning. His anti-intellectualism—defensive at first, and self-justifying—became in time self-congratulatory. "If you want theological niceties," he would say in effect, "go to the Jesuits. But if you want the basic truths of the faith, and experience out among the people, then come to the hardworking pastor, who knows—like his parishioners—what it is to pay bills every month." He even found a way to be proud of his jejune sermons. Catholics came to Mass to participate in the miracle of transubstantiation, to be mystically present at Calvary. The rite accomplished something of itself (*ex opere operato*), apart from the merits of the priest as singer or speaker. Even so fine a prelate as Bishop Spalding faced the hard facts of the situation: "The ecclesiastical seminary is not a school of intellectual culture, either here in America or elsewhere, and to imagine that it can become the instrument of intellectual culture is to cherish a delusion."

If a young Jesuit, brought in to hear the extra hordes at confession before a feast day, got up at his allotted Mass the next morning and actually said something, the pastor would warn his congregation next Sunday that it is sinful to want one's ears tickled with novelty, or to come to Mass in pride as if it were a classroom where one argues or debates. "We come here to pray and be humble," he would say, to humble the "Jebbie." Seminaries seemed to have taught the ordinary priest only two passages from Thomas a Kempis, the famous ones that say "What doth it avail thee to discourse profoundly of the Trinity, if thou be void of humility, and consequently displeasing to the Trinity?" and "I had rather feel compunction than know its definition." These became, in the memory of many pastors, proof that humility would result from mere inability to discuss the Trinity, compunction from mere inability to define it. . . .

The whole enterprise came to depend on shared ignorance. Escape from that ignorance was betrayal of a sort—nun betraying priest by departing from her expected role, betraying the priest to her students if she questioned any child's serene acceptance of the faith; curate betraying nun if he encouraged her to take a less submissive attitude to their pastor; people betraying pastor if they appealed to a bright young curate or nun for more intellectual nourishment than was contained in Sunday's mumbled five minutes of sermon. An unconscious conspiracy was entered into, each person secretly promising not to embarrass the next by knowing anything. We all took each other's hands and sat down together in the dark.

And there, in the dark, oddities of belief were bred.

Theological metaphors, imprecisions, suggestions took on the aggressive life of superstitions, their inadequacy only partly disguised by a learned overgrowth of Latin phrases. Religious life was presented as a crude hydraulics of the soul. Mortal sin emptied the reservoir, instantly, of all grace (grace being a quantifiable store of fuel not burned in any known activity, just collected for its own sake, like stamps). Confession pumped grace back into the reservoir, but in lesser measure than before. Venial sins put leaks in the tank. Meritorious acts patched the leaks, added little jets and spurts of fuel. Manning the locks in this pipe system of the soul, one tabulated, stores of grace, of merit, of indulgences, with prodigious feats of spiritual bookkeeping.

Actually, this picture of religious life was the sophisticated one, presented at later grades. First images were more rudimentary—the soul as a reverse blackboard, sin the chalk that "writes black" on it, confession the eraser to wipe out black spots. Communion as hygienic cannibalism— "Indian braves used to cut out the heart of their bravest leader and eat it," the nun would say (this led to her hissed injunction, as one came back from communion, "Don't chew the baby Jesus!"). . . .

Time could only make such a faith more vulnerable. The majesty of the priesthood dwindled as parishioners, awed in the sacristy, saw collarless priests deferring to bankers in the country club locker room. The dignity of theology dwindled to the level of the most mawkish story told one's children by a senile nun. Church history shrank to a series of background changes behind the same dreary parish church one knew—this church was the church as it had been, unchanging, down the ages. One took the mixed bag as a whole, or not at all.

So everything came to depend on immediate, unquestioning, total acceptance. Anything said or done in one's neighborhood church was the belief and practice of Rome, of the Pope's church, of historical Catholicism, of "Peter." Any discontinuity between this church and the church would represent a breaking of the bond, dissolution of the circle, parting of hands. The urgency not to know increased, in quiet ways, as one came nearer to knowing—knowing not only about "the world," but about the church itself. Educated Catholics' ignorance of their own church's past history and teachings was amazing—it led to such things as belief that "the Pope" had "always" condemned contraception. The first papal mention of the subject came three decades into the church's nineteenth century of existence—that is, forty years ago, as recent as the Depression. . . .

The church of other ages would have been unrecognizable to such Catholics. Few Catholics knew what language the Bible was written in, what languages the early church used; how Latin came into the liturgy as vernacular, then froze, excluding all later vernacular usage. Few knew the character and separate purpose of each Gospel. The Old Testament was an exotic book of stories blessed, for some reason, by tradition—a holier Arabian Nights (from parts of which nuns subtly diverted their students' attention).

The barest acquaintance with history would have destroyed most Catholics' image of the church—which was the reason (a suppressed one, unadmitted, even to oneself) why few Catholics learned any but the simplest outline of their own religion's past. One learned the list of Popes, without any idea of the difficulties involved in constructing that list. It was easier to pretend that the church had no past, only an eternal present. The church-then was just the same as the church-now; and we already knew the church-now, so we had nothing important to learn about the church-then. This Catholic ignorance of all other faiths and of Catholicism made the entire field of history dangerous, a rich source of satire in the Gibbon manner. And the wittier the satire, the more insistent the church was on preventing Catholics from seeing it. . . .

It is typical of Catholics that they knew very little about what kept them knowing very little—knew little, for instance, about the Index. For several reasons. It was published in Latin (Index Librorum Prohibitorum). No one a Catholic knew had ever looked at it—including the parish priest. No one was ever likely to. The only "working rules" familiar to confessors were the ban on non-Catholic translations of the Bible and on non-Catholic works of theology (i.e., all religious books—all books dealing with the church, theology, or the Bible—which did not have an Imprimatur on the opening left-hand page), and the ban on "dirty books" as ex natura on the Index. That last rule is a beautiful example of the Catholic urge to codify reality and capture it in rules: evil books were not rejected because they were evil (if they were evil) but because, being evil, they were implicitly legislated against by the church. . . .

Robbed of its past, the church existed in a present of precarious immediacy. Faith bound one's whole life up in ties of communal teaching, habits, discipline, authority, childhood assumptions, personal relationships. The church was enclosed, perfected in circular inner logic, strength distributed through all its interlocking aspects; turned in on itself, giving a good account of itself to itself—but so vulnerable, so fragile, if one looked outward, away from it. It had a crystalline ahistoricity; one touch of change or time could shatter it—and did. No wonder we protected it as long as we could, with a latent sense of its brittleness, and wept when it broke.

For though it was an enclosure, we lived there in most pleasant captivity—unless memory, with softening Dickensian touches, has romanticized our father's debtors prison. But, no, it was more than that. Unlikely things, even then, surprised us with meaning where we expected none. In fact, that which had least to do with reason seemed the least irrational parts of our lives. The liturgy, for instance. It did not, as it promised, take us outside time; but to some degree it pitted us against our own time, put us in an adversary posture toward the here and now.

Since the sermon was so bad, the best Mass was the early one on a weekday when there was no sermon, only the odd mixed rites so familiar we could mumble proper responses in our sleep. . . . But eight o'clock Mass on a Monday "in the old days" did have a feel of the catacombs about it, of underground good rendered to a world still bound in sleep. We came in winter, out of the dark into vestibule semidark, where peeled-off galoshes spread a slush across the floor. We took off gloves and scarves, hands still too cold to dip them in the holy water font. Already the children's lunches, left to steam on the bare radiator, emanated smells of painted metal, of heated bananas, of bologna and mayonnaise. Inside, we had an almost furtive air about our cramped genuflection and inhibited first crossings of the day—as if virtue were a secret we feared to confess even here. The priest's words came to us disjointedly through a hiss and protest of harshly awakened pipes. Girls without hats hairpinned Kleenex to their heads—it fluttered as they strode to the communion rail, like a raffish dove ill-perched on these sharers in the mystery. At the rail, as one knelt on the hard marble step, there was first the priest's quick murmur over each communicant (Corpus Domini Nostri Iesu Christi custodiat animam tuam in vitam aeternam), then the touch of his thumb wetted down the line from tongue to pious tongue. . . .

The whole thing clearly did not mesh with what we did afterward. It stood apart in shadow, as if we re-entered some oracular cave to puzzle meaning out of phrases both foreign to us and familiar. Isolated so, apart from the world, we could almost believe this was our own "last supper" —or, in John Donne's phrase, "the world's last night." But then the scuffling resumed; all the coughs and sniffs held in during consecration and communion formed a firecracker series of soft percussions. Back into the vestibule. And when, galoshes resumed, we came out, day had broken after all. The world was saved again. . . .

To remember such mornings is to start one pigeon of a muffledly screeching flock. Memories throng back, each of them stirring others:

Altar-boy assignments at odd hours, when God was a morning woozily begun under candles, a sweaty afternoon of games ended in the incense-tessitura of preprandial Benediction—the crusty and unwieldy monstrance, spangled cope, and Tantum Ergo.

Or midnight Mass—the first time one has been out so late, and farewell to Santa Claus—a pompous affair served with twenty or so other altar boys: endless high candles to light (the long lighting-tree makes young arms ache), biretta of the celebrant to dispose of (it drops on the marble step with a cardboardy pop), as the organ undulates "When flowers blossomed in the snow . . ." The crib is dimmed-blue, suggesting Christmas night, and banked evergreen trees give off a rare outdoors odor inside the church as one extinguishes candle after high candle. The three kings will come in pineneedled silence (Epiphany is not a holy day of obligation), hooves of their camels unheard—already they inch over the sanctuary; they must arrive punctually by Twelfth-night.

A lenten procession, cross carried in front (swathed in purple), no organ to support the a cappella groan of "Pange lingua." The purple cloth is folded back, exposing the feet on the crucifix for people to kiss (priest making quick passes with a clean handkerchief, wiping the feet between each kiss).

An oddly jazzy lilt to Flectamus genua, sung over and over on Holy Saturday. All our food-chiseling during Lent (ne potus noceat) will end in a Saturday afternoon orgy of candy and stored-up sweets. May procession in the warm night air of summer, "Hail Holy Queen enthroned above," as a girl in her prom "formal" teeters up a ladder with flowers to crown the plaster brow.

It was a world of quaint legalisms. Looking up a movie in the Legion of Decency list (if one had to look, it was probably "Condemned"). Wild surmise on the contents of a Friday soup—did it have gravy or meat products in it? Long debate, as midnight approached on Saturday, over using Mountain Standard Time to begin the precommunion fast. Priests groping their way to the pullman lounge, for light to finish the breviary. Dies Irae on All Souls' Day as J. P. Morgans of the soul accumulate indulgences in purgatorial vaults by ducking in and out of church all day. . . .

Holy cards of saints with eyes so strenuously upturned as to be almost all white. The Infant of Prague bulkily packaged in "real" clothes. The sight, in darkened churches, of a shadowy Virgin with hands held palm-out at the level of her hips, plaster cape flowing down from those hands toward blue votive lights unsteady under her like troubled water. Sand under the votive candles for putting out tapers; and a box of kitchen matches, for lighting tapers, stuck into the sand. The momentary waxen strangle of St. Blaise day, as crossed candles bless one's throat.

Certain feelings are not communicable. One cannot explain to others, or even to oneself, how burnt stuff rubbed on the forehead could be balm for the mind. The squeak of ash crumbled into ash marked the body down for death, yet made this promise of the grave somehow comforting ("Rest, rest, perturbed spirit").

There were moments when the weirdest things made a new and deep sense beyond sense—when Confession did not mean cleaning up oneself (the blackboard erased again) but cleansing a whole world, the first glimpse of sky or grass as one came out of church. When communion was not cannibalism but its reverse, body taken up in Spirit. Being inwardly shaken by unsummoned prayers, as by muffled explosions. Moments of purity remembered, when the world seemed fresh out of its maker's hands, trees washed by some rain sweeter than the world's own.

All these things were shared, part of community life, not a rare isolated joy, like reading poems. These moments belonged to a people, not to oneself. It was a ghetto, undeniably.

But not a bad ghetto to grow up in.

69. Albert Ottenweller, "A Call to Restructure the Parish" (1975)

Somewhat unusually for an American bishop, Albert Ottenweller had thirty years of experience as a parish priest before he became auxiliary bishop of Toledo. The new prelate was thus well-placed to comment on the effect the reformist ethos of Vatican II was having on U.S. parishes—and the effect it ought to have been having. Pressure on individual priests had mounted as they struggled to translate the liberating but sometimes vague directives of the Council into practical instructions for a new kind of parish life in which they would be "servant-leaders" rather than the autocratic, though often benevolent, dictators of days past. Meanwhile, the sudden exodus of Catholics from their physical and intellectual "ghettoes" (see No. 68) meant, in part, a decline in their participation in parish life. The tensions between institutional and communal models of parish life which Ottenweller pointed out to the U.S. bishops remain in many American parishes today.

I feel very honored to be able to present to this body of bishops a concern of mine for the future of the church. I will try to be brief and to the point. From the outset I must admit that I have a prejudice in favor of priests who are in pastoral ministry.

I see the parish as the key to renewal in the church. I am not a theologian, nor a scripture scholar. For more than 30 years I have worked as a parish priest. I see myself as a journeyman pastor experienced in dealing with people and problems at the grass roots.

I think a pastor's expertise is taking theory, theological principles, and making them work on the level of where people are. I think this was Martin Luther King's genius—he drew the principles of civil rights out of the textbook, Jesus' teaching from the gospels, and took them down to a crowded basement of a Baptist Church in Selma, Alabama and brought them to birth in people there; and they marched through the streets, and theory became a movement.

I think priests do this in parishes. Under the guidance of the Holy Spirit the bishops at the Second Vatican Council saw a vision of what the church of our time ought to be. But that vision must be brought to life in the churches and in the market place. It is one thing to formulate guidelines for the new rite of penance—it is quite another thing to put those guidelines to work so that ordinary Catholic people may celebrate penance as a deep and satisfying faith experience.

This said, I would like to propose that a study be made of the model of parish as presently structured compared to other possible models. I think restructuring is critical because parish priests are finding it extremely difficult if not impossible to bring the directives of the Second Vatican Council to life in their parishes (especially the large parishes) as those parishes are now constituted.

I will not take up your time going over the problems of declining mass attendance, alienation of youth, lack of communication, etc., that beset large parishes in this day. They are only too well known. I would like to mention, however, the frustration of pastors and others working in parish ministry.

I see talented priests avoiding parish work in favor of specialties such as campus ministry, counseling, religious education, etc. I see pastors of larger parishes transferred to smaller parishes, having breakdowns, just waiting around for retirement. I believe that a substantial part of the problem lies in this fact that, at least, the large parishes are not fitted for the job the council is asking them to do. To coin a phrase—we're trying to put new wine into the old bottles.

Institution/Community

What do I mean by restructuring the parish? Mostly when we talk about models we think in terms of church in general.

Instead of talking about the institutional church, and church as community I would like to speak of the parish as institution and the parish as community. For our purposes I would like to define institution in this way: Institution is a grouping of people organized to put out a product, or deliver a service. For example, at General Motors people are organized as workers, sales people, etc. to produce and market automobiles. In an institution the product is important not the person.

I would define community as a group of people banded together not to put out a product or to deliver a service, but to grow in relation to one another. Example: the family. A family does not put out a product or deliver a service. Members are responsible for each other. They care for each other and in loving relationships they grow as persons.

Now let's refer these ideas to the parish situation. A parish is an institution. And this must not be minimized. A parish delivers services. It educates, cares for the poor, helps the missions, etc. But a parish is also a community. Members of a parish have a need and a right to be like an extended family, to know each other, care for each other and so grow in the love of God and of one another. My contention is that right now, organizationally, parishes are very heavy on institution and very light on community. We think institution. We think programs. We think service.

For example, suppose in the parish we are worried about our religious education program. It is not effective. Young people are not showing up. How do we meet the problem? Institutionally we must put out a better product. We will improve CCD teacher training. We'll buy the best film strips we can find. Perhaps, we'll even invest in a director of religious education. We'll give it one more try. After all this effort, maybe, children stay away in even greater numbers than before. Why? They are hungry for community, but we keep giving them institution. We emphasize product more than person.

The movements that seem spiritually alive and appealing are such groups as cursillo, marriage encounter, charismatic prayer groups, comunidades de base—groups that are person and growth oriented. It seems very odd that in most cases parishioners must go outside the parish structure to be a part of one of these movements.

My proposal is that parish structure be studied to find a model more adaptable to our times and to the vision of the council.

Both the crisis and the challenge it seems to me lie in the parish. We can strengthen commissions, conferences and departments on both national and diocesan levels, but unless their programs are able to be absorbed and implemented on the parish level, not much is accomplished.

I know a pastor who reads it like this. He says, "I feel like there is a big funnel above me. All kinds of programs are dumped into it from the top: new rite of penance, bicentennial observance, Holy Year, fight against abortion—and he listed some more—and they come down through the narrow end of that funnel right on my head."

It seems to me that beautiful programs have been developed for use in parishes. I call them secondary programs. Many of them, ideal as they are, never see the light of day, or at most only dimly, because the primary structure of the parish is faulty. It is not adapted to do the job we ask of it.

If we can say with Pope Paul, "The church is a mystery," we also can say, "The parish is a mystery." It is a reality imbued with the presence of God.

It lies, therefore, within the very nature of the parish to be always open to new and greater exploration. It is my proposal that the structures of the parish be explored so that it truly can be God's little flock.

70. Judith Tate O'Brien, "Presenting My Entire Self to God" (1984)

Since the 1960s, the numbers of ordained clergy, as well as the numbers of male and female religious, have dropped precipitously in the United States. Simultaneously, the Second Vatican Council's renewed emphasis on the dignity of the lay (married) state and the responsibility of all believers within the church caused many laypeople to contribute their talents as full and part-time ministers, both volunteer and paid. Lay ministers in the United States range from parish coordinators (in the absence of a full-time pastor) to religious educators to pastoral counselors to extraordinary ministers of the Eucharist. As of 2006, they held well over 30,000 half- and full-time paid positions; more than 80 percent were women. Many serve with an intense sense of personal vocation, as Judith O'Brien's reflection demonstrates.

I knew I wanted to serve people. This desire was complicated by the fact that I also wanted to marry. I struggled between these two futures.

I knew, of course, that they were mutually exclusive! I'd learned the catechism lesson. I knew that only men could choose the highest vocation. Women couldn't be priests, but they could choose one step above marriage by becoming a sister. Sisters could minister. Married women couldn't. . . .

Could I be lay and still serve? I began to realize I could. And I have for the better part of the last sixteen years.

My first job as a lay minister was that of pastoral assistant. I had an old Dodge Dart that went on spontaneous honking sprees, a shabby furnished apartment, and a salary of $500 a month. I felt noble about my poverty and my low salary until a jobless layman with a degree in religious education pointed out that people like me kept people like him from being able to work for the Church and support a family.

People in our parish seemed hungry for Scripture. At this point I began graduate study in theology. Through Bible study in the parish, I was able to do what I best knew how to do—teach. More importantly, I was able to deepen my own religious understanding and to find a lay style of prayer. I believe that no amount of skill and no number of degrees is sufficient to make a job into a ministry. Genuine lay ministry must, I believe, be grounded in genuine prayer. Although people came eagerly to Scripture classes they didn't seem too interested in other courses and workshops unless those workshops dealt with family life.

I quickly noticed that ordinary people seemed to be more interested in learning how to rear an adolescent son, keep a marriage healthy, or adjust to divorce than they were in, say, learning about the early history of the Church. People in the pews were also people in families. There—in kitchens and cars and back yards—is where families live and that's where people work out their salvation.

My parish work soon led me to full-time family-life ministry. I helped create and direct Oklahoma's first diocesan Office of Family Life. I went back to school and got a degree in counseling psychology. . . . I find it fascinating to reflect on the ways God uses all these past experiences. Ministers (and isn't that every caring believer?) seem to seek to serve those who've had similar experiences. Social scientists might call it finishing unfinished business or doing vicarious emotional work. I suppose that's so. I also believe it's a kind of divine economy in which God moves us to use our own pain to help others. Perhaps only the wounded can really understand the similarly wounded. . . .

Currently I work as coordinator of family life in a large inner-city parish. My work includes counseling and education. I find that some people more easily trust a counselor in a church setting than one in an agency. Some persons who come to me would probably not go for counseling at all if it weren't offered in the church. I sometimes pray with my clients, and I always pray for them. I make sure I don't substitute prayer for skill. I try simply to integrate the helping process so that it may accurately be named counseling and described as pastoral.

I believe that this particular ministry of professional pastoral counseling will be more keenly called for in the future. Priests are too scarce and too busy to add this time-consuming job to their schedules. Many of them lack professional training in counseling. Catholic parishes, at least in Oklahoma, are just beginning to see pastoral family counseling as a possible part of parish ministry. It's exciting to be in on the ground floor of this new and needed Church work.

As a lay minister, I generally feel well accepted by both laity and clergy. For one thing, people in Oklahoma know me. I've lived and worked here for the better part of fifty years, and although the Catholic population has shot up to four and a half percent, we're still few enough that many of us know each other. For another thing, this land of oil derricks and wheat fields is marked by a frontier spirit that sets an open and welcoming climate for just about anybody, including lay ministers.

Even here, however, the old taint of clericalism has caused some occasional frustration. I've been passed over for a diocesan leadership job because it "had" to be filled by a priest—even though I was better qualified by both experience and education. I've had to cancel a retreat because I had scheduled it to be held in some diocesan cabins used often for retreats. A notice from the chancery explained that lay persons (lay ministers) could not reserve the cabins.

Events like these infuriate me. What I find even more frustrating is the silence on the part of my clerical and lay friends about these kinds of injustices. That noxious idea that lay persons are inferior citizens in the Church seems still to linger among us. So, yes, I've experienced some frustrations as a lay minister.

In general, though, working in the Church has been good for me. I am instinctively religious, and I think God has given me the ability to make religion real and God personal to people who might be inclined to see religion as a Sunday event and God as an uninvolved overseer.

I find intense joy in helping children grieve when they need to, in helping single-again persons find new life, in helping stepparents give the lie to the Cinderella story, in helping couples improve communications and freshen love. I've found that Church work generally permits more creativity than non-Church work. I guess what pleases me most is that the work I do allows me to bring together my past and personal experiences and my professional skills. It's like presenting my entire self to God through service to God's people.

FURTHER SUGGESTED READING

Joseph Chinnici and Angelyn Dries, eds., *Prayer and Practice in the American Catholic Community* (Maryknoll, N.Y.: Orbis Books, 2000).

David Hall, ed., *Lived Religion in America* (Princeton, N.J.:Princeton University Press, 1997).

Timothy Matovina and Gary Riebe-Estrella, eds., *Horizons of the Sacred: Mexican Traditions in U.S. Catholicism* (Ithaca, N.Y.: Cornell University Press, 2002).

Paul Marx, OSB, *Virgil Michel and the Liturgical Movement* (Collegeville, Minn.: The Liturgical Press, 1957).

Robert Orsi, *The Madonna of 115th St: Faith and Community in Italian Harlem,* 2d edition (New Haven, Conn.: Yale University Press, 2002).

Robert Orsi, *Thank You, St. Jude: Women's Devotion to the Patron Saint of Hopeless Causes* (New Haven, Conn.: Yale University Press, 1996).

James O'Toole, ed., *Habits of Devotion: Catholic Religious Practice in Twentieth-Century America* (Ithaca, N.Y.: Cornell University Press, 2005).

Ann Taves, *The Household of Faith: Roman Catholic Devotions in Mid-Nineteenth-Century America* (Notre Dame, Ind.: University of Notre Dame Press, 1986).

Marina Warner, *Alone of All Her Sex: The Myth and Cult of the Virgin Mary* (New York: Random House, 1976).

Source List

Part I: Frontiers and Encounter

1. *Sublimus Deus* (1537)
   Francis Augustus MacNutt, *Bartholomew de Las Casas* (New York: G.P. Putnam's Sons, 1909), 427–431.
2. Meeting of a Spanish Missionary with a Navajo Apache Chief (1630)
   Peter P. Forrestal, trans., *Benavides' Memorial of 1630* (Washington, D.C.: Academy of American Franciscan History, 1954), 48–50.
3. The English Jesuits Establish the Maryland Mission (1634)
   E. A. Dalrymple, *Narrative of the Voyage to Maryland by Father Andrew White, S.J. An Account of the Colony of the Lord Baron of Baltimore* (Baltimore, Md.: Maryland Historical Society, 1874), 10–43.
4. Brebeuf, "Instructions to Our Fathers Who Shall Be Sent to the Hurons" (1637)
   Reuben Gold Thwaites, ed., *The Jesuit Relations and Allied Documents* (Cleveland: Burrows Brothers Co., 1898). Volume XII, 117–123.
5. *Maryland's Act of Religious Toleration* (1649)
   William Hand Browne, ed., *Archives of Maryland. Proceedings and Acts of the General Assembly of Maryland, January 1637/38—September 1664* (Baltimore, Md.: Maryland Historical Society, 1883), 244–247.
6. Hennepin's "Description of Missionary Difficulties with Natives" (1697)
   Rueben Gold Thwaites, ed., *Louis Hennepin: A New Discovery of a Vast Country in America* (Chicago: A. C. McClurg & Co., 1903), II, 457–474.
7. Massachusetts's "Act against Jesuits and Priests" (1700)
   The Acts and Resolves, Public and Private, of the Province of Massachusetts Bay (Boston: Wright and Potter, 1869), I, 423–424.
8. Report on Catholicism in the English Colonies (1773)
   American Catholic Historical Researches, XXI (July 1904), 118–120.
9. First American Report to the Propaganda Fide (1785)
   An Address to the Roman Catholics of the United States of America by a Catholic Clergyman [John Carroll] (Annapolis, Md.: Frederick Green, 1784), 59–60, 113–115.
10. John Carroll's Letter on Lay Trusteeism (1786)
    American Catholic Historical Researches, XVII (January 1900), 1–4.

11. Report on Catholic Life in New Orleans (1795)
    John Tracy Ellis, *Documents of American Catholic History, 1493–1865* (Wilmington, Dela.: Michael Glazier, 1987). I, 177–179.
12. First Council of Baltimore (1829)
    Concilia Provinciala, Baltimori Habita ab anno 1829 usque ad annum 1849 (Baltimore, Md.: John Murphy and Company, 1851), 76–77, 79–81. Translation by Francis Dombrowski, OFM Cap, and Margaret Klotz, OSF.
13. Benedicta Riepp Defends Nuns' Autonomy (1857, 1859)
    First selection: Benedicta Riepp, O.S.B, to Archbishop von Reisach, "Points on Which I Cannot Agree with the Right Reverend Lord Abbott Boniface Wimmer," no date, 1857. Second Selection: Letter of Benedicta Riepp, O.S.B., to Alexander Cardinal Barnabo, January 4 1859. Both in *Behind the Beginnings: Benedictine Women in America,* ed. M. Incarnata Girgen, O.S.B. (St. Joseph, Minn.: Sisters of St. Joseph of St. Benedict, 1981), 110–113, 135–137. Reprinted with permission.

Part II: Inside/Outside

14. Alexis de Tocqueville on American Catholics (1835)
    From *Democracy in America* by Alexis de Tocqueville, translated by Henry Reeve, copyright 1945 and renewed 1973 by Alfred A. Knopf, a division of Random House, Inc. (I, 300–302; II 26–30). Used by permission of Alfred A. Knopf, a division of Random House, Inc.
15. John Hughes Condemns the New York Public School Society (1841)
    Complete Works of the Most Rev. John Hughes, D.D., Archbishop of New York, ed. Lawrence Kehoe (New York: For the Compiler, 1865), I, 275–284.
16. The American Protestant Association (1842)
    Ray Allen Billington, *The Protestant Crusade, 1800–1860: A Study of the Origins of American Nativism* (New York: The Macmillan Co., 1938), 438–439.
17. Archbishop Hughes Explains American Liberty to Rome (1858)
    Henry J. Browne, ed., "The Archdiocese of New York A Century Ago. A Memoir of Archbishop Hughes, 1838–1858." *Historical Records and Studies* XXXIX–XL (1952): 168–174.
18. "Roman Instruction on Catholic Children in Public Schools" (1875)
    Latin text: *Acta et decreta concilii plenarii Baltimorensis tertii* (Baltimore, 1886), 279–282. English text: The Pastor IV (June 1886): 232–237.
19. Isaac Hecker on Catholic Scholasticism in America (1887)
    Isaac Hecker, *The Church and the Age: An Exposition of the Catholic Church in View of the Needs and Aspirations of the Present Age* (New York: Catholic World, 1887), 181–187, 189–191, 204–205.
20. John Ireland, Introduction to the *Life of Father Hecker* (1891)
    Walter Elliott, *The Life of Father Hecker* (New York: The Columbus Press, 1891), vii–xvii.

21. Testem Benevolentiae Condemns "Americanism" (1899)
    John J. Wynne, S.J., ed., *The Great Encyclical Letters of Pope Leo XIII* (New York: Benzinger Bros., 1903), 441–453.
22. "Report on the Religious Conditions of Puerto Ricans in New York" (1951)
    Encarnacion Padilla de Armas et al., "Report of Some Catholic Women on the Religious Condition of Puerto Rican Immigrants in New York City," 1951. Personal archives of Jaime R. Vidal. Reprinted with permission.
23. John LaFarge on Race Relations (1956)
    John LaFarge, S.J., *The Catholic Viewpoint on Race Relations* (Garden City, N.Y.: Hanover House, 1956), 77–86. Reprinted with permission.
24. Patty Crowley and the Birth Control Commission (1965)
    Patty & Pat Crowley, "Statement of Mr. and Mrs. Patrick F. Crowley Made to the Committee on the Study of Problems of Population and Birth Control, Working Under the Supervision of the Supreme Sacred Congregation of the Holy Office, March 1965." Photocopy in the archives of the University of Notre Dame, Patrick and Patricia Crowley Papers, Box 5, Folder 18. Reprinted with permission.
25. U.S. Bishops on "The Challenge of Peace" (1983)
    Excerpts from *The Challenge of Peace*. Copyright © 1983 United States Conference of Catholic Bishops, Washington, D.C. Nos. 2–7, 8, 10–12, 32–33, 36–39, 41–43. Used with permission. All rights reserved. No part of this work may be reproduced or transmitted in any form without the permission in writing from the copyright holder.
26. Hispanic Deacons to Cardinal O'Connor (1988)
    Confraternidad de Diaconos Hispanos de la Nueva York, 15 August 1988, photocopy from the personal archives of Jaime R. Vidal. Reprinted with permission.
27. Michael Novak on the "Spirit of Capitalism" (1993)
    Michael Novak, *The Catholic Ethic and the Spirit of Capitalism* (New York: Free Press, 1993), 132–136. Reprinted with permission of The Free Press, a Division of Simon & Schuster, Inc., from *The Catholic Ethic and the Spirit of Capitalism* by Michael Novak. Copyright © 1993 by Michael Novak. All rights reserved.

Part III: Catholicism and the Intellectual Life

28. John Tracy Ellis, "American Catholics and the Intellectual Life" (1955)
    John Tracy Ellis, "American Catholics and the Intellectual Life," *Thought* 30 (spring 1955): 363–365, 367–368, 374–375, 376–377, 385–386, 387–388.
29. John Courtney Murray, *We Hold These Truths* (1960)
    John Courtney Murray, S.J., *We Hold These Truths: Catholic Reflections on the American Proposition* (Kansas City: Sheed and Ward, 2005), 48–52, 53, 56. Reprinted with permission.

30. Madeleva Wolff, "Educating Our Daughters as Women" (1961)
    Sister M. Madeleva, C.S.C., "Educating Our Daughters as Women," Chapter
    VII. In *Conversations with Cassandra: Who Believes in Education?* (New York:
    The Macmillan Company, 1961), 48–52. Reprinted with permission.
31. "Land O' Lakes" Statement on Catholic Universities (1967)
    "Statement on the Nature of the Contemporary Catholic University, Land O'
    Lakes, Wisconsin, July 23, 1967," reprinted in Neil McCluskey, S.J., *Catholic Ed-
    ucation Faces Its Future* (New York: Doubleday, 1969), 298–300.
32. Flannery O'Connor on Being a "Catholic Writer" (1969)
    Flannery O'Connor, *Mystery and Manners: Occasional Prose* (New York: Straus
    and Giroux, 1969), 172–173, 174, 177–182. Reprinted with permission.
33. Andrew Greeley, "Models for Viewing American Catholicism" (1977)
    Andrew M. Greeley, *The American Catholic: A Social Portrait* (New York: Basic
    Books, 1977), 28–30. Reprinted with permission of BASIC BOOKS, a member
    of Perseus Book Group.
34. Elizabeth Johnson, "To Speak Rightly of God" (1992)
    Elizabeth A. Johnson, C.S.J., *She Who Is: The Mystery of God in Feminist Theo-
    logical Discourse* (New York: Crossroad, 1992, © 1992), 3–4, 5–6, 7, 8, 18–19, 33–
    35. Reprinted with permission of Crossroad Publishing Company.

Part IV: Politics

35. Bishop John England on Slavery (1840)
    Ignatius Reynolds, ed., The *Works of the Right Reverend John England,* Vol. III
    (Baltimore, Md.: John Murphy and Company, 1849).
36. Cardinal Gibbons Defends the Knights of Labor (1887)
    Henry J. Browne, *The Catholic Church and the Knights of Labor* (Washington,
    D.C.: Catholic University of America Press, 1949). Reprinted with permission.
37. John A. Ryan and the Bishops' Program for Social Reconstruction (1919)
    Bishops' Program of Social Reconstruction [reprint] (Washington, D.C.: Na-
    tional Catholic Welfare Conference, 1950).
38. Joseph Nevins, "Education to Catholic Marriage" (1928)
    The Ecclesiastical Review 79 (December 1928): 625–632.
39. Dorothy Day, "Loaves and Fishes" (1933)
    The Catholic Worker, May 1967. Originally printed in *Loaves and Fishes* (New
    York: Harper & Row, 1963). Courtesy of the Dorothy Day Library on the Web:
    http://www.catholicworker.org/dorothyday/
40. Katharine M. Byrne, "Happy Little Wives and Mothers" (1956)
    America (28 January 1956). Reprinted with permission.
41. John F. Kennedy, "Address to Southern Baptist Leaders" (1960)
    http://www.jfklibrary.org/Historical+Resources/Archives/Reference+Desk/
    Speeches/JFK/JFK+Pres/Address+of+Senator+John+F.+Kennedy+to+the+
    Greater+Houston+Ministerial+Association.htm.

42. "Dignity and the Priest" (1961)
    The Pilot, 1961. Reprinted with permission.
43. Dr. John Rock, "The Pill" (1963)
    From *The Time Has Come* by John Rock, M.D., copyright © 1963 by John Rock. Used by permission of Alfred A. Knopf, a division of Random House, Inc.
44. Kay Toy Fenner, "American Catholic Dating Guidelines" (1963)
    American Catholic Etiquette (Westminster, Md.: Newman Press, 1963)
45. Sister Jeanne Reidy, C.H.M., "A Nun in Street Clothes—Theory and Practice" (1967)
    The National Catholic Reporter, January 11, 1967.
46. "Statement by Catholic Theologians" and "Dissent in and For the Church" (1968 & 1969)
    Charles E. Curran and Robert E. Hunt, *Dissent in and for the Church* (New York: Sheed and Ward, 1969). Reprinted with permission.
47. Phyllis Schlafly, "What's Wrong with 'Equal Rights' for Women?"
    Phyllis Schlafly Report 5, no. 7 (February 1972). Reprinted with permission.
48. Joseph Cardinal Bernardin, "A Consistent Ethic of Life" (1983)
    Archdiocese of Chicago's Joseph Cardinal Bernardin Archives and Records Center. Reprinted with permission.
49. Richard John Neuhaus, "The Catholic Moment" (1987)
    Part VI: The Catholic Moment, 283–288 from *The Catholic Moment: The Paradox of the Church in the Postmodern World* by Richard John Neuhaus, Copyright © 1987 by Richard John Neuhaus. Reprinted with permission of Harper-Collins Publisher.
50. Andrew Sullivan, "Alone Again, Naturally" (1994)
    First published in *The New Republic*, November 28, 1994. © 1994 by Andrew Sullivan, permission of the Wylie Agency.

Part V: Worship & the Spiritual Life

51. Preparing for Confession (1792)
    The Pious Guide to Prayer and Devotion: Containing Various Practices of Piety Calculated to Answer the Various Demands of the Different Devout Members of the Roman Catholic Church (George-Town [Potowmack]: Printed by James Doyle, 1792).
52. "Sunday Morning Mass" (1868)
    James Parton, "Our Roman Catholic Brethren," *Atlantic Monthly* (21 April 1868).
53. The Baltimore Catechism (1885)
    A Catechism of Christian Doctrine, Prepared and Enjoined by Order of the Third Plenary Council of Baltimore (New York: The Catholic Publication Society Company, 1885).

54. James Cardinal Gibbons, "The Invocation of the Saints" (1876)
    Faith of Our Fathers (Baltimore, Md.: J. Murphy, 1876).
55. The Sodality of the Blessed Virgin Mary (1897)
    Manual of the Sodality of the Blessed Virgin Mary (New York: Apostleship of Prayer, 1897).
56. "Litany for the Conversion of America" (1908)
    The Missionary 12 (December 1908); republished in Anthony Freytag, *The Catholic Mission Feast* (Techny, Ill.: Mission Press, 1914).
57. "The Passion Play of the West" (1910)
    L. B. Jerome, "The Passion Play of the West," *Rosary* Magazine 36 (March 1910).
58. "Youth and Catholic Leadership" (1936)
    Catholic Action 18, No. 2 (February 1936), 15–16.
59. William Leonard, S.J., on the *Missa Recitata* in Wartime (1943–45)
    William J. Leonard, S.J., *Where Thousands Fell* (Kansas City, Mo.: Sheed & Ward, 1995). Reprinted with permission.
60. U.S. Catholic Bishops, "Regulations on Fast and Abstinence" (1951)
    Archives of the National Catholic Welfare Conference, Archives of the Catholic University of America.
61. Patrick Peyton & the Family Rosary Crusade (1951)
    Patrick J. Peyton, *The Ear of God* (Garden City, N.Y.: Doubleday, 1951). Reprinted with permission.
62. American Catholics from World War II to the 1970s: Photographs from the Collections of the Library of Congress
63. "How the 'People of God' Want to Worship" (1964)
    Rev. Robert Dougherty, "How the 'People of God' Want to Worship," *ACT* 17, no. 9 (July-August 1964): 3–5. Reprinted by permission of the Christian Family Movement, Ames, Iowa.
64. Father Gommar De Pauw, J.C.D., "The Catholic Traditionalist Manifesto" (1964)
    Father Gommar De Pauw, *The Catholic Traditionalist Manifesto* (1964). http://www.latinmass-ctm.org/
65. Thomas Merton, "Fourth and Walnut Vision" (1966)
    Conjectures of a Guilty Bystander (New York: Doubleday 1966).
66. Daniel Lowery, CSSR, "A 'Piety Void?'" (1966)
    American Ecclesiastical Review 154 (January 1966): 31–38. Reprinted with permission.
67. Mary Papa, "People Having a Good Time Praying" (1969)
    National Catholic Reporter, May 17, 1969.
68. Garry Wills, "Memories of a Catholic Boyhood" (1972)
    Garry Wills, *Bare Ruined Choirs: Doubt, Prophecy, and Radical Religion* (Garden City, N.Y.: Doubleday, 1971), 5–37. Copyright 1972 by Garry Wills, reprinted with the permission of The Wylie Agency, Inc.

69. Albert Ottenweller, "A Call to Restructure the Parish" (1975)
   Origins 5 (December 11, 1975): 394–396. Reprinted with permission.

70. Judith Tate O'Brien, "Presenting My Entire Self to God" (1984)
   Excerpt from "Presenting My Entire Self to God" by Judith Tate O'Brien. In *Why We Serve: Personal Stories of Catholic Lay Ministers,* ed. Douglas Fisher, preface by Rosemary Haughton. Copyright 1984 by Paulist Press, Inc., New York/Mahwah, N.J. Used with permission. www.paulistpress.com.

About the Editors

Mark Massa is the Karl Rahner Distinguished Professor of Theology and the Co-Director of the Curran Center for American Catholic Studies at Fordham University. He is the author of *Catholics and American Culture* and *Anti-Catholicism in America*. Catherine Osborne is a doctoral student at Fordham University.